THE GREY MAN

Order this book online at www.trafford.com
or email orders@trafford.com

Most Trafford titles are also available at major online book retailers.

© Copyright 2010 GARY ,S, LYNCH, AB, MM.

All rights reserved. No part of this publication may be reproduced, stored in a retrieval system, or transmitted, in any form or by any means, electronic, mechanical, photocopying, recording, or otherwise, without the written prior permission of the author.

Note for Librarians: A cataloguing record for this book is available from Library and Archives Canada at www.collectionscanada.ca/amicus/index-e.html

Printed in Victoria, BC, Canada.

ISBN: 978-1-4269-1961-9 (sc)

ISBN: 978-1-4269-1962-6 (dj)

Library of Congress Control Number: 2009939958

Our mission is to efficiently provide the world's finest, most comprehensive book publishing service, enabling every author to experience success. To find out how to publish your book, your way, and have it available worldwide, visit us online at www.trafford.com

Trafford rev. 3/31/10

Trafford PUBLISHING   www.trafford.com

North America & international
toll-free: 1 888 232 4444 (USA & Canada)
phone: 250 383 6864 ♦ fax: 812 355 4082

To my son, Jim
A fine young man and my two angels
Catherine and Cheyanne

SOLDIERS
FATHERS   FRIENDS
ALWAYS

Col Chapman (R.I.P)

Contents

Acknowledgements	xi
Foreword	xiii
Our Spirit	xiv
Introduction	xv
Preface	xix
Second Place! You Mean First Loser	1
Train Hard, Fight Easy	15
It's Character Building	31
The Leading Parachute Battle Group	38
Doing Time The First Time	46
Survival The Ten That Got Away.	65
It's An Anti Tank Mine Mate.	71
Badm317	79
The Orphans	85
Good Idea Brigade	91
Northern Ireland	104
The Low Level Parachute Trials	112
Mrs Turnbull	122
Brevet Militaire De Parachutiste	124
It Seemed Like The Thing To Do At The Time Sir!	130
The Brotherhood	139
Extreme Sports	146
Judo	158
Chechnya	166
Running Guns	185
Rules Of Engagement	194
Alternative Agendas	205
The Firms	230
Close Protection	248
The Khmer Rouge	256
Banged Up Abroad	269
Abu Sayyaf	278
Hunting With Giants	303
Light At The End Of The Tunnel	311
End Ex	320
Glossary	329

Acknowledgements

I WOULD LIKE TO USE THIS PAGE TO THANK MY WIFE ANGELA,
THE KENYAN FAMILY, MARK FLEET, YAN COOPER, COL CHAPMAN, & MIDLAND MICK FOR THEIR SUPPORT.

ALL THE MEN OF THE FIGHTING 63RD AB TP
THE MEN OF 1 PARA A COY 3PLT.
THE CO AND RSM LOG BN 90,
MARTIN WELSH, PHIL C,
THE 1ST CHECHEN ARMY, 3RD INFANTRY,
GENERAL URWELD 1RCP, NATIONAL GEOGRAPHIC.
OLIVEBRANCH PMC, GLOBAL CRISIS MANAGEMENT PMC,
IAIN AND HIS FIRM,
THE BRETHREN OF 7820 PHEATHEN
FOR THE OPPORTUNITIES.

SI FERRIS, AND ALL THE STAFF AT THE VICTORY IN HEREFORD, BIG VENUE SI, PHIL C, STU DOW, SAS MARK P, BIG MIKE AND GED. DAVE T, TAFF T, BOB, BEZ, SEAN M AND DODGE. H, RITCHIE P, BIG JOHN AND MAGS, WOODY, AND THE OUTLAWS
FOR THE GOOD TIMES.

MY SON JIM, BIG JOHN C, SANDLINE PMC, PATHFINDER PLTN. BRITISH SPECIAL FORCES, RENZO GRACIE, ROBIN HORSFALL, KEN FOLLETT AND RAY MEARS, FOR THE INSPIRATION.

DEL COPE, BIG TED, DAVE SCARBOROUGH, MARK WOOLDRIDGE, CHRIS KNOX, PAUL DEAN, RICHIE DOVE, MARK EARL, ARMY JUDO SQUAD 93 95, JOHN

MORTON, PINEWOOD & LE HABANA CUBA JU JITSU CLUBS, ALDERSHOT BOXING CLUB. CHECHEN TSAMBO TEAM, LANCASHIRE WRESTLING CLUB, BORDEAUX & LE MANS JUDO CLUBS,
FOR THE TRAINING.

Foreword

This book is written not only from memory but from notes taken at the time and meetings and interviews with old colleagues. Due to the accuracy of some of the anecdotes many names and places have been changed unless I've had expressed permission from individuals to use their real details.

The opinions and feelings written, reflect the emotions and atmosphere at the time of events and are not necessarily the same now.

I also make no excuses for my grammar, I am a mere Soldier, I am not Politician.

Our Spirit

I CHOOSE NOT TO BE A COMMON MAN.
IT IS MY RIGHT TO BE UNCOMMON.
I DO NOT WISH TO BE A KEPT CITIZEN,
HUMBLED AND DULLED,
BY HAVING THE STATE LOOK AFTER ME.
I WANT TO TAKE THE CALCULATED RISK.
TO DREAM AND BUILD
TO FAIL AND SUCCEED
I WILL NOT BARTER INCENTIVE FOR A DOLE.
I PREFER THE CHALLENGE OF LIFE TO THE
GUARANTEED EXISTENCE.
THE THRILL OF FULFILMENT TO THE CALM
STATE OF UTOPIA.
I WILL NOT TRADE FREEDOM FOR A SENTENCE.
NOR MY DIGNITY FOR A HANDOUT.
I WILL NEVER COWER BEFORE AN ENEMY.
NOR WILL I BEND TO ANY THREAT.
IT IS MY HERITAGE TO THINK AND ACT FOR MYSELF.
TO ENJOY THE BENEFITS OF MY CREATIONS WITH
MY FAMILY.
FACE THE WORLD BOLDLY AND SAY,
"THIS I HAVE DONE"

Gaz Lynch

Introduction

Inspiration for any goal comes in many different forms and it has taken a series of meetings and events over the last three years to convince me to put pen to paper. Funnily enough one inspiration for this work is a Military book given to me by a good friend of mine Mick H. The book was written by a former Blade (not Andy Mcnab or Chris Ryan believe it or not), a man I've never met before only heard about. I've always avoided Military books purely because of the bullshit factor, there's a lot to be said for the saying:

"The older I get, the better I was"

That applies heavily to Military books in general but to be fair that applies a little to all of us.

The book I read was from start to finish filled with the brutal honesty of the feelings, emotions and hard decisions that face a British Special Forces Operative and the quite often "Forced" profession that follows. Like the author, how I felt about some of the people mentioned in this book is not necessarily how I feel about them now, I've tried to put across how feelings were running at the time of events. It takes time and a certain maturity and a wealth of experience to understand some people and their ways and a lot of the people mentioned I have met since and put old tensions to rest.

My best friend of twenty years JFK had a baby girl with Downs Syndrome last year. I flew from Southern Africa to the UK and drove to Hereford all within twenty hours to support him and his family. The Downs Syndrome was never an issue but baby had a bad heart and JFK was, for the first time in all the time I've known him, worried and asked if I could be there with him in Hereford.

"What can you do?" I was asked "Why fly literally half way round the earth, just to be in a situation you can do nothing about?"

All I could think to say was:

"If you have to ask, you'll never understand and if the shoe was on the other foot he'd do the same for me."

When I got there, JFK and I spoke candidly as friends can do about his new baby girl, her heart and her Downs Syndrome, the condition, the care, what next, that kind of thing. It was curiosity on my part as I'd never had anything to do with Downs before. As the conversation came to an end and the answers to my questions sank in, JFK said:

"I'm glad this has happened to me and not some 19 year old with nothing, I'm gonna have a baby girl to love me forever and I've got all the means to provide for her for all her days".

The words tugged hard at my heart and I found myself trying to breathe through my eyes as I fought back the tears.

He's a great man, who time and time again has had great influence on the important points in my life.

Another strong influence is my friend Mark Fleet. He is the finest friend any man could wish for. The support I've had and the support my children have had from this man is unprecedented and I can say in all honesty, this man taught me to smile.

Other influences I'm sure will become apparent throughout the book. I've changed names, places and had to leave guys out because everyone has a life after the Army. Some work nine to five, some sell themselves abroad. Some work for themselves on the open market, others the black market. Some work pure organised crime. Whatever the case, all soldiers look for another family, a group to conform to, a group to work for. There is an inherent need for a soldier to belong. All the guys I couldn't contact, I've left out or given different names. I've also done the same out of respect for fallen friends.

My biggest single influence for this work is my wife Angela. Like so many of my kind, I've known evil in its truest form, have witnessed human brutality beyond that of fiction, and injustice that only the western world, the supposed civilised world lets happen. This woman, my wife, has shown me that there is more and that it really is better to be loved than feared. Also, men like us really can find a true sense of family and home.

Within this book I use quotes, with authors if you like. They may seem random, but at the time they were enough to change my way of thinking and with that my actions. Sometimes it worked out well, other times it just fucked my life up but I believe you have to take the rough with the smooth and it's easy to fight, when you believe you're right.

Other big influences for this book, I've known only a few years. I speak about them but only in the latter parts. My only regret is I never met them years ago, but as my wife Angela pointed out

"Would I have been ready for them and would they have been ready for me?"

With that in mind I believe we met at exactly the right time, they are firm and good friends not only to myself but to my family as I hope I am to them.

Not all my inspiration for this book comes from friends. A lot comes from tragic and humorous events, people and factions, along with Governments and Government departments I find hard to stomach. All of which to my mind are guilty of injustice, malice, treachery and other heinous crimes, against myself, my kind and humanity. I'm certainly no bunny hugger but some things are just wrong.

On the subject of rabbits (you'll understand at the end), unlike so many other Military books, I've focused a lot on the good times and not just the dramatic and tragic. Military life is fantastic and full of opportunity. Its true that 80% of a soldier's life is spent training and waiting to do your job, but to think we sit around doing fuck all in that time while we wait, is ignorance. It's in that time your character is built. It's only tested in combat and adversity.

I also believe that character can, if used right, empower a soldier in Civie Street. I made my second million at the age of twenty-nine and put it all down to my character. It wasn't my academic ability that's for sure.

In our chosen profession, it pays to be a "Grey Man", keeping those you know and love in the dark, and feeding strangers and even potential friends, well practiced lies in order to give answers to the most innocent of questions without drawing unwanted attention. We spend our lives in the grey areas of society. We seek no credit and this book serves to give none. I have left out a lot of people and events, some for their protection some for mine, others because they're not very important to me or my life in the grand scale of things.

My life's been a long, violent and challenging journey, full of good and bad situations and decisions, but I feel I have found peace. I have the love, support and responsibility all men search for. My future is clear to me and I aim to use all my experience to keep me and mine safe and well to enjoy it.

Preface

The counter attack was coming in fast, hard and unorganised, as it had been all night. They were more like a barbarian rabble than a Unit from the world's second largest Army. An RPG hit the bedroom next door to my position, flooding the first floor with a smog of dust and heat. A few more bricks fell into the room and the ceiling lost another layer of plaster. The sudden flash and the tremendous noise nearly made me shit myself. This building I was in had taken some extreme punishment during the night, these digs were built to last.

From the hole in the wall that used to be a window, I could see the advancing troops. I counted their numbers as about ten, for our building alone and, for the first time that morning, they weren't all moving like a rugby scrum, huddling together in the vain hope they'd be safe in close numbers. They were learning.

We'd been hitting them hard all night and it had cost them dearly, but true to Russian tactics since the dawn of time, they just threw numbers at us and kept on coming.

With the fact that our supply lines were drying up, I couldn't help feeling that we might not get out this time, and in the same breath thinking "Fuck em". That was my answer to everything when the shit hit the fan, "Fuck em".

I heard heavy, quick footsteps coming up the stairs, one maybe two men. In the next second or two, things would get messy. My ears still were ringing from the blast, my throat was full of dust and my heart felt like it was about to burst out of my chest.

Night was now surrendering to the day. It had been a long night but there was no time to let my guard down. They could see us now, we'd have to change positions shortly. All night we'd expected the big guns, but they never came. It was too much to ask to get that luxury during daylight.

I'd deliberately left the door open, what was left of it anyway. I didn't want to slow their momentum, I wanted to stop it. A closed door would make them gather strength and come in full bore. I wanted them to bottle neck and stumble in, it would even the odds.

I was concentrating so hard on the open door, I almost missed a young Russian conscript entering my observation point, using a wooden ladder he must have brought with him. I cursed myself for missing it. As he stuck his head though the shattered brickwork, I put eight rounds in his head and chest. His helmet might as well have been a flat cap for all the good it did him at that range. He fell lifeless in the opening, dropping his rifle on the floor in front of him. "Good job" I thought, I might need that. His climbing partner close on his tail leapt from the ladder in an act of pure self preservation. It wasn't a particularly high jump but it was onto rubble and hot warped metal. It wasn't going to be an easy landing but it was the right thing to do. He was next.

I turned my attentions back to the open door. The reason for the quick steps on the stairs was now stood in the room, trying to get a clear view through the thick dust cloud. I needed no such sight alignment, I knew exactly where my guys were. I unloaded the remanding rounds from my AK47 into the centre of his body. Not a very disciplined move but my arse was going ten to the dozen, that and I knew I had another two rifles propped up against the wall next to me, all loaded and ready to go. The last intruder kindly left his in the room aswell. My victim fell violently backwards onto the landing, lifelessly lying spread out.

I reloaded. As I did, another inexperienced conscript came rushing in from the room next door. He too must have got in through one of many holes made during the night via a ladder or grappling hook. The booby-traps I'd left around the first floor had been going off all night. I had barely enough time to re-rig the room I was in, let alone renew the other devices in the other first floor rooms. One thing was for sure, I knew he didn't come up the stairs.

He stood in the doorway and froze, like a rabbit in the headlights of a car. Too close to shoot, I swung at him with my rifle, hitting him with my head at the same time. He went crashing back and fell over his dead comrade.

I kicked him in the chest as he tried to sit up, pushing him back, then smashed him repeatedly in the face and throat with the heel of my boot till he went limp, all the time looking for the next target to come rushing onto the landing. I was tired and hadn't eaten in twenty four hours, my reflexes were slowing. I'd managed to avoid hand to hand conflict all night by being quicker; I knew I was going to have pull myself together if I was to keep avoiding it.

I could hear more commotion downstairs. Sean was hard at work with his own arcs. I called out to him, and he called back. He was doing alright.

The counter attack was on the retreat for the fifth or sixth time that night. The support we'd put in place across the street was ruining their offensive. Picking them off on their way in, and doing the same sterling job on their way out. They were being hit so hard and from so many angles they didn't know where it was coming from or who best to attack next but the rising daylight would change that.

I quickly checked round the first floor, hitting every room as if it would be full of Russian troops. My heart still thumping rapidly and hard in my chest and, even though now ten feet away, I could still feel the softness of my enemies throat under my left foot. I felt sick.

I looked out of my west facing OP to see three T-72 tanks forming up on a field at less than a hundred meters away. Sean must have seen the same thing:

"Get out" he screamed.

I needed no second words of command. An RPG was one thing but rounds from a seventy two ton road block was another thing altogether.

The three Soviet made tanks were pointing in our direction and the remaining attacking force was fleeing at a great rate of knots. It was the quickest I'd seen them move all night. I turned and ran straight through the house and, without hesitation, leapt out of an OP on the other side. As I landed, Sean, also running at full pelt out of a door directly underneath my OP, ran straight into me. We hit each other hard but without a second thought or hesitation, we picked ourselves up giggling like two school boys at our collision and continued running, using a well planed and practiced exit route.

Less than two minutes later the small row of three houses and the three houses with our support in, were under heavy tank fire. The tank section blew great holes in the old Chechen houses that had looked after us so well during the night and, in less than fifteen minutes, they were little more than rubble and dust.

There was a hard frost on the ground and mist filled the air in front of me every time I exhaled but I never felt the cold. My blood ran through my body at a hundred miles an hour as it had done all night. As Sean and I ran, the adrenaline subsided and tiredness set in. A short while later my body started to let the extreme cold in. We worked hard that night to hold ground we knew we'd lose in the daylight hours, a tactic we adopted purely to slow the Russian advance, and it was working, but now we were as far out of harm's way as we could be in the bombed, machine gun riddled streets of Grozny. Tiredness and hunger was taking a firm grip. I was physically and mentally spent.

It wasn't the first time I'd engaged the Red Army and it wouldn't be the last in that campaign, but it was the first time I realized how young the average Russian conscript was. A lot of our battles had been, and would continue to be, very close quarter. A lot of hand to hand combat that always got very brutal very quickly.

Having to go from a fairly relaxed state to extreme violence in less than a heart beat takes its own emotional toll and I found a sick comfort in the enemies' youth. Prepped and prepared to fight their best, a less seasoned soldier was easier to outwit and easier to kill and, if that's all they had, I might just survive the winter and see our part in this war out alive.

WHEN EVIL STRIVES TO
OVERCOME GOOD.
WHEN FIREPOWER IS GREATER
THAN THE SPOKEN WORD.
DEATH RIDES A WINGED HORSE.

5's Bar T-shirt

My Pegasus flash from 5 Airborne Brigade

Second Place!
You Mean First Loser

I'm the oldest and smallest of three. My mother is Scottish from the large crime riddled city of Glasgow. It is true what they say about the Jocks. They are tight, with money, with time, with the air in the room, if it were possible and whenever they can, they fight like fuck. Fight anyone and anything and as so many New Years Eves proved, they love to fight each other.

For some reason, we'd travel from wherever we were stationed all the way to Glasgow by train (which was the best bit) to spend a week with my grandparents over the New Year period. Without fail, it was always a shit time for us boys. My folks would go off to the pub leaving us with my Granny who was a demon. The woman hated us kids. She would get pissed up every night on neat whiskey then turn the TV off and bang on at us about any random subject and no matter what it was about, we were to blame. It was a blessing when she finally lost her temper and fucked us off to bed.

The cropper of the whole holiday was always and without doubt New Year's Eve. My brothers and I would be shifted off to bed around 1930. I remember the time because the music for Coronation Street would start and that was always time for bed, even at home. We'd always be awake though mainly because we were all stuck in the same hundred year old double bed, which only led to arguments and us all knocking the shit out of each other. After about 2200, the same would be going on downstairs.

Basically, my other four Aunties would turn up with their respective boyfriends or girlfriends, get snot flying drunk, fall out and bash the life out of each other.

I'd go down in the morning to find my Mum and Grandma still awake drinking and talking and, every time, Grandma had the mother of all black eyes and we'd get fucked off upstairs again and told to come back in an hour. It was without fail, the New Year's routine.

I'm sure there were good times too, the odds tell me that, but for me they were overshadowed greatly by the remarkable level of family violence. Looking back it's no surprise BJ and I found our own lives of violence, what else did we know?

My mother did have a short fuse but, bless her, life wasn't easy with us lot and a husband with no fuse at all, who always put his career before his family. In all, she was a good old girl, our mum, and as kids we always felt loved by her.

Welsh, my father. An RSM in the Army, selected for the Olympics at 17 for gymnastics but broke his back training so that ended that. He boxed and played rugby for his Regiment but his physical and sporting career was over by about 21, leaving nothing more than delusions of a past grandeur that didn't last long enough to really exist. I think that frustrated him all his life. He was pissed off at everything all the time. Generally, he was a large emotionally cold man. No opinion other than his was allowed. Sure he'd listen, but he never really cared what you thought. He just used the time to perfect his next argument, which, if flawed (and it usually was), he'd reinforce and dominate with an I'm bigger and better than you intimidation approach.

He was so fickle with his moods we never knew how to take him and in time we stopped caring. As much as we wanted desperately to know how his day was when we were younger, him being the action man, most of the time we were too afraid to ask. He would always start things with us with good intentions but he would lose interest and his temper in a heart beat and he wouldn't think twice about throwing his weight about. Knowing this made enjoying time with him almost impossible and even when we did get a few moments of acknowledgement, we knew it would end angrily and shortly.

After a twenty year career in Her Majesties Forces, he settled in Scotland in a small village called Kirkcolm just outside Stranrear. He had a good job with the DRA, nice house and a good circle of friends. Then, in 1996 he was found being "Inappropriate" with a very young girl. If it hadn't been for poor police procedure that the judge jumped all over, he was definitely going to prison.

I'd like so say from my mind that he was innocent, but I can't. The man that never ran or backed down from anything. The man whose favourite phrase was

"When you're right you fight"

Turned on his heels, left his house and his job and ran, ran like a COWARD. That to me meant there was more to the whole affair than he was telling me. It put such doubt in my mind that now a father of two girls, I won't let him near them.

* * *

I was about ten and we did a caravan holiday in Wales. A run of the mill campsite with an entertainments hall that everybody would go to at night. We'd go on local walks during the day and when the old man wasn't telling us how grateful we should be to be on holiday, it was a nice time. One night they had a disco. Me and the boys spent a lot of time on the arcade games and not so much dancing. Like all boys that age you want to kill aliens more than you want to bop with your folks. Despite this my mum asked me if I'd dance.

Why oh fuckin why didn't I just say yes and do it. It would have lasted three minutes and saved a ton of shit. Instead, I said no and made up some bullshit excuse about being next on the asteroids game.

My old man was pissed off about it all night and stopped giving us money for the arcade so we ended up sitting with them watching them drink till the end of the evening.

When we got back to the six berth caravan the shit hit the fan in a big way. Once again, the boys and I were in the one room with the double bed and all things being equal the normal happened. We started arguing and fighting the sort of thing that normally led to a quick slap and vain threats of being grounded the next day, followed by lights out.

But not tonight. It was almost as if my old man was waiting for a reason to lash out. He came flying in the door and sent BJ (my brother) who was standing behind it, flying. Mart and I stopped whacking lumps out of each other and got up to help him, he'd taken quite a knock. He had a fuckin great lump on his head, I yelled at my dad to call him a "Bully" but the words "Fat Bastard" slipped out somehow.

With that he hit me, and fuck did he hit me. To this day I've never been hit that hard. My mum was all over him like white on rice. She pulled him back and put herself between him and me. He'd never hit her, he'd never dare. She'd kill him in his sleep. My mum could put up with a world of shit but she had zero tolerance for that. The old man proceeded to call me a

"Useless worm" for not dancing with my mother. Once again I yelled back. This time to point out that he should've danced with her, but somehow the words:

"Fat, idol fuckin twat" slipped out.

As my mum turned to give me a slap she stopped dead in her tracks. The look on her face was one of complete horror and after a pause she said to me:

"Sort the boys out, I'll be back".

She turned again and looked at my father. He stopped dead in his tracks. Whatever look my mother had given him worked a treat. She motioned him outside with a nod of her head and in complete silence he turned. She followed and closed the door.

It was a frightening time and it was difficult settling the boys. They wanted to be anywhere but there, we all did. We were just very scared boys stuck in that caravan and praying the old man was done for the night.

I said to the boys in a whisper: "Let's sleep guys and hope for a better day tomorrow."

As I tucked them in BJ said to me "Are you OK? I never seen him hit you that hard before"

Until that point I'd not given it a second thought but the swelling had come up on both sides of my face from my ears to my chin. We found out later my jaw was all but shattered, broken in three places on one side and two places on the other. I wish even now that that was the last blow of the night but as we all lay in bed the conversation next door got a little louder. We'd already heard my mother say "You ever hit that boy like that again, next time you're away, you'll come back to an empty house. " My old man's reply was something along the lines of

"He's had it coming all week."

The neck breaker came as my mother was pointing out to my dad that if the job he had within his career was going to cause high blood pressure and with that the violent streak, then he might want to find an alternative and that's when he said it:

"I'm sorry Liz, but my career means more to me than my family."

They'd been talking at this point for about half an hour and I prayed the others were asleep but as I looked across BJ started to cry. Poor little bugger had heard it all. I reached over and hugged him. I couldn't think of anything to say. I wish the old man had just burst in the door and hit me again. It would have hurt a lot less than hearing my brother sob himself to sleep like a beaten child.

The old man flat out denied what he'd said years later when I mentioned it on one of the very few occasions I went home on leave but, whilst he was giving a babbling back pedal my mum said'

"I knew that would come back one day."

Once again the old mans opinion was the only one. I didn't chase it. My Mum withered under his dominance yet again and I didn't need the fight, so I let it go. The evening ended and the next day it was as if I'd never posed the question. I should have seen then what a manipulative liar the old man was.

BJ is now 32, can't hold down a regular job, has an obvious steroid abuse problem and is what's commonly know as a bully and a nasty bit of work. He's beaten the mother of his child to within an inch of her life, takes pleasure in bullying smaller guys and wrongfully believes everyone fears him. I pity him and I've often wondered if any of that stems from that night.

I never hated my father even though he was a bit quick with his fists and harsh pointless criticism but after that night I would never respect him, his job, his thoughts or his wishes again.

* * *

For as long as I can remember, according to my old man I was always too old or too late to start something:

"Dad, can I do gymnastics?"

"You're too old to start now son, you need to start at three if you want to be any good."

"Dad, can I start Judo?"

"You're too old now son, my boss's boy started at five, you'll never beat him."

"Dad can I stay after school for rugby training?"

"What's the point son, you've started half way through the term, you're too late they won't want you now"

"Dad can I start motor cross? What about Boy scouts? How about extra maths?"

You can guess the kind of replies I got.

The only thing outside of school I was allowed to do and only if the old man was in the mood to let me, was boxing, and I did. I must admit I loved it from the start but I wanted to do other things too. My brothers could do what they wanted without the old man's interference but he was on my case about everything.

Like so many other things, against his advice I did join the school gymnastics team and made the Hampshire county team in less than a school term. At the final meet of the year I came second in my selection of disciplines, the floor, vault and the rings. We only had to do three disciplines back then. I'm told it's five now for juniors.

When I told the old man he looked at me and said:

"Second place, you mean first loser"

Why bother? I remember thinking and at the same time thought "Fuck him!" I didn't do it for you, you old bastard. I don't know if I did it because I wanted to or because he told me I couldn't, either way I learned right then:

"If you can motivate yourself, you'll always succeed!"

We moved again a few months later and I haven't done gymnastics since.

* * *

So what does a teenage boy do when the things he wants to do are out of bounds? Mischief, that's what. When a teenage boy has no hobby opportunities, no pastimes or short term goals he creates mischief or havoc as it's more commonly known.

My old man being in the Army meant we moved every three years, sometimes every two. We never saw much of him because of his job. He could be away up to six months and that suited us boys fine. What made it better was my mother worked full time and for a few years did nights at an airport. For a little of that period we had a nanny. A fat Scottish bird who was all but useless and I mean useless. She was asleep by 1800 and didn't get up till we'd gone to school. With or without her we were what you'd now call "Latch key kids".

I cooked for the boys after school, made sure the house was clean, put the boys to bed, saw off bullies and calmed parents. Indoors the boys and I fought like cat and dog but when we were outside we always fought together. We never planned anything it just worked that way. If one of us got a slap, a push or a hard time the doors of hades would open and the offender would get a fuckin good hiding and as all of us were accomplished boxers, it really was a good hiding.

My school career boasts seventeen different schools. Even during my all important final two years, we moved twice more.

Moving so often we never got to make firm childhood friends or have a home town, things that are of such importance to young soldiers as I found out later in life.

I was never short of work though. I always had an earner on the go, some way of making money or getting money earned for me. I worked at the local market and the arcade in Aldershot, I worked three paper rounds which I in turn sub-contracted to my brother and two of his mates for a 60% take of course. When I was at school in Germany I had a contact that could get heavy metal patches of groups like Iron Maiden, AC/DC and Scorpion that I'd sell in school for 100% mark up. However, the best biggest money earner I had was when we lived in north London.

We lived on the Sweetsway Estate in Whetstone, around the corner from us was a Greek restaurant and I used to wash the dishes for £3.50 an hour from 1800 till 0130 Friday, Saturday and Sunday. I loved that job. I had to work my arse off but it was for all the food I could eat and £3.50 an hour. In the early eighties that was a shit load, especially for a 14 year old. With that money and money from other little ventures I had going on, I was making enough to support myself, so I made my first attempt to leave home.

The old man was away and when I approached my mother with the idea she instantly tried to call my bluff saying "If you go you can never come back." Unlike BJ and Martin who ran away from home a couple of times over the years, only to be dragged back by the law for stupid things like having no money yet trying to get on a train to anywhere or carrying my old man's kit bag with his machete strapped to the side of it and a list of other comical give aways, I was not bluffing.

I had a plan. I'd found a flat to rent above a corner shop that I could afford. I could pay my bills, eat, work and stay in school for my last year or so to finish off my secondary education. I put a lot of effort in and did a ton of research to leave home for two reasons. The first was to get away from the old man, the second was I knew the only chance I had of a future was to get good exam results, something that wasn't going to happen following my father through his career. However, despite my efforts the old man came home pissed all over my idea and moved us to Northern Ireland.

Not to say he was wrong. I wouldn't let any child of mine leave home at 14 either but at that time it was a lot of shit to take from someone who turned up four or five times a year just to fuck your life over on the notion he wanted to play dad that week and not soldier. The truth was my home and social lives were better when he was off round the world playing Rambo.

* * *

Northern Ireland! It must have seen me coming. I was 15 when we got there. School had all but finished. I had no exam results to show potential employers and the situation out there was one of complete paranoia. We couldn't talk to people in case they were the wrong people. If we did talk we couldn't tell them anything, which is hard to do as a kid if you're trying to make new friends. We couldn't leave the shitty Army estate we were on and with an English accent getting a job was almost impossible. The Irish love to stick together. Even possibilities and potential I would create myself became impossible to execute with my old man tightening the reins at every turn.

Life was boring and bordering on lonely! I had no mates, no job and the boys were at school all day. Life was grim and for the first time in our lives us boys were apart. They were at school and I was bumming around at home. With all this going on the resentment for my father and his career grew daily.

The only thing holding my sanity together was a friend of my old man's, Mr Sharp. He was a bodybuilder and he had a great gym in his garage and better still, he let me use it anytime I wanted.

Mr Sharp was a short Scottish guy built like a brick shit house. He drank coffee like he breathed air and spoke at a hundred miles an hour and to top all that off he was a great guy. He loved the bench press and always said:

"If they could put the world on a bar, I'd lift it."

He was magic. He not only gave me something to do during the long and lonely days but training with him and talking to him about training gave me a new found confidence. As sad as it may seem, he was my first real father figure. On his advice I signed up at the local college and did a year's course that would qualify me to be a personal trainer. He also let me baby sit for his son so I could earn a few bob and he wrote me a glowing reference to go along with my forced Army application.

The training was going great and I could see good personal development from week to week but like all boys that age I craved a social life, a girlfriend, some kind of interaction with other human beings my age. The training was ok during the day. Mornings or afternoons, whenever I decided to go but I still found myself with a lot of down time and with an old man putting up more and more barriers life was becoming very claustrophobic.

I'd gone from a young man of friends and means in North London to a solitary and isolated boy in a very short space of time so when the opportunity to make money and friends came along stealing state of the art high performance motor cycles, I was well up for it.

All us boys could ride. Mart was the best, he was in the kick start finals on the telly. We all did it but could only afford one bike so Mart got it. If myself or BJ banged it, it could mess things up for Mart and he was the best by far. I never had a licence back then but who fuckin cared. The bikes were nicked and we'd be doing 120mph from Larne to a chop shop in Lisburn. If I got caught, not being on the road legally would be the least of my worries, as I would find out 6 months later. But all risk aside it paid well and I made some mates my own age and the rush was unbelievable.

The job was straight forward. I'd get a lift from my new employer, Bones (a guy I met at college) from the college in Lisburn to the docks in Larne. Once there we'd take delivery of anything from two to six bikes then ride them to a chop shop either in Lisburn or Bangor. There were five of us in total. Bones always drove the car and the rest of us shuttled the bikes. If there were any bikes left behind, Bones would do a second run to clear them away. Nothing was ever left on the docks over night. I only ever did one run a day and it was worth fifty quid to me.

All seemed to be going well. My folks thought I was at college all day and who could tell them otherwise. They never came to the college and because I was sixteen now the college were under no obligation to inform them of my movements. The old man had a philosophy that he loved to quote time and time again:

"I don't care what you do outside this house as long as it doesn't come back to my doorstep."

And it was paying dividends. He didn't want to know and as long as it didn't interfere with his career, he didn't care.

Nothing lasts. At the peak of it all I was spending two days a week at college studying the human body and playing sports and three days a week running the stolen bikes earning a few quid. Then one beautiful summers morning a great day for riding a high performance bike it all ended, for me anyway.

As I was pulling out the gate at Larne docks an RUC car with full Military escort stopped me. Reality entered my world with a bang. I was arrested and taken to Larne nick. My father was called in and was there within the hour. He must have really been motoring because it took me that long on the bikes.

When he got there he was cool as a cucumber. He had me out that cell within minutes of his arrival and was quizzing the custody Sergeant as to what was to happen to me next. It should have been obvious but things rarely are to a sixteen year old. The bikes we were moving were part of a larger operation within the Northern Ireland underworld. The authorities wanted me to give evidence in open court in exchange for not charging me with anything and I point blank refused as did the old man. A grass is a grass no matter how old or ignorant you are. If in doubt, keep your mouth shut. That's how life is especially in Ulster. With that they put me on trail.

Thankfully, because of my age they tried me as an individual. It started with a list of charges as long as your arm, but after a fortune in legal litigation (paid for by the old man) the charges were whittled down to "Moving / Receiving Stolen Goods". Any mention of my involvement with Organised Paramilitary Crime or Fundraising was left out due again to my age and the fact the authorities believed I was ignorant of the bigger picture.

One month after my arrest I was in court escorted by the old man who'd not talked about the incident since my arrest other than to say very sternly that I wasn't to talk to anyone, not even my brothers as to what had gone on.

When we got there I was expecting a jury and men with wigs using twenty syllable words I'd never understand. What I got instead was a seat in the Judges chambers and to my jaw dropping surprise the old man and the Judge were on first name terms and seemed to know each other quite well. How?, I never did find out.

The Judge pointed out the seriousness of the charges and my whole involvement, then he lectured me for a good half hour on the bigger picture in Northern Ireland and how my actions could affect my family. It was a no punches pulled reality check. I was so scared I listened to every last word. As the Judge appeared to be rounding up it occurred to me that there had been no mention of any kind of punishment. I optimistically thought "I'm gonna get away with this" but no such luck. The Judge leaned forward onto his desk at the end of his pep talk and said:

"Young man, I'm going to give you a choice, either you go down to the Army Careers Office at Palace Barracks today and find yourself a job (by that, he meant enlist) or we can go into the Court room right now and I can pass sentence based on the evidence at hand. What's it to be?"

Instantly, I thought of enlisting and pulling out a month later. The idea of joining the Army had never crossed my mind. I had other plans and polishing floors, ironing kit and being yelled at all day weren't part of them. BJ on the other hand was mad about it all his life and seemed destined to do nothing else, but it definitely wasn't my cup of tea. Then, as if reading my mind, the Judge said:

"And in case the idea of dropping out half way through enters your mind, be advised, if you don't serve a minimum of three years, I will lock you away for five."

"Where do I sign" I said.

"Your father will drop you off with the recruiting Sergeant today and he will inform me of your progress directly" he said.

And that was that. Two months later I was in Aldershot marching round a parade square. Even though I trained hard with Mr Sharp, who wrote me a blinding reference, I could never tell him how my decision to join the Army came about. I couldn't tell anyone. I don't even think my mother knew the whole story. I knew even then the old man had pulled a lot of strings and asked a lot of favours to get the result we got and he insisted that I kept things to myself. So I did. I found it strange that the old man hadn't been there for me my whole life then he trumped up for this. I found out later it was a career saving move for him to have me out the way. I should have known.

* * *

Overall my childhood wasn't a bad one but only because I chose to take control of it. I'm even sure my folks thought the way they did things was right.

In the Army my father was a proud, respected man and it was always Army first, family second but civie street took its toll on him quickly and with going from "Sir" to "Mate", he found it harder and harder to cope.

In the Army he could get his way because of his rank and the hard work he'd put into a twenty year career but civie street offers no such respect. It took about five years for the old man to turn into a self righteous, power tripping drunk, who'd do anything to get his own way.

My mother, bless her, spent that twenty years following and supporting him, raising us kids and picking up the pieces. She too took to ending each day by drowning it in whiskey. She got so bad that I had to tell the old man she wasn't welcome at my house alone, purely because she got bitter and angry when she drank and became rude and uncontrollable. The old man, embarrassed, agreed to always accompany her. But as usual he took it to the extreme and stopped coming round altogether, which suited me better.

We are not a close family. I have no regrets about not keeping in touch especially with my father him having developed an unwelcome interest in young girls. My adult life, as my childhood seems to go smoother without them in it.

Mart was murdered in Newport South Wales in 1998. His arms and legs were broken and he was thrown into the river Severn on a Saturday night. He was washed up alive the coroner said on the Sunday on the mud banks by an industrial area but with no one at work to hear him cry out, he was stuck fast in the thick, cold, polluted mud for twelve hours. Unable to help himself due to his broken limbs, he was drowned that evening by the tide of the Severn and was found at lunch time on the Monday by a passing factory hand.

BJ, after a failed Royal Marines career became a steroid addict and in turn a narcissistic bully. He takes easily to beating his girlfriends and pushing his weight around on the door of the clubs he bounces at but has never been seen toe to toe with someone of his own stamp. I feel BJ is a true victim of our upbringing.

I've had no significant contact with my family for the past ten years and my life is all the better for it.

A MAN THAT KEEPS ONE EYE ON THE PAST IS
BLIND IN ONE EYE,
A MAN THAT KEEPS TWO EYES ON THE PAST,
IS BLIND IN BOTH

Polish folk proverb

Thanks to good friends, I see clearly in both eyes.

Train Hard, Fight Easy

It seemed that from the day I joined the Army I was learning and constantly training, and on days I didn't train, I learnt. It was a rollercoaster ride of education unlike anything I imagined.

Basic Training was the sharpest learning curve of my life. I'd never had any interest or intention at all in joining the Army and if a Judge hadn't pushed me that way I never would have. To go from hell raising school boy to smart conforming soldier was a short sharp shock to say the least.

The subjects went from Drill and Weapons through First Aid and into NBC (Nuclear biological and Chemical Warfare / Defence). With Map Reading, Survival and Infantry Tactics thrown in, all this to bring you up to a basic level for your new career; SOLDIER.

All subjects at the time required a proficiency pass mark of 85% or thereabouts.

British Airborne Forces is unique in that it has no pass quota. If a Craphat Regiment Training Depot is given a hundred recruits it has a pass quota of about 70%. That means the Instructors, who are usually the best the Unit has to offer have to take the best seventy out of the hundred, even if they're all shite.

Airborne Forces doesn't have that bind, the Instructors can fail a 100% of the class if they don't meet the grade. The British Airborne warrior is the finest soldier in the world. He is not the best of a bad bunch, but rather the best there is.

* * *

P-Company is:
"Arguably the hardest course in the British Army"

To quote the P-Company OC. This course really does separate the men from the boys. Those that want it from those that are not sure and don't. It pushes the individual to his physical and mental walls, then it pushes you through them. Its geared to make sure that when you get the command:

"STAND BY……. GO"

That you are gone, without reservation or hesitation. Both can cost lives. It also confirms your ability to get from A to B on a Battlefield on foot carrying everything you need to go to work, instigate or greet the fire fight, win it then survive the elements.

Tabbing is how we get to work. It's a combination of forced marching and running, quite simply force march up hills and run down them, then share the two speeds on the flatter surfaces with an Airborne shuffle. The first three miles of any Tab are the worst. Your shins burn and the skin comes off your back while your Burgan settles down. After the first ten miles your sweat turns to pure salt and your knees feel like they'll buckle underneath you at any moment. All this is made more adventurous by the freezing rain, mist and eighty mile an hour winds that come free with the lovely views of the Brecon Beacons.

The best comes later in the form of blisters that bleed, a skinless back and tender bleeding lumps on the back of your head where you fell head first and got smacked on the back of your neck by your Burgan that then took another three miles to settle down again.

But you have to ignore all those slight inconveniences keep your head down and your arse up. Stay with the squad and get where you're going. Until you get the hang of Tabbing the real mind fuck was not knowing when it ends. Once you have got the hang of it though you don't care you just keep going.

No matter how hard you are, no matter how many fights you've had in bars or playing fields, the MILLING is guaranteed to make your arse twitch. You don't know who you're going to fight or how its going to go. The only way to sum up the event is to quote the P-Company CSM:

"The object of milling gentlemen is to extract as much blood and snot out of your opponent as physically possible. To do this we give you two things, a pair of boxing gloves and a minute"

That really is all there is to say about it. You put your nineteen twenty's horse hair, eighteen ounce gloves on, then on the word of command "FIGHT", smash the fuck out of the guy in front of you.

The Log Race and the Stretcher Race have the same thing in common. Everything seems to be going faster than you want it to. There's no let up from start to finish and you'll do anything but let your team down, anything to stay on the apparatus. Even if it means getting dragged down hill for thirty feet face down over wet mud and gravel with the log smacking you on the back of the head every inch of the way. If you come off the Log at anytime over the three mile sprint or don't keep up with the Stretcher on the seven mile incline, you Fail.

The Assault Course and the Steeple Chase are individual events that find you digging down to the very soul of your being to find more, guaranteed to get wet and whacked you have to keep going. Nothing less than an absolute 100% will cover the cost of a pass mark. No matter how fit you are, you finish both events blowing out your arse, bumped, bruised, shaking and light headed to a point of passing out and if you swallowed any of the stagnant water in the Steeple Chase a good vomit and case of the shits is a sure thing. The pass mark is total commitment. All four events test both your individual and team participation ability well above the limits you thought you had.

The Trainasium is a sadistic test of coordination and balls and you need them to run across scaffolding five stories high. Even the slightest wind moves the whole structure with the greatest of ease. As if that wasn't enough, the Seesaw, a child's toy at forty feet that has to be taken in no more that two steps at high speed, even boasts a fatality rate. The illusion jump. Don't tell me four feet's not a lot until you've done it forty feet in the air with the plank you need to land on twelve feet below you. From up there it might as well be Cheddar fuckin gorge. The trick is not to think about it, just do it.

If you can do all that in "A smart soldier like and uniform manner" and cope with the Beasting's PT sessions, lessons, bullshit and discipline in between, you might pass.

One thing's for sure, the P-Company staff reveal the man you are inside. Since I passed P-Coy I've felt almost invincible. I believe I can achieve anything, take on any man or challenge and win. I believe in my abilities and training. I believe in myself and there's no stronger adversary than a well trained man that has an unshakable belief in himself.

STAND BY ………..GO

* * *

The Jumps course crowns the Airborne warrior. Four weeks graft at RAF Brize Norton in Oxfordshire. It's a Military culture shock of note. The RAF's on camp life is a lot more comfortable than the Armies that's for sure. Their accommodation was nice and new and the tables were laid in the mess hall. They had nominated parking and someone else did all the Guard duties. But so as to make sure we didn't get too comfortable our accommodation was a row of prefabricated, wriggly tin huts at the end of the camp. We shared the mess hall but that was about it.

The course was as physically demanding as everything else done to date. Before we adopted the "Parachute Position", we were warmed up vigorously for a good half hour and as the days went on the steps we jumped off got gradually higher.

The fan was the first real test of faith, a harness, a bar, a fan to control the descent velocity and a platform twenty metres off the ground. I could have built it in my back yard crude as it was but it worked.

From there onto the Nacker Cracker. A box that simulated a C130. It too was about twenty meters off the floor and the idea was to leap from the box (C130) in your parachute harness which was attached to a steel cable coming away from the make shift plane and slide to the end. This tested your plane exit and your three count as well as your ability to keep your balls on the right side of your harness straps.

On from there you get to earn your first T-shirt with the balloon jump. Its an old WW2 barrage balloon with a five man cage swinging underneath it with room for four jumpers and the dispatcher (PJI). It rises to eight hundred feet over Western on the Green and as you're dispatched one by one you test your new found exit skills, three count and landing drills. As soon as you've done that you can buy the T-shirt from the PRI that says "JUMP BALLOON" across the front.

Then the real thing. A static line jump from the side doors of a C130 Hercules aircraft. To pass the course you must complete eight jumps. In that eight at least one must be at night and at least one with equipment. This is very important because when you get back to Battalion they're mainly all at night in full kit.

The pass out parade was a simple affair. We lined up and the PJI's handed out the prize. The coveted Wings, The Blue Badge of courage. The badge that defines the act that sets us apart from others in our field.

My first set of issued wings

TIGHT IS RIGHT, LOOSE IS NO USE

PJI Woodward

* * *

Infantry Tactics is our bread and butter. It's always challenging and constant hard work and pulls men together unlike any other discipline. It's our attention to detail and the constant dedication to the subject that keeps us alive and together as a fighting force in a time of conflict.

Trying to hold a straight line during a Company attack on the wet cold slopes of Senibridge or Otterburn is not the easiest thing to do for the tenth time in one day. Exercising pair's fire manouver and section attacks is knackering and serious work but the thrill of fulfilment is its own reward even in the harshest of environments.

Infantry tactics from individual skills to Platoon to Brigade is the very core of what we're about.

We trained hard, to fight easy.

Unfortunately the instruction of infantry tactics is open to massive abuse outside of Her Majesties Forces. I took a job in Ghana in West Africa working for their Government, teaching the subject. After a long hot journey to a training camp on the shores of lake Volta I was presented with my class. Out of the fifty men I had to instruct twenty three of them were no older than ten years of age. I pointed this out to the Camp Commander who thanked me for bringing it to his attention, then said he'd sort the matter out. I slept easy that night knowing that my concerns had been addressed.
The next morning I was taken to my class room to start the instruction of section attacks only to find it was outside. The walls of the classroom were no more than single logs on the ground and on the outside of those logs sat the very children that were the cause of my concerns.

I left the class sat in the coolness of the morning and went to find the camp CO. When I found him, I explained what I thought was the problem. He was quick to dismiss me with the explanation that these younger warriors were not "IN" the class and I should only be concerned with who was in the class and not with who was listening.
I was pissed off at this mans contempt for my case and for the youth of his country but not surprised after the events of Somalia and Rwanda.
The continent of Africa is constantly plundered by the rest of the world and its tribes kept at war all for the good of the Green Back. It's a sad fact that we get involved in the training which ultimately leads to the genocide and the atrocities that blacken Africa on an hourly basis. But as a soldier I couldn't get work in my own country so I did what so many of us had done before. I found a war and joined the side that paid the best. I didn't know whether to be proud

that I could find work or be ashamed of my part in the big picture, but I had bills to pay so the Green Back won.

* * *

No matter how hard we trained or how meticulously we drilled, there was always room for accidents.

On an exercise in France we laid out an ambush for our French counterparts who were playing enemy for us. We'd been laying in wait all night when all of a sudden a loud bang broke the silence. Billy had accidenlty struck a thunder flash. He tried to get the fuse out but ran out of time. Then as he threw the ordinance away it went off just as it left his hand.

I saw him the next day in the first aid post. His eyes were wrapped up, he had no skin on his nose and his hand was quite badly burned. He just laughed it off. Apparently, he couldn't get a good enough grip on the fuse with his fingers, so tried to bite it out. Billy is one of life's stronger characters.

On another tour in France, we played enemy for an intake of Officer Recruits from Sandhurst. Our job was to defend a small village while they attacked it. Myself and two others hid in an old hay loft. The Officers cadets tried hard to take our position but everytime they stuck their heads through the door, which was a good eight feet off the ground, I just kicked them back out and shot them. On their fourth assault on the same door, I misjudged my kick and instead of hitting the potential Rodney on the shoulder and pushing him out, I hit him on the helmet and tipped his head back, I dropped my rifle down to take the shot and he was still there. The BFA (Blank firing attatchment) rested on his nose and I pulled the trigger. He fell back to the ground in no end of pain. When the attack of the village was over I stuck my head over the edge and he was still on the floor holding his eyes,

"You alright mate?" I said.

He replied "Did you know the safety distance of a BFA is a hundred meters? And it's Sir to you".

I had no reply. He was right on both counts.

* * *

Fighting and Defence in built up areas, or FIBUA and DIBUA is a breeding ground for accidents and learning the hard way. Guys fall off roofs walls and window ledges, get stuck in sewers and chimneys and are left hanging upside down when an absail goes wrong and for all the practice we do, they do still go wrong. Guys get burnt by smoke grenades punctured by grappling hooks and are left 100% deaf for days by the intense noise from the pyrotechnics. Assaulting a building, train carriage or aircraft from multiple points of entry is aggressive, loud and fast. Keeping constant momentum and communication is key and personal fitness is massively important, but when the attack comes together, it's hard on material.

On Salisbury plain in the South of England the Army has a purpose built FIBUA Village called Cope Hill Down. It's designed around old European villages. On a big Brigade Exercise I was asked to take a pallet of rations to the village from the BMA. A Gurkha Regiment was held up there waiting to be tasked. I landed the job because I was the only guy available who could drive an ATMP, a six wheeled overlander that the Logistic Battalion had been trailing for a while. It was a good half hour drive across the plain and I had to take an Ordinance guy with me, but that guy turned out to be a splitarse (a woman). All the way there she bitched and winged "Slow down, are we there yet? Are you sure you know where you're going?"

It was endless, it wasn't even a long journey but She just wouldn't shut up. We didn't work with women so this was a bit of a first for me and a last I hoped.

When we got there, she shot off to find her counterpart and hand the rations over. While she was running around the treefrogs (Gurkhas) unloaded the ATMP. I was stood watching when a Gurka private asked me if the splitarse that I was with was my woman, all the time pointing at her. I said she was but he could have her for twenty quid.

Obvious, to me anyway, I was joking.

The Gurkha shot off and came back a few moments later with three five pound notes and some change. His guys had had a whip round for the split.

I don't know why, I just did. With the ATMP empty and the split nowhere to be seen, I drove off.

When I got back to the BMA (Brigade Maintenance Area) all hell had broken loose. The SSM called me in and asked:

"What the fuck have you done? I've got four Gurkhas claming ownership of Cpl Atkins (the split) and her Boss screaming sexual harassment"

He then ordered me to go back to the village and sort the mess out. I got back to the village in about forty minutes. I was having a great time tearing around the plains in the ATMP.

When I did get there though the split was foaming at the mouth. I'd never seen anyone that mad before and she was going for it. Ranting on about me prostituting her and how I was a Para low life, blah blah blah. The list of insults was long, but nothing new.

I must admit I wasn't really listening. I was too busy trying to negotiate her cheap return. I had to buy her back from the Gurkhas I sold her to, but they wanted fifty quid for her and if I thought she was pissed off before, you should have seen her after I asked to borrow the money from her. The only money I had was the score I charged them for her. With a bit of help from their Platoon Commander and a new negotiated rate of forty quid, I got her back.

The earache on the way back to the BMA was not worth the prank. Her level of moaning went up ten fold, so did the volume. Her pitch got so high at one point only dogs and small deer could hear her.

When we got back to the BMA I was called in by her SSM who warned me of the seriousness of what I'd done, then asked why I did it. What was I to say, I didn't know why. I just thought it'd be funny. The only reason I had for leaving her there was:

"It seemed like the thing to do at the time Sir"

The SSM just smiled at me and told me to fuck off back to my Unit while he cleaned up my mess.

On another occasion a farmer in Senibridge gave our Unit permission to use an empty house he was building to practice attacking a house at night. There was nothing in it, it was just walls, roof and windows. One of the conditions of use was that we didn't use Chorley grenades or thunder flashes, as the farmer had only just had new windows put in. The idea was he would leave all the windows open and we could enter through them if we chose, but whoever gave the attack brief forgot to mention that.

An open window is a bottle neck and a possible ambush point and entering a room without first throwing some kind of pyrotechnic in was all but unheard of. We weren't some poncy SIS, slowly slowly catchy monkey Unit, we were Airborne Forces. So without the "No Go" brief, we hit that building as we would any other building in battle. With everything we had.

By the time we'd finished there wasn't a single window or window frame left anywhere in the building. I don't know who got the bill or the shit but it wasn't us.

* * *

Great Britain has some of the most diverse training areas in the world. The Brecon Beacons has the wonderful ability to give all four seasons in twenty four hours. I've patrolled in the snow there and got back to the harbour area and had to sleep in my shorts.

The training areas in Scotland house some of the largest mosquitoes found anywhere in the world and although they don't pass on diseases, on more than one occasion guys have been CasEvac'd due to the massive swelling a bite gives round the eyes.

Otterburn, on the Scottish English boarder guarantees to soak you to the bone as soon as you get there and keep you that way until you leave and the Salisbury plain gives that constant paranoia that you'll be hit by a tank anytime now, and that's just to name favourites.

Even though Britain doesn't have big game to contend with as they do on the Kenyan ranges, anyone who'd accidentally knocked down a new dry stone wall with the farmer watching, would argue if we needed it.

As distinct as each training area is they all have two things in common. They'll all get you really wet and really cold and you can get lost on any of them. It takes a lot of practice to stay dry, warm and on track but there is never any shortage of practice.

Each training area is used to enhance different skills, be it fighting patrols, ambush, recci patrols, Fib and Dib or defensive exercises and each one can cater for a Brigade, Regimental, Company or Platoon. Long before my career took me abroad I was confident in warfare on all terrains thanks to the training areas Britain has to offer. Even after leaving the British Army I used these areas to assess and build teams to work for my Company Olivebranch, on the private military circuit. A lot of the time I didn't have to weed out the ones that really didn't want the work a simple Fan Dance and the terrain would do it for me.

* * *

A four man Fire Trench comes in different forms. The two most popular are a box U shape and an L shape. The Box U shape breaks down into three parts; two sleeping bays and a main fire trench. The L shape breaks down into; one fire trench and one sleeping bay.

On a defensive exercise in Senibridge South Wales, I shared a trench with a giant of a man Steve L. He was an Army boxing champion and an Army Judo champion and weighed in at at least seventeen stone. He was a good guy Steve but he was definitely in charge and he liked me to know it.

From our trench I could see the Welsh mountainside for miles. I could also see the guys in the trench on my left flank and just about make out the trench on the right. Bob, one of the guys in the trench on my left and I had a bit of a game going on. Basically, every time

I needed a shit, I'd pinch it off on my digging tool (a short spade), then I'd catapult it as close as I could to his trench. Bob in turn would do the same. It's gross and unprofessional but at seventeen it quelled the monotony of trench life.

After a while the game like our metabolisms slowed down thanks to good compo rations. But on the third day Steve was off getting orders for the next twenty four hours and I was left alone as the other two in our trench were picked for some other random daily task.

I used my alone time to take my first dump in three days. As per the rules of the game I shit on my digging tool then stood at the far end of the fire trench and spotting Bob who also stood alone launched proudly my giant stool sample.

It must be the compo because this hadn't happened before. The solid mass that had been clogging my bowel for the past three days stuck to the shovel a little longer than usual and instead of flying through the air towards Bob it shot into the hood of Steve's sleeping bag which was laid out in the sleeping trench in front of me.

The irony was we built those trenches to withstand a major Artillery offensive and yet, Steve's sleeping area hadn't survived an adolescent shit flinging game.

Irony aside, now I had the problem of cleaning it up. I had a bit of time but not loads so I got to work straight away.

Cleaning fresh shit off green nylon is not as easy as you'd think. It doesn't wipe off, it smears on. I needed more time so I swapped Steve's doss bag for mine in the hope he wouldn't notice. They were identical in every way. Almost every way.

Steve came back and I told him I was going to clean my rifle and get my head down. He had no problem with that so I folded myself into the other sleeping bay and proceeded to try once again to clean the hood of Steve's maggot. After a good hour I managed to get it back to a state I would return it in. Unfortunately for me the opportunity to return it never came. I needed Steve to leave the trench to return his wank sack, but he never did. No real problem I thought, I'd just return it the following day. He'd been lying on my doss bag all afternoon and not noticed any difference. But there was a difference and he noticed it that night when he tried to get in it. The bags were standard Army issue identical in every way, except one. SIZE.

Steve was a fuckin giant and I was ten stone wet. Steve came out off his sleeping bay with my tactically replaced doss bag on one leg.

"Who's the fuckin joker" he said, with half a smile.

Now here was a short lived conundrum. Did I own up to the practical joke and ride that wave? Or did I own up to flicking shit into the big guy's sleeping bag? No contest.

"Me Steve, thought it'd be good for the laugh" I said and braced for the outcome.

After the lads had a laugh at the comical sight of the big man using my maggot as a sock, we swapped bags and Steve went to bed none the wiser.

The next day Steve and I were alone in the trench looking out over our arcs. Without even looking at me, Steve said in a cool, calm, almost friendly voice:

"Next time you've got shit on your shoes, don't walk on my doss bag".

I was stunned, I was expecting a good left hook at least.

"I'm sorry," I said sheepishly "I did my best to clean it up"

"Don't worry about it" he said "When we live like this things like that do happen, now make us a brew and we'll forget it eh."

We drank the tea in the cool of the morning air and as the real reason and Steve's concept of events were both pure accident I chose not to say what had really happened.

* * *

As a military career progresses a soldier is required to study other subjects such as languages and methods of instruction, man management and then move on to instruction itself.

The study of enemy transport. (AFV Recognition) was a favourite of mine as it becomes to many Snipers and Anti Tank Specialists. I always enjoyed the Chemical element of NBC training and the practical side of First Aid and everyone had a hard on for a day on the ranges.

Quality training and the repetition of that training is vital for keeping a soldier and his Section alive. Britain breeds the finest soldiers in the world and does so due to that very concept.

The opportunities the Army gave me were endless and for every one I missed I took full advantage of ten others. My Military career only really started after I left British Airborne Forces but the training and its quality has kept me alive for the last fifteen years.

For all the aspects of my life that take any form of discipline and training I hold true some wise words from, RSM Col Chapman:

"Practice, does not make perfect. Perfect practice makes perfect"

Airborne Ethos

AIRBORNE ETHOS IS A STATE OF MIND

IT IS THE AIRBORNE WARRIORS
UNSHAKEABLE BELIEF IN HIS UNIT AND
HIS OWN ABILITY TO STRIVE FORWARD
AND OVERCOME ALL OBSTACLES.

IT IS A SENSE OF FAMILY AND BELONGING
OUTSIDE THE BLOODLINE.
FOUND UNDER OFFENSIVE ATTRITION

IT IS THE RIGHT TO STAND FIRM IN THE FACE OF
ADVERSITY AND FIGHT FOR WHAT YOU BELIEVE IN

IT IS THE PHYSICAL AND MENTAL AGILITY TO
PUT A FRIENDS NEEDS BEFORE YOUR OWN

IT IS THE MINDSET TO SEE A GOAL AND ACHIEVE IT.

IT IS THE NEED TO STAND ALONE
AND OVERCOME GREAT ODDS

IT IS THE CAPABILITY TO DEFEND YOUR FAMILY

IT IS THE ABILITY TO LIVE YOUR LIFE

AIRBORNE

It's Character Building

It's a fact, any time served with British Airborne Forces builds character. "Character building" is the ultimate answer to all a soldier's questions and when there's no one to answer questions, it's the quickest way to boost moral:

"Why are we digging this hole in the freezing December rain?"
"It's character building"
"Why is the DZ always full of rocks and wet mud?"
"It's character building"
"Why are we Tabbing through the night in thick fog?"
"It's character building"

And for the latter:
"Why do I put myself through this?" and:
"What the Fuck am I doing here?" Yes it's all Character building and for as long as there's a reason, you don't mind going though it, whatever it is. I once heard a new lad answer back with:
"When will I have enough character Corporal?"
Phil, a full screw of more tours and wars than half the Battalion replied:
"You can never have enough character."

A smart insightful answer. Is it possible to have enough character? Is there a time to stop testing yourself? Can anyone ever say, I'm good enough? I've done enough! For the Airborne warrior the answer is, No. Life and combat can throw what it likes at a British paratrooper and no matter how hard or how lost he gets he'll put it all down to character building and keep going. It's the Airborne way.

That's not to say that the concept is not open to a bit of harmless abuse, usually for the greater good. When I first got to Battalion it was a Monday and I was only seventeen so not allowed out on the piss. I was allowed to have a pint in the NAAFI but I was a bit shy at the time so chose to stay in the block. The lads would come back around 1100 all pissed up obviously and they'd wake me and get me to sit with them while they had a night cap.

Andy M drank gin, he was also our room senior. He'd fill my black Army issue one pint mug with gin and I could leave the party when I'd finished it. I wasn't allowed to join in with the conversation. I just had to sit, listen, laugh and finish my gin. Andy was an animal, he could drink all night and still run ten miles every morning with the Unit cross country team. I asked him one morning why I had to drink the gin. His answer was a straight and simple one:

"It's character building" he said.

This happened every night. It was a great way to get to know the guys. Every night was hilarious. They joked about life and pranked each other endlessly. Then the weekend came. The lads came back on the Friday night later than usual, about 0100, and as per the rest of the week, they woke me up, only this time with a mission. Lee P the guy that woke me up said:

"Right young un, go and get chips for everyone"

"Yes Corporal" I replied.

I didn't have to ask where from, Tony's was the only place open. He only opened at nine on weekends and didn't close till four in the morning but as I went to get dressed, Lee said:

"What you doing?"

"Getting dressed Corporal" I replied.

"No you're not" he said "Go down like that."

I was stood with my boxers on having just got out of bed. It didn't even occur to me to argue the point. I just took off down the town, I didn't even have my shoes on.

When I got to the door of Tony's chip shop the queue was long and drunk. Tony had a big grin on his face,

"Hello my mate" he said in his Mediterranean accent. "How many bag o chip you want?"

He called me to the front of the queue.

"Ten please Tony" I said.

I was shitting myself. I hadn't really looked into the queue I'd just jumped and I could hear girls giggling. I was getting embarrassed and was about to run out when someone in the queue shouted out:

"It's character building mate"

I looked up to see who it was. I didn't recognise him. He was wearing a Support Company T-shirt, but as I looked up into the queue every man in it was just smiling. Then a man two or three down from me said with a laugh:

"We've all done it son."

I didn't know him either. He had a C Company T-shirt on. As I looked up the rest of the queue all the men were nodding in agreement.

"Yer, they made me walk round town naked strapped to a blow up sheep" another man said. With that the place erupted with laughter. After that I didn't care about the women laughing. My embarrassment was replaced by a new emotion, a new feeling, I felt like part of a team.

Tony agreed to let me pay later and I ran back to the block. The back gate guard had seen me go out and didn't ask for ID. They treated it like an every day occurrence.

Back in the block I joined the guys and handed out the bags of chips then took my usual position next to Andy with my black mug.

"Where's your chips?" asked Phil

"I didn't get for me" I said gingerly.

With that they all put some chips in my empty mug. I felt proud.

"Right, sit shut up and eat them" Phil said.

I said nothing I just sat and ate and enjoyed the night. No sooner had my chips finished and Andy filled my greasy mug with Gin as usual.

On the Saturday the lads stayed in and we partied in the block doing Character Building exercises. They made an arena and I had to fight other new lads from other Sections. I say fight but it was really just king of the ring, wrestling followed by drinking games and all four of us new lads being sent out once again in our underwear for chips. It was a great first weekend at Battalion. The next day I was sick as a dog but the guys left me to sleep it off.

The evenings of the following week were the same apart from now when I sat with the guys, they would on occasion ask me questions. It started with things like. Did I have any loose sisters? Did my mum put out? and was I a virgin? Those and all other manner of response orientated questions. Then they went on to more normal enquiries like; Where did I come from? Why choose Airborne Forces? and do you want a fight? I still wasn't allowed to talk freely but I enjoyed it as small as it was. It was good to be in a part of the conversation.

Every anecdote told by the lads had one thing in common. At some point the power of resourcefulness and improvisation came into it. No matter what the problem, if you couldn't fix it you got round it, but things had to move forward. These men were respected on that basis. I aspired to them and for the first time since Stu in Northern Ireland I respected someone enough to want to learn from them.

After a week of this and a new found ever growing confidence and with the weekend upon us, I made a plan. On the Friday night before I went to sleep I put a pair of trainers and a track suit in a tesco shopping bag and put it outside my window then went to bed. The idea being, that when I was woken for the weekend mission, I would go down the town for chips dressed. Then when I came back the lads would ask where the clothes came from and I would tell them, hoping for points for resourcefulness.

Unbeknown to me the guys had gone to another block that night for a party, which let me sleep. That would have been great but at 0200 that morning the Guard found my parcel next to the block and called a full Garrison Bomb alert. In short time the whole Brigade was called out. Picture it! two in the morning, freezing their arses off and forming up on the Drill Square.

I stood on the square in my boxers because I couldn't find my track suit. There were women, girl friends and Aldershot dogs. Some stood in knickers and bra at best and guys stood in nothing more than towels. These scenes went on for nearly four hundred men. We all had three things in common. We all lived on the same Barracks, we were all Airborne, and we were all very cold, pissed and pissed off.

EOD was called in to "Inspect and Dispose" of the suspect package and after an hour and half of freezing our bollocks off an EOD operative walked up to the Brigade Orderly Officer with a small bag. The BOO looked through the carrier bag and pulled out a track suit top. He looked into the collar then shouted out a last four and a name. It was mine.
I stepped forward to claim my property. I was not popular to say the least.
The Brigade was dismissed and I was called in to answer questions after which I was sent back to the block.

The next morning the guys I'd been drinking with for the last two weeks had a meeting and to no great surprise, I was invited.
"What the fuck were you playing at?" was the first question. I told the guys my intention and my plan as I'd done earlier that night to the RSM, the SSM, the OC, the CO, the RMP, the EOD and a whole host of other abbreviations not to mention the civie police. Once I'd told them my plan they all calmed down and the likelihood of me having my head kicked in went away. Then Andy said:
"Know next time your actions left us cold and wet for a long time"
"It's Character building" I replied and in the same breath learned the hard way that the Character building concept like shit, only rolls downhill. I sponsored a black eye for the next week with no hard feelings. Phil, my Section Commander loved my ingenuity.
"I see hard times ahead with you" he said with a smile.

* * *

Every now and again things go better for the participant of a character building exercise than one might expect. One Saturday afternoon Lee and Phil called all the new lads into the corridor then sent them away with orders to be back in the corridor within five minutes dressed in full Combat Batman suit.

The Combat Batman suit consist of your Respirator (Gas Mask), Poncho, (for the cape), Webbing belt (For utility belt), small mess tin at the front to cover your balls and large mess tin at the back to cover your arse and of course your boots.

Once back in the corridor they were made to run out the Block, over the road (Queens Avenue,) passed the Gym, across the green. By this time they'd run about a kilometre and then the good bit, they had to run ten times round the female accommodation singing the Batman theme tune.

At that time I'd been in long enough to be excused such exercises but not long enough to instigate them but it was great to watch.

From our windows in the block we could see everything. After a good ten minutes laughing at the expense of our new intake, Billy pointed out one of the lads climbing into an open window of the female block.

"Does he know it's an instant twenty eight days in the nick for being caught in there?" I said,

"Find out a month from now won't we" Phil said,

The guys arrived back a short time later one man down. None of them could explain what went on. Thinking nothing more of it we all got ready and went down town on the piss. A few hours later, Nobby our AWOL Batman turned up in the Traf.

"What happened to you? Lee said.

Nobby went on to explain that one of the Splitarse's took pity on him and invited him into her room. When he refused she pointed out that she was a higher rank than him. With that he did as he was told and took full advantage of the situation letting the split sympathy fuck him for the rest of the afternoon.

It was a great turnaround of the event and a talking point for the rest of the day on the piss.

The next day Phil and Lee didn't turn up for breakfast. They joined us later in the 5's for cabbage rugby. I asked Phil what he'd been up to.

"Lee and I were arrested last night" he said "and only let out this morning."

"What for?" I asked.

"Running round the female block in Batman order" he replied.

* * *

The time and effort taken by your peers to develop your character in the Army should not be taken lightly. The difference between bullying and building a man's character through miscellaneous tasks is the intention. An outsider will almost certainly always view the task as bullying and abuse as will the man that refuses, fails or cannot rise to the task and if the intention is to single out and humiliate the individual then they'd be right. But 90% of the time the intention is to build the wall of a mans inner strength, to give him tolerance and teach him not to take life too seriously and that life does not revolve around one individual.

It is not always academic education or money that carries a man through his life but rather his individual character and like anything worth having and keeping that's built from a solid foundation.

IMPROVISE, ADAPT AND OVERCOME

Clint Eastwood

The Leading Parachute Battle Group

An LPBG's objective is to put the sharp end of 5 Airborne Brigade, the Teeth Arms of the British Army on the ground behind enemy Lines in the smallest space possible and in full fighting order. The phrase non-combatant is never used in the Brigade. "Every man fights".

We are selected on the basis that we can and will. If you've got a trade or a skill outside of Infantry man it can wait. When the Brigades on the ground and the shit hits the fan, when all you have for support is the kit you've got and the man, the colleague, the friend at your side:

>   We stand   We fight.

* * *

We ruck up at the UK's Form Up Point (FUP) in South Cerney just outside Gloucester. Over the next few hours the whole Brigades Leading Parachute Battle Group will arrive. Then we'll sit for a jump and mission brief. The "Green Light Warning Order" will also be given, then we'll wait for the jump window to open. Full alert for three days plus. At any second in that time we'll be called forward and onto the busses to make the short trip to RAF Lynham. From there we'll DFC and the jump will be imminent. We'll land somewhere round the world, none of us knows where, none of us knows when, but we'll go with a single purpose, COMBAT.

The LPBG arrives in full. We parade on the unused airstrip on the Barracks and the CO gives us a brief on his personal expectations. It's a magnificent sight, the whole Brigade from the Pathfinder Platoon the 1st Battalion Parachute Regiment the Logistic Battalion, 216 signals, 9 Sqn Royal Engineers and 23 Parachute Field Ambulance, fifteen hundred men armed, prepped, fully equipped and ready to engage an enemy force anywhere on the planet.

Eight hours into the jump window the Pathfinder platoon is called forward. They're a quiet lot, keep themselves to themselves. Even though a breeding ground for the SAS some would confidently argue they exceed the skills of their Hereford counterparts in the infantry field.

All details are "Top Secret", not even they know where they're going yet. They'll go in HALO, from thirty two thousand feet using oxygen to breath. They'll descend with confident stealth and the enemy won't even know they are there.

Once they've landed it'll be their job to be the eyes and ears for the Brigade Commanders, the men that will play with our lives from thousands of miles away. Then they'll mark and secure the DZ and then as they hear the distinct sound of a Squadron of Hercules aircraft they'll light it up just before H Hour. Then they'll slip back into stealth mode and using militia tactics to assassinate the infrastructure of our enemies country with our Allies.

The call is given, its 1400 hours. After a short bus trip we arrive at RAF Lynham. As well as the 105lbs of my own gear, I've been given two Greenies (mortar bombs) and a thousand rounds of Link to drop off with Support Company on the DZ, I can only hope they're not too far from where I land. My mate sits on my container as I pull the securing straps tight to a point of snapping. My 120lb container now looks like something from a bondage mail order catalogue. Returning the favour for my mukka we recall the words of our first PJI, Sgt Woodward:

"Tight is right, Loose is no use".

Parachute fits, reserve fits, boots fit, container bracingly heavy.
I love this job there's nowhere else I'd rather be and nothing else I'd rather be doing.

I run a last minute kit check in my head, not that it matters if I'm not carrying it now then I can't have it.

We load onto the C130's, sim 45's. Ninety men per plane and a two ton wedge ready to slide off the back, I'm number eighteen on the starboard stick. With all the planes in the air and there still being a little daylight left I can see a line of six Hercules behind us.

This is what it is to be Airborne. This is what it is to make that grade.

We're packed in like commuters on a London tube train, we're flying low level over the sea and it's like being on a fuckin roller coaster. My mate next to me throws up when I offer him a sandwich I proff'd from the Mess, poor bastard he's always found the turbulence a bit rough. In the best traditions of Airborne sympathy, we laugh at him, some doing so trying hard not to join him.

We're in the air for nine hours when the order comes to:

"STAND UP-----FIT EQUIPMENT"

It's dark outside, another night jump, my favourite. Must keep my wits about me on the ground.

We remain standing for the next forty minutes then the dispatchers open the doors put the foot plates out and close the doors half way. A rush of cold air swirls around the aircraft, it's not till that point you realize how hot and stuffy the C130 can get. We're all stood now, each man doing his best not to lean on the guy in front. It's all about carrying your own weight.

Half an hour later we get the command:

"ACTION STATIONS"

The door is opened and we are called forward and the count begins. Forty five OK forty four OK forty three OK, all the way past me at eighteen and down to the first man who yells at the top of his voice: "starboard stick OK"

The first man is bought to the door and the Red Light comes on, we wait, braced and gripping our containers.

RED ON--------GREEN ON-----------GO.

The first man goes and with no gap between us we step down the plane, the port stick jumping at half second intervals to us. I get to the door and thrust myself out into the hundred and twenty knot slip stream and the blackness of the night, my chute deploys as it does a trooper from the port stick shoots straight though my rigging lines, it's a fuckin miracle he didn't get caught up in them. No time for praying or cursing, got a job to do.

As my chute settles I smack into the guy next to me, we both try and steer away from each other but there are troopers covering every inch of free air space so I settle where I am, happy that my chute's open.

As I descend I can see the next wave coming in to my front, they're not a threat as long as all their parachutes open, I'll be on the ground before they get to where I am. I release my container and wait for the ball breaking jerk as it yanks off the bottom of the fifteen foot drop cord. Then I brace myself for the landing, its pitch black I can't see the ground to get the rush, but its coming that's for sure.

"FEET AND KNEES TIGHT TOGETHER AND TAKE THE LANDING AS IT COMES"

That's the advice given at RAF Brize Norton on the jumps course and that's pretty much all you can do. I pull myself in tight trying hard not to hold my breath and wait.
Then it comes,
"Thud,"
It's the only way I can describe it, I land with no finesse whatsoever, all the rolling techniques taught at Brize yet I always land like a five hundred pound bomb that didn't go off. But I don't care, I'm down and I can walk. I collapse my chute and start to gather it in.

For less than half a second my mate took his eyes off the sky and got side swiped by a container still attached to a descending trooper, it sent him flying sideways across the DZ, as amusing as it was I run to help him up.

I watch the planes flight path to get my bearings on the DZ, I have to find Support Company before I can join my own guys. The moonlit DZ is well organised pandemonium, the sky is a falling ocean of dark canopies and every inch of the ground is moving in a different direction.

I find a grateful Support Company getting themselves together on the port side of the DZ. They've pulled themselves just inside the tree line which will give them good cover if they're still here at dawn.

I hear a loud crashing sound coming from a clearing on the other side of the woods no more than fifty feet away, it's the heavy drops, the Landrovers, light artillery, trailers, ATMP's, eager beavers and other logistical kit needed to feed the inevitable fire fight. It can't be easy for the guys that have to maintain and drive that shit. Is there an insurance company in the world that would insure a vehicle that had just been thrown out of an aircraft in the middle of the night and landed on its side on a marshland DZ? Probably not.

I find my way to my Company and once all together we start to make ground. Apart from the fact we get to work via a plane that doesn't have to land the thing that sets us apart from the Hats, is our ability to cover any ground on foot carrying all we need.

It's a long night and an equally long day. We march for just over ten hours stopping briefly every two for water. My burgan stopped being heavy five hours ago, about the same time my feet stopped hurting and my back stopped aching. I've been like an android since. I'm aware of everything except my own discomfort, I'm not even hungry anymore, chocolate and boiled sweets have kept me going since I ate the sandwich my mate didn't want.

My mate, I hope he's ok, he must be fuckin starving and more dehydrated than me with all that throwing up, I know he'll be ok though, he's a warrior.

We arrive late afternoon at the location we'll call home for the foreseeable future. We set up a harbour area and wait for further orders. A heavy frost sets in as the night falls. After two hours: "Stood to"
in silence, each section is given its arcs of fire and told to dig.

We dig four and six man fire trenches. The ground is full of slate and the going is slow but we dig, we dig all night. One man makes his scran and the others dig, when he's eaten and changed his socks we swap, no one takes the piss there's a job to do. If the shit hits the fan now the only cover we'll have is what we're digging now. Best to get it dug.

Just before dawn we climb into whatever we've dug and "Stand To" again.

We wait. I've not slept now for nearly thirty eight hours, I've only had one meal in that time and a shit load of tea, coffee and chlorine treated water, I'm tired. It's silent and dark, I watch my arcs and pull myself back into line, pushing the tiredness and fatigue to one side using my place for the safety of my Unit as incentive.

Once we're stood down the digging continues, over the next day or so we'll make this place a home away from home as we have done so many times before. With the LPBG now in play and all dug in, with the logistical lines open and the comm's lines set up, we can get to work. We came to fight, if the fight won't come to us, we'll go and find it.

Selected Sections leave the safety of the entrenched positions at night on fighting patrols. "Search and Destroy" is no longer politically correct, they replaced that mission objective with "Search and Assess". But a fighting patrols job remains the same whatever you call it. Even if you called it a Military Swan Lake, that wouldn't stop people being discovered and dispatched or sought out and killed. It's a great way to thin out enemy troops and crash their moral to an all time low.

After five to ten days of living in the freezing wet mud and enjoying the rain, snow and drizzle that comes with each day, drying wet feet and putting back on wet boots, and trying to invent new meals from the same five ingredients you've had since you arrived at Lynham, a re-supply arrives.

Some poor bugger gets the job of running around the whole Battalion location handing out mail. Delivering it's not the problem, delivering it dry enough to read is the problem. Rations are handed out and gratefully received and the Vicar might even pop round to your comfortable mud dwellings to see how life is. He'll always ask the same questions and the answer no matter what, is always the same:

"Boots fit? Mail getting through young man?"

"Absolutely Sir"

Things quickly settle into a routine. The nights on patrol are long and cold, moving at a snails pace to find an enemy that might not even be there. The days are filled with personal admin and daily chores and in between, orders and mission briefs you may even get a moment to sleep.

5 Airborne Brigade was created for the soul purpose of war. A war fought behind enemy lines. Our Officers are some of the finest Ground Commanders in the world, they study war and conflict and we execute their orders without question or hesitation. Nothing in a British paratrooper's training tells him that when he becomes operational he is not in harm's way. We are always in harms way. The only troops covering our arse in a combat zone are our own men, the men we took with us, the men chosen from a far superior selection process than that of any other Airborne Unit in the world. Nothing we do in our training is peace orientated. NATO wont use us and the UN cant. But the Great British politician sleeps better, knowing he can.

> We stay awake for as long as we need to stay awake,
> We Tab, for as long as it takes to get there,
> We fight, for as long as it takes TO WIN.

IT'S NOT ABOUT DYING FOR YOUR CAUSE

IT'S ABOUT MAKING THEM DIE FOR THEIRS'

Freezing my arse off, in an OP on the West Side of Grozny.

Doing Time
The First Time

Airborne Forces weekend in Aldershot. It was one of the years highlights. Every living paratrooper did his level best to be there. Aldershot's not a big town, from the Alexander Hotel at the top, down passed the Pegasus to the Rat Pit (or Royal Exchange) then across passed the 5's Wine bar and up to the George via the Traff (or Trafalgar) was no more than a mile give or take. But on ABF weekend the streets were packed. An ocean of maroon T-shirts as far as you could see. It didn't matter if you knew the guy next to you or not, we all had one thing in common, we'd all taken off in a plane more times than we'd landed in one.

The 5's Wine Bar. Fuckin place never sold a bottle of wine in the ten years I drank there. All drinks were served in plastic cups from a bar that a six foot man might be able to see over. There were no optics and no bottles or canned beers, just draught. The DJ was in a different room and the speakers were up high so no one could pull them off the wall and swing them round and all the furniture was nailed to the floor. Every Saturday at five o'clock we'd all congregate on the place to play: "Cabbage Rugby".

The rules of this urban legend were simple. The landlord would throw the vegetable into a crowd of waiting hairy arsed, half cut, topless paratroopers, from there the idea was to get the husk of the cabbage to the bar anyway possible and claim a free half pint.

I once tried to swap two cabbage leaves for a coke but the bar wench wouldn't have it.

The civie police during Airborne Forces weekend were always great. I never saw a young copper on duty on any ABF weekend. It always seemed to be the older boys, the Bobby with a sense of humour and a career's worth of experience who wouldn't shit himself every time a glass broke or two troopers had a drunken stand off.

Younger coppers have a way of fuckin things up real quick. They panic and try condescendingly to enforce unnecessary conditions or arrests. We could police our own and as long as it didn't get to out of hand they let us do just that.

The MP's (Military Police), on the other hand loved to throw their weight around. It frustrated them that they didn't have the power the civie police did. In fact if it wasn't for traffic control an MP probably wouldn't have any authority at all outside of events like ABF weekend and even then if you weren't a squaddie there was pretty much fuck all they could do. I'd been caught a few times by the monkeys (MP's) scrapping and arseing about, as you do as a young trooper and bluffed I was a civie living at the other end of town, they didn't have stop and search powers then so as long as I stuck to my guns they had to let me go. They say you meet good and bad in all trades, but I never met a good monkey.

This ABF weekend was particularly wild. Maybe because I was a little older and had seen and done a bit more since the last one and wasn't worried about getting stuck into the festivities. A year is a very long time in British Airborne Forces.

Over this particular weekend Andy had smacked a Military Police horse in the mouth for staring at him, not such a big deal but the monkey was still on the horse. By the time the two MP's (they worked in pairs) settled the horse, Andy had shot into the nearest pub and hid amongst three hundred other troopers, all dressed the same.

Phil had kidnapped a local female civie copper and was hiding her from her partner in the Traff plying her with drink, and some guy from 2 Para had climbed up the side of the Nat West Bank and jumped off into the arms of his mates. He was then arrested for his own protection from himself and later released without charge.

It had been a great weekend. I'd taken the Sunday slowly, not because I had work on the Monday but because I'd over done it Friday and Saturday and my seventy kilo frame was struggling with the fast alcohol intake. When I left the town at 1600 that afternoon the weekend was still in full swing but I had no regrets swapping the festivities for a shower, food and an early night.

For years after I always told myself I made "ONE" mistake that day walking back to the block taking the route I took, but the fact is I made about a hundred mistakes in a very short space of time.

From the Rat Pit (another great drinking hole) there are three ways back to the block. The first was straight across the road and up Hospital Hill to the top, hang a left at Cambridge Military Hospital and walk onto the Lines back gate. Another was to walk to the other end of town, to the Princess Hall hang a right at the lights and walk up Gun Hill and into the back gate of the Lines. Any of these two routes would have done and although both of them the long route back to Lines, either of them would have saved me a ton of shit. The other and my chosen route was a short cut through the Married Quarters and up Middle Hill.

* * *

The Married Quarters.
They're purpose built housing estates for Army families and a complete "No Go" area for single soldiers. If you want to go and see one of your mates and he's married, you're supposed to have the permission of both parties. The guy you visit and his wife and if you get stopped by the monkeys you have to prove it. The idea is to stop single guys shaggin the wives when the husbands out of town. Not so much troopers with other troopers wives, we all know each other too well and I'd like to think have too much respect for each other. It happens but it's rare. But Craphats wives are "Un Fuckin Real". 27 Regiment was a Hat Regiment up the road from us in Travis Barracks and as soon as that Regiment went away anywhere the town would flood with women, every one of them looking to take a young squaddie home for the night. As if to take revenge for the fact the husband had to go to work. It was always safe to say, when 27 Reg were away, you were guaranteed a piece of ass that weekend.

* * *

The innocents of me being on the Married Estate stood me in no favour whatsoever. I wasn't after getting me leg over with some Hat's slapper but only trying to get home quicker.

No more than thirty meters onto the estate, an MP car pulls up besides me and stops.

"Shit" I thought. I knew I was in the wrong and on account of me being pissed chose not to run, but to play it out. I heard the window wind down.

"Hold it there mate" said a young monkey not much older than me.

I stopped and turned towards the car but stepped away to give him room to get out. He was young and small to. He was my size and that for an MP was small.

"You got any I.D mate" He said.

Running was out. The monkey was stood right next to me and with no head start and me being pissed he'd most certainly catch me and I didn't really want to ruin a good weekend by fighting with a Monkey. Denying I was in the Army was out with my crew cut, desert boots, blue jeans and maroon T-shirt on. I'd be hard pushed to bluff that. So I said:

"Yes mate, here you go" and handed him my I.D card.

"Where you going" He quizzed

At that point, not wanting to be any more wrong than I was, I confessed all.

"I'm off back to Lines mate" I said "Look I know I should have gone round the other way and if you let me go, I'll walk straight off back the way I came and go the long way"

With that, he handed me back my I.D card and said:

"OK" Then he added "Next time though, it might be a different story"

I nearly shit myself. A decent monkey willing to give the benefit of the doubt.

"Thanks very much" I said "You're a star"

Then I turned and started to walk back the way I came.

I'd walked no more than ten yards when an older voice broke the Sunday silence.

"Get your arse back here sunshine" it said.

I turned to see for the first time the young monkeys partner. A great big fat Sergeant. This man couldn't have passed a BFT (Basic Fitness Test) in years. I'd have no trouble out running this fat fucker, going uphill, pissed on a moon hopper, but I chose to meet his demands and walk back to him in the vain hope of avoiding trouble.

"Who the fuck do you think you are?" He yelled, so close to my face I could smell his lunch.

"You What" I said in total confusion

"Who the fuck do you think you are calling a Military Policeman MATE?" He screamed.

As I tried to answer, he interrupted. I tried again and again he cut me short and continued with an onslaught of loud condescending insults.

Then it happened.

Fed up with taking shit from this fat bastard, I rolled my eyes and dipped my head looking at the floor. This disrespectful action drove my verbal assailant to a new level of rage and he slapped me lightly but stiffly under the chin to lift my head up.

But my chin stayed down and my right fist came up. With speed, force and accuracy that amazed even me, given how pissed I was.

BANG!

and the monkey hit the floor. Out cold.

I stood there shocked just staring at him lying there in the star fish position. I almost missed the young monkey coming round the side of the car with a baton. But I didn't. As he came towards me baton in hand, all his inexperience came out. He lashed out at me over balancing himself. Picking him off was an easy reflex. A short combination of two punches and a good knee strike to the heart and he was out the fight, over on all fours wondering if he was ever gonna breath again.

The fat fucker or the youngster must have got a message out at some point before the action. Because as I was turning to leg it another car with another two monkeys in screeched to a halt right next to me. At this point I was in full swing. As the car door opened I kicked it shut as the monkey was stepping out, it was a close shave for him it would have knock him out if the door had hit him, but he wasn't coming out that car till I'd gone, that was for sure.

On the other side of the car a short fat Scottish female Sergeant got out and came waddling round the car screaming:

"Stop Military Police".

* * *

Even in the heat of the whole incident the comment made me smile. Were they taught that as a standard response? "Stop Military Police," as if it wasn't fuckin obvious who they were, even with two lying on the floor and one hiding in his car waiting for his overweight female Sergeant to make the situation safe. The other thing that came to mind was how and why did the Military Police have so many fat people in it? Even traffic control must take some effort.

* * *

I was in no danger of being caught by any of this lot. So I decided to run and if the young monkey remembered my name and if they could find me I'd ride that storm then.

So I legged it.

I ran straight across the front gardens. The only fences were six inch privet hedges and within two gardens I was in full flight and far beyond the reach of the large arse monkeys I'd left behind.

But unbeknown to me one of the gardens I was approaching at full speed had had its privet hedge replaced by a very ornate, very solid, white iron bar fence, also six inches high.

And I hit it. At full pelt.

My face hit the grass a millisecond after both my shins connected with that bar. I didn't even have time to put my hands out. The pain was immense. I couldn't have stood straight up after that if my life depended on it. How I didn't snap both my legs I'll never know.

I rolled around the lawn grasping both my shin bones in so much pain I almost forgot about why I was running. Then as I lifted my head it all came flooding back.

WHAM!

All three monkeys dived on me. It was like a school playground, "All pile on." and I was at the bottom of it. Not now wondering but wishing to God the MP's hadn't employed so many fat people.

As the MP's restrained me they giggled and laughed. Despite the adrenaline and injuries of the event the sight of me sling shotting into the ground was enough to break their composure.

* * *

The Airborne Forces weekend fiasco saw me doing seven days in the nick. The MP's wanted to hang me for ABH, GBH, Assault, Failing to stop when challenged, Damage to an MP vehicle and I'm sure the list went on. But we had a great OC, Major Kirkbride who managed to plead and argue my case and keep it in house. That is to say he would deal with me directly and not let them take charge of the outcome.

It was a good month after the incident when I went on Orders. The CSM marched me into the OC's office with my escort Whinny as he was known to us, and I stood to answer the charges. What they were exactly I didn't know. I just knew I was in deep shit.

Stood there in my two dress, no belt and no beret, Major Kirkbride spoke:

"Well young man, you've excelled yourself this time."

I was no stranger to being on orders hence the "this time" but it was usually just for scrapping in the town or general pissing about nothing serious. Punishment usually amounted to a couple of shitty jobs. I'd never been up for anything like this before, I was beginning to worry.

"We'll keep this brief" He said "All the evidence is documentary, do you wish to accept my award or elect for trail by Court Martial?"

What that means is; do I want to take in on the chin right now. Or drag it out piss a whole load of people off and take it up the arse later. The choice was simple;

Accept the OC's award.

It was the best thing to do. I'd already been briefed on that over the month leading up to this. I'd expressed interest in a trail by Court Martial. On the grounds that the charges they wanted to sting me with would most certainly see the very end of my career. My start at the Battalion had been a rocky one. Having freedom money, beer and women for the first time naturally comes with problems, especially when in the hands of a testosterone filled seventeen year old. But I love my Unit and every guy in it, even the ones I didn't get on with and I wasn't going to let some fat bully boy fuck that up. So had the MP's retained the case I would have elected for the Court Martial. My defence being even though out of bounds they provoked the hostilities after I'd been released and sent on my way.

"Sir I accept your award" I said

"Good" He replied "Because of the severity of the charges you cannot possibly escape a custodial sentence. Do you have any thing to say?

"No Sir" Was the only thing for me to say.

With that I was marched out over to the CO's Office where I was awarded a seven day custodial sentence. The OC didn't have to say any more. He'd said his bit to me over the month it took to get this far. What had just happened was the formality for paperwork and sentencing.

Whinny marched me up to the Block to box all my stuff and put it into storage for the time of my incarceration. Then we went back down to the Lines to find out what nick I was off to and get there.

Not so surprisingly all the jails at Montgomery Lines were full. The only nick in Aldershot Garrison with a vacancy was Buller Barracks which was handy because it was close but not so handy because it was a Craphat nick and Hats hate the Maroon Machine.

***

By lunch time that day I was at Buller Barracks signed in and standing in my cell folding my kit and laying it out on the bed, as per the instruction leaflet I was issued. I was also given a wad of wire wool to scrape all the paint off my boot polish and shaving foam tins. Then locked in till Dinner when I'd get to meet the other inmates for the first time.

They weren't a bad bunch. I hadn't had a lot to do with Hats. But they were pretty much what I expected. All of them were on the sick and they moaned about absolutely everything and they saw nothing but obstacles in their lives.

There were five of us;

Geordie, a very tall driver doing two years for giving some one the hiding of his life, I thought that a bit steep until he explained it was his former Troop Commander. Normally anyone with a long sentence would go straight to the Glass House in Colchester the main British Army Prison, but Geordie suffered from back pains apparently, so they were floating him round local nicks till his time was up, at which point he was to be dishonourably discharged.

Dickie was a South London gob shite. A poky little urchin, he too was a driver. He was in for theft. Steeling off the new lads in his Troop, taking their kit into the local town and pawning it. He came unstuck when a surprise inspection found kit in his locker that he didn't have time to get rid of. He was half way through his fifty six day stint.

Bill was a Medic and a lot older than the rest of us. He was doing fourteen days for kicking the life out of his wife's boyfriend. I didn't ask anymore. It doesn't sound like much but he was a Full Corporal before the incident and was bust down to Private and locked up. That's a jolt for a single man. It was a fuckin disaster for a Pad (Married Soldier).

Then there was Taff. This guy was a fuckin nightmare and I knew from the second I met him, we were gonna end up having it out. He was in for desertion and in the last week of his twenty eight days. He was a big man in his late twenties and he was a natural bully. The minute I walked into the small mess area in the nick that doubled as a general area he was on at me. I fucked him off straight away making sure he understood I wasn't gonna be taking any shit from the: "Lard arse Welsh cunt" as I so elegantly put it, but I knew that wouldn't be enough.

The routine was simple;
Reveille at 0500 giving us one hour to clean our cells the block, ablutions and ourselves. Then just before breakfast the Orderly Officer would come in to see each prisoner, and that's the first time in the day we were allowed to talk. As the Officer entered the room with the RP Staff, you had to come to attention and say:

Sir I am, State your Number Rank and Name, Of
, State your Regiment Company Platoon.
I have been sentenced to. Give your Sentence, By,
Give your CO's name and Regiment.
I have been sentenced under. Give the Army Act (Law)
they got you on.
Then my favourite bit,
I have No Requests and No Complaints Sir.

But if you had a request or complaint that was the time to mention it, and God forbid not getting that right word for word.

Breakfast at 0600. It was delivered from the cook house and I thought that odd. On our Lines the prisoners got there own grub under RP supervision.
Then from 0700 till 0900 was personal and Guardroom admin time. Bulling boots, polishing floors and brasses pretty much anything the RP staff wanted you to do really.

Then at 0900 Drill. On the Drill Square for forty minutes, marching at high speed, which I quite enjoyed once I got the hang of it. It had been a while since I'd done any real Drill and I needed prompting a few times. On one occasion the Drill Instructor gave the Command:

"Salute to the Front" Then a pause "Salute"

I came to a halt and stood fast.

"What do you think your doing? Maggot" He yelled as he marched over to me pushing his face into mine.

"It's been a while Staff" I replied "I forgotten the Drill"

"Oh" He said in a calm softer voice "On the command Salute. Its, halt check one two, two three UP, two three DOWN, two three UP, two three DOWN, two three ABOUT, two three IN, two three LEFT RIGHT LEFT. Remember now?"

That's exactly what he said and I did remember the Drill. All that Drill Instruction in Basic Training came flooding back.

"Yes Staff, Thanks" I said

"Good, let's carry on" He said marching back to a better position to give commands.

For the next forty minutes the Drill Instructor yelled a series of commands with perfect audible clarity and timing. I'd always enjoyed Drill. As regimented and annually retentive as it is there's something proud and disciplined about marching as a body of men under competent command.

From there it was back to the Guardroom to get changed into PT kit, then off to the Gym for a forty minute beasting. I loved the PT. Army PTI's all have a God complex. They all have that: "Twice round my bronze God like body …. GO" attitude.

Their always confident and always stand with their hands on their hips and their feet shoulder width apart. I'm sure that's the first lesson they get at the Army School of Physical Training, but that aside they are good at what they do. No matter what your level of fitness you always leave the lesson blowing out your arse, feeling sick but looking forward to the next session.

After that it's back again to the Guardroom for a shower the lunch time head count and lunch, again delivered.

The afternoon program varied. Thursdays the Vicar would visit, so all afternoon all we did was bull boots, iron kit and scrub our cells and clean the Guardroom. Anything to keep us busy because no one knew what time in the afternoon the Sky Pilot was coming, but we had to be on hand to listen to the old boy.

Other afternoons we'd have to clean all the weapons in the armoury or sweep up round the camp. Generally any shit job that needed doing the prisoners would do.

I say prisoners but what I should say is prisoner. The Hats I was locked up with all had sick chits for everything. Dickie was even excused from standing in line for the lunch time Nominal Role Call. I was the only one on the Drill Square in the mornings and the only one in the Gym after that. So it goes without saying who got the shitty jobs in the afternoons, but I didn't mind it got me out the nick and it meant the time went quite quickly, but the others just sat round all afternoon in the general area talking or in the exercise yard smoking and bragging to each other about fuck all.

At 1700 it was teatime, that to was delivered. After that a bit more down time till about 2030. Then a visit from the on coming Orderly Officer, where we have to give the same "Request and Complaint" spiel, quickly followed by lights out.

After only two days of this I decided to ask the Orderly Officer for more PT in the afternoons. I wasn't doing anything else and the PTI's were always keen. That lot loved their work. Their like fifteenth century torture masters that way.

The earliest time I could request this was on the third morning of my incarceration as I only got the idea lying in bed the night before.

The next morning the Orderly Officer was late because of an incident during the night. Something to do with someone who'd been AWOL for a month being seen and caught on the Married Quarter

Estate. He was in custody at another nick but as this was his Regiment he had to be transported back to Buller Barracks.

So we did our morning chores had Breakfast and hung around till he got there, a lot like waiting for the Vicar. The Orderly Officer turned up about 0930. We were all put back in our cells ready to go the motions, come to attention and give the prisoners speech. I could hear the other inmates give their speeches, all ending with:

"I have no requests and no complaint, Sir"

My cell was the last cell on the left and the last cell to be inspected. When the Orderly Officer came in I came to attention, gave my speech and at the end said:

"I have one request and one complaint Sir"

There was a silence right the way through the Guardroom and the Officer in front of me look at me as if to say:

"What now?"

It was obvious he'd had a very long night, he looked knackered and still had a days work to do.

He gathered his composure and said:

"Let's start with your complaint shall we"

"I'd like to complain about the lack off PT Sir"

"Well that's a first" He said "And your request"

"I'd like more PT Sir, I don't want to fuck anyone about" I said "but this is a Training Depot if I could join in with the intakes, I'd be happy with that Sir"

I should have stopped at "I'd like more PT" but I was on a roll and the bitching that came from Taff's cell made me, the officer and the escorting RP staff smile.

"I'll see to it your request and your complaint are satisfied young man" he said still smiling. Then he walked out.

I went up to the general area to sit with the other guys and wait for someone to put us back onto our routine. I walked in to see Taff throwing chairs around and kicking the walls.

"What's up?" I said with no idea what was going on.

"You're up, you fuckin gobbie cunt that's what" He spat the words out at me.

He was real pissed off about something and I had absolutely no clue what he was on about. Whatever it was had Geordie and Bill in fits of laughter and that was pissing him off even more.

"If I can't get out of this, you're fucked Pal" He ranted pointing and walking at me.

I was gonna hit him then and with good reason, but he put his head down and barged passed me. He was a big lad, well a fat lad, and I felt it but it wasn't enough to go toe to toe over. That and I still didn't know what was going on.

He stormed out bitching and winging all the way. I took a seat with the others who were still pissing themselves laughing. Everyone of us thought he was a right wanker so anything that wound him up made for good humour.

"What was all that about" I asked

Bill explained:

"Taff and the Orderly Officer we had last night had a big fall out. Taff took the piss out of him and his wife. He was openly rude and crass to her and just fucked the Officer off when he piped up to say something knowing that he couldn't be touched because not only was he in jail, but he's also on the sick."

Bill took a breath and continued:

"Taff's sickchit ran out yesterday and you can only get on the Sick Parade between 0800 and 0900 after you've seen the Orderly Officer. However the Officer was late this morning and the sick parade over by the time he got here. So Taff couldn't renew his biffchit."

Now things started to come together, Bill went on:

"So now he has to do the Drill and the PT this morning but not only that, you've requested more PT. Something the Officer couldn't do, its not part of the jail program and the RP Staff can't be seen to be doing favours. It gets better. The Orderly Officer we had last night is the senior Gym Instructor at this Gym."

As everything fell into place I could help but smile, today was gonna be a very physical day.

* * *

The Orderly Officer returned less than half an hour later. The RP staff came out to the general area and told Taff and I to be in PT kit and formed up out the front of the guardroom in three minutes. As usual the others were excluded they had valid sick chits. I was already in my kit so all I had to do was run out to the front.

As I got there I saw the Orderly Officers stood on the steps talking to the SSM. I came to attention in front of them and announced myself:

"Prisoner, number, rank, name, reporting for PT Sir"

"So you're our Airborne visitor are you son" Said the SSM

"Yes Sir" I replied, not once making eye contact. Sergeant Majors don't like that.

"Enjoy your day!" He said. The SSM was looking at me but he was talking to the Orderly Officer, who answered

"Thanks Oz"

The SSM then walked off with the swagger and presence you learn to expect from the cream of a Regiment.

The Orderly Officer stood in front of me as we waited for Taff to emerge. He was a big man with dark skin, a bit of Mediterranean in there somewhere. Not dressed now in his combats as he was for his duty the night before but in the ever familiar white PTI's vest with red trim, lightweights and boots. The tired man that walked into my cell less than an hour earlier was gone. He'd been replaced by a PTI on a mission. The mans excitement was all too obvious.

Out the blue and with smile, He said, "I've a personal interest in your request"

"I've heard, Sir" I said.

"So you know what went on do you?" He asked, not as a formal question but as you would in conversation.

"Not really Sir" I replied "But I know enough to know your gonna use my request to educate him today."

"Educate. I like that" He said.

With that Taff came running out the RP staff on his heels like Jack Russell on a postman's leg.

He came staggering to attention on my right already out of breath and sweating. He was gonna have to pull out something special to survive today, I thought.

"As there are only two of you" Said the PTI "Your goal is to beat each other in any given task, the winner will rest the loser will be punished.

"IT PAYS TO BE A WINNER GENTLEMEN"

As he said it he stared at Taff with a massive grin. Taff was always gonna suffer a bit today but now he was real fucked. He was an overweight slob who prided himself on how many different skives he knew. I was an eighteen year old paratrooper whose soul goal in life at the time was to get, stronger faster and fitter. Add to that the "Regimental Pride Factor" that being me the trooper not being beat by a fat Hat. Put that sum together and poor Taff truly was fucked. I had no intentions of losing any event that day and short of a pie eating contest I'd get me wish.

The PTI played with us all morning on the assault course and when we weren't on that we were doing sprints. After an hour I was knackered and Taff was on deaths door.
The times I was beating Taff by on the assault course and sprints were getting embarrassingly longer and longer and I got to rest and watch the fat Welsh twat fall over the line. As soon as he did the next task was given and off we went again.

When we were finally given a water break Taff was throwing up and falling all over the place and I wasn't even sweating or out of breath. I'd beat him on the last assault course laps by over five minutes. He was at his end. I passed him a cup of ice cold water. Even though I couldn't stand him the Army had instilled in me a staunch sense of team work as it did in all who wanted it. I didn't pity him, I was just in a position to help.
Then the cheeky fat bastard said, "You're making me look like a cunt."
"Ten years of self abuse and picking a fight with the wrong bloke is making you look a cunt" I replied.
"When this is over, it's you and me" He said.

I wasn't worried in the slightest by the Welshman's threat. The water break ended and the morning continued in the Gym, an indoor assault course and a set of exercises to complete in a given time. This PTI was a genius, even when stood still we were working. When our lungs were spent our legs worked, when they were spent our arms worked. It was amazing a true beasting. It was great.

After an hour of this we broke for a shower and lunch. I was starving and ate like a horse. Taff was almost too tired to shower. He collapsed on his pit and fell into a deep deep sleep.

Dickie suggested sharing out his food. But Geordie said not to.

"Don't give him any excuses not to go out again this afternoon" He said

Everyone was happy with that.

That afternoon was just as brutal for Taff. We started with a CFT, (Combat Fitness Test). Eight miles in one hour forty five minute, in full kit, over undulating ground. For me it was as easy as walking into town on a Friday night. At Airborne Forces we did the same CFT but in one hour ten. We religiously had a Sergeant Majors Tab every Friday and that was ten miles in less that one forty five. That aside I was Airborne Force's we Tabbed everywhere. It was our bread and butter.

Hats do it once a year as part of there ATD's (Annual Training Directive). Some take pride in it but for the most they'd pull a sicky or body swerve it another way. Just as Taff did and now Taff was paying for his idleness and lack of self respect, he felt every step. The staff dragged and beasted him every yard and it still took him two and a half hours.

I was a bit embarrassed. All the way round the PTI and I chatted as if we were on a Sunday stole and another two PTI's dragged Taff along.

Once the CFT was finished it was back in the Gym for more of before.

About twenty minutes into the next set of tasks Taff collapsed. He was taken up to the Cambridge Military Hospital (CMH) emergency room and treated for dehydration and exhaustion, not a big deal but the insult to injury was when the Doctor wanted him charged for self inflicted wounds on the grounds Taff didn't have lunch and as a trained soldier should know better. The Regimental Police at Buller Barracks were more than happy to oblige the Doctor.

They kept the fat boy in over night and the atmosphere in the nick was lighter to say the least, even amongst the staff. Not only that they let us share out Taff's food and have the TV on that night till lights out.
The next day the routine continued, I asked for more PT and got it and I was still the only one on the Drill Square in the morning. Everyone was happy.

When I got back from the afternoon PT session Taff had rejoined us. He was pissed off, embarrassed and out to save face and out for revenge.
The staff knew it as did the other inmates, Bill and Geordie pulled me to one side and offered to keep him at bay. I was a lot younger than the rest and half their size. It was good of them to look out for me but I didn't want that. That would follow me through my career like the colour green. I knew how to sort it out and I needed to sort it out and sooner rather than later.

I walked into the exercise yard and asked Bill to keep everyone else away. Then I asked Geordie to tell Taff where I was. They looked at each other then at me. I smiled. I always do when I'm nervous, then the two of them went about their tasks.
In less than a minute Taff burst into the yard he was fired up and as vulgar as usual. Stomping over to me, saying,
"You Fuckin this" and "You Fuckin That".
I let him rant on. Then just before he reached me I took one step towards him and smacked him in mid sentence. I wasn't there to talk and neither was he, but he was talking, more fool him. He went down harder than I expected, but like all his kind he went down fast.
I stepped back and let him up, lip split and bleeding profusely he spat on the floor. As he bought his head back round to look at me, I hit him again and down he went again.

Once again I stepped back to let him up but he stayed down and began yelling.

As he did the yard door burst open, Bill and Geordie rushed in behind the RP staff. I was sent to my cell and told to not to move. Taff went back to the CMH for the second time in twenty four hours and was given twelve stitches, eight in the mouth and lips and four above the right eye.

A while later the Orderly Officer came to my cell. It was the Sergeant Major the PTI called Oz earlier that day, I stood to attention.

"So what did you see?" He said

That threw me, surely he should be asking what happened or what did I do.

"It's a simple question young man" he said walking behind me. "Did he fall off the door step, slip on his fag packet. What?"

Now I understood.

"He fell off the step lighting his fag Sir" I replied

"Ok" he said "Get yourself into the general area, its radio night."

No more was made of it than that, Taff was kept in overnight again for observation and the prison routine resumed. When Taff came back the next day he was confined to his cell and I was released the following day Back to Battalion and straight out on Exercise Black Lanyard.

The time spent in the nick wasn't hard time more of a waist of time. Even though it was only a week, I'd missed so much back at Battalion. I promised myself from that point on no more fuckin about. I loved the Army and enjoyed Unit life and if I wanted to keep that I would have to stop trying to become a good drinking story and practice what was said to me before I was incarcerated:

*"BEING HARD, IS A STATE OF MIND"**

CO, Log Bn 5AB Brig

Survival
The Ten That Got Away.

Survival and bush craft has always been a personal favourite of mine. It was a subject I always excelled at and later went on to teach, both in the Army and in civie street. Our Units dealt with personal survival a lot more than most others. The whole idea of having an Airborne Forces is to land behind enemy lines in the dark and usually in shit weather, so the possibility of being split up from your Unit and having to go it alone is always a very real one.

We trained Escape and Evasion avidly and of course, once you've escaped and evaded capture you have to feed, navigate and live, you may even have to patch yourself up. Being alone and pulling yourself back from being cold, wet, hungry and scared, is a true test of a mans training and educated properly it can be done confidently and with relative ease.

I've always loved the outdoors, the forests and woodlands of Europe, all the lush greenery of the temperate zone. These are lands I grew up in as a small boy, building shelters camping out overnight enjoying the stars, and lighting fires to cook sausages on green sticks, the simple lessons learned in play stay with us all our lives.

The different types of jungles took some getting use to, each different eco system poses its own special obstacles and they have a unique way of tuning your fears, especially at night. The only ways to conquer those fears is through knowledge.

The dry harshness of the summer African savannahs, offer challenge unknown anywhere else in the world, where the land is as abrasive as the temperature and the constant threat of big game is a very real one.

Then there are the Arctic conditions of the far north and south, places God forgot about a long time ago. It is by far the most unforgiving territory. Mistakes made there promote extreme punishment.

All of these areas have challenged not only the best of men, but the best equipped of men, and even though they have been the birth place of some extraordinary tales of survival, for everyman that made it through, the land has claimed a thousand more.

Over the last thirty years, hundreds of books have been written on the subject. The most popular is probably any one of the revised SAS survival handbooks, written by Lofty Wiseman. A legend in some circles.

There have also been a few arseholes on the TV selling the subject under the guise they were Ex Special Forces. How?, God only knows. Some of their techniques are criminal and would put you in more shit than you were in, in the first place. For me and most people I speak to about survival and bush craft, the outdoor Guru has to be Ray Mears. You can't help but love this mans approach to his craft in his programs and his books. One of the greatest instructors I ever had, RSM Col Chapman, said to me:

"When you teach and demonstrate, you have to make it look easy, so your pupils know it can be done with ease, with practice".

Mr Mears has that ability. He is truly a master of the outdoors and it's always good to see his guests sweating away, trying to light themselves a fire or build a shelter. It's a true reflection of the work that goes into staying alive in the wild.

* * *

Once or twice a year a guest speaker would come to the Lines and talk about, and teach survival techniques that had kept them alive. Not just soldiers, but adventurers and pioneers that found themselves lost, stuck or injured. They spoke about their feelings at the time and how they conquered their fears more importantly, how they created options for themselves and how they kept up their moral.

We had a civilian survival expert come in one year. He was an Ex Para Reg Sergeant with connections on the Lines that's how he got the job. He'd left the Army and set up his own survival training school and used his connections for business. Good on him we all thought. He took us for a two day carder. The first day was all theory and the second day was to be practical, but to be honest it was less than revision, he had nothing new and he left a lot out. We had to bring the newer lads up to speed ourselves.

The first lesson of the second day was rabbits. The catching, skinning and eating and other use's for a dead rabbit. Even though we went over the basic snare our Instructor didn't want to wait to catch anything, he had a short cut.
JFK and I were pulled out of the last lesson, "Foraging and Gathering" and sent to a farm near Hook, a small rural village about twenty five miles outside Aldershot to buy rabbits. Ten wild rabbits, one rabbit between two troopers. We collected the money from our Instructor, who was obviously gonna bill Her Majesty for them and went to the MT to collect a Landrover to complete the task.

The MT fucked around for ages to get us transport and by the time we left the lines and reached the farm the bloke we needed to see was gone and wouldn't be back till the morning.
We started to head back and on the way stopped off at a quaint little country pub just down the road from the farm and popped in for a pint and a bite to eat. It was too late to get back in time for dinner at the cookhouse.
In the pub the landlady asked what we were up to, we told her that we'd missed the guy we needed to see at the farm up the road and were on our way back to the Barracks.
"Don't do that" she said "He'll be in here tonight, he comes in most nights, I'm sure he'll get you sorted"
That news put us both in a great mood so we ate and waited, and waited. Then the pub filled up slowly with wonderful local people who chatted to us and bought us drinks. It must have been the uniforms. We bought drinks back and chatted some more but still no sign of farmer Giles. After three hours we'd both had too much to drink to make our way back so made a plan to kip in the back of the Landy and get a fresh start first thing in the morning. The conversation and drink flowed till closing time and still no sign of the bloke

we needed. We left the pub and got our heads down in the Landy parked in the pub car park.

The next day we got up at sparrows fart, it wasn't long before we realised we'd spent all the money we had for the rabbits in the pub the night before.

The new plan was to get back to the Shot, get money from the block and back to the farm ASAP, buy the rabbits and get back for the first lesson.

But that never went to plan either, the second we got back to the Lines the MT took back the Landrover. All we had at this point was hangovers, no money and no rabbits.

JFK's new plan was a long shot, and an expensive one but it wouldn't be the first time a night on the piss cost more than I planned.

Aldershot had a pet shop at the bottom of Grovesnor road. It was one of the few places that sold puppies and kittens, it also did rabbits. We clubbed all our money together and ran down there.

The shop opened at nine and the first lesson was at nine, we needed a delay tactic for the Instructor, being late for anything in the Army is a big deal and brings on all kinds of bother. We had an excuse to miss the parade (we were meant to be looking after rabbits), but not the first lesson. JFK ran back to the Training Wing to buy us some time, and I stayed to buy the rabbits. I ordered a cab too in an effort to keep my lateness to a minimum.

The shop opened five minutes early and with luck from the Gods I was less than fifteen minutes late for the lesson. When I entered the classroom, everyone stopped what they were doing and looked at me, it was blood and guts time and the blood and guts had arrived. Some of the lads loved that bit.

"Good" The instructor said "You're here, put the box on the front table, and hand them out, one between two".

I put the box down, and did as ordered. I reached into the box and pulled the first two out. The class fell into complete silence. The instructor had his back to the class and was writing on the board. A minute later everyone had their "Prey for the day" as our would-be expert put it. Then he turned and looked at the rabbit on the desk in front of him. He walked over to the helpless prey and picked it up. With the rabbit sitting in the palm of his hand he looked at JFK and me and said'

"What the fuck is this?"

JFK looked at me for the answer.

"It's a long haired long eared dwarf rabbit" I said. Well nine of them are, ones a Guinea pig."

The class roared with laughter, as for JFK and me we tried to offer some kind of explanation, but it fell on deaf ears The men spent the next half hour petting and stroking their new pets. The sweet little long haired long eared dwarf bunnies were in no danger of dying that day or any other day. No one had the heart to murder such an innocent sweet creature, they would get off Scot free and become pets for the married guys kids.

As for me and JFK, we had a few shit jobs coming our way, but if it hadn't been for the humour of the Training Wing Staff we could have been in a ton of shit.

* * *

Those two days came and went with nothing new learnt. It was a bit of a let down to be fair, our own guys did a better job and did it on a regular basis. The incident with the dwarf rabbits happened in the early days of my career and was good for a laugh, but I've put into practice many of the skills taught in those lectures and lessons, not only in exercise and training but to save my life and the lives of comrades in the jungles of Central America and the mountains of Eastern Europe.

They are skills I hold dear to me and when their not saving my life, I practice them with my son Jim whenever I can create the opportunity. He loves the outdoors as much as I ever did.

Today, living a stone throw from the African bush I look to the locals for knowledge and I learn more and more every time I venture out. We eat out in the field a lot here and I love to start fire in as many different ways as I can and usually do so to the smiling face of a loving wife, who will stand patiently with a box of matches in her pocket just in case, waiting for me to start the Barbeque.

ANYONE CAN BE COLD WET AND HUNGRY

It's An Anti Tank Mine Mate.

We'd been long range patrolling in the Middle East on and off for over two months, dropping in by Chinook, sometimes with landy's but for the most part on foot. Given a patrol route an objective and an extraction point then picked up a few days later. To my surprise when I first got there the desert wasn't an ocean of soft sand thankfully, but hard like concrete with the occasional sand dune and large litter of random rocks, some bigger than others. It was hot as hell during the day and cold and exposed at night. The star patterns were unbelievable, billions and billions of them blanketed the sky from one horizon to the next, interrupted only by the silhouette of mountains in the distance.

The patrols were largely routine, the gathering of intelligence and updating of old intelligence. Not a lot of time for the "Hearts and Minds" aspect of things purely because the idea was to keep our heads down and our arses out the way. That said, when we did cross the path of the occasional nomadic tribesman, we were always respectful and exchanged gifts of water and food when appropriate, then called our encounter in so the Int boys could undate their files. It was always a daunting moment meeting such people. They know no boarders, and answer to no western authority, you never knew for sure how any one encounter was gonna go.

We had a great section at the time. Most of us had been together almost two years and we knew each other inside out. Phil C was our Section Commander, he'd been in forever, and was proper old school, we were lucky really to have him, Phil came from a background of practice and execution of task, that and fifteen years of experience some senior ranks wished they had.

So from a soldiers point we were blessed. Phil insisted on practice and rehearsal again and again and again. If we as a team were getting it wrong or he didn't think us ready we went nowhere. He was a good soldier and we are better soldiers for it.

It was the middle of June and we'd been out four days, we moved largely at night fighting the intense cold working from one point to another then laying up during the day moving as little as possible in order to control the life sucking heat, that and it was easier to maintain a low profile. This particular patrol had been quite uneventful which is never a bad thing in light of how things can get. We'd covered a lot of ground and reviewed and amended old and out of date intelligence.

The sun was on the rise on the morning of the fifth day, it had been another very productive night and all our objectives had been reached. We were looking to lay up in the next hour and were moving smartly for a dry river bed a few kilometres to the north. When in the middle of nowhere we happened upon a T-64 (T for Tank and 64 was the year NATO first spotted it). Seventy two tons of Soviet made hardware just sat there, seemingly undamaged. Instantly we went to ground in order to assess and evaluate the situation. With this obstacle in the way we'd never make the river bed, a new plan would have to be made to get our heads down, if that opportunity arose at all. If the T-64 still had its crew that would mean the rest of the tank Regiment would be near by. Had we just walked right into the middle of an enemy Brigade?

Each man knowing his individual task we secured an immediate perimeter and with a 360 degrees all clear given, Phil handed things over to Sean our Section 2ic so he could take a better look himself. At the time I thought it strange, surely the idea was to send someone else so that if anything happened Phil could still remain in command.

The T-64 could easily turn out to be an Artillery marker. We could be being watched by an enemy Forward Observation Team that would call an Arty bombardment the second we came within half a mile of the thing.

Or it could be there as a marking point for a garden verity ambush that would be set off the minute we touch it, then any survivors picked off by killing groups anything up to 500 meters away, hidden somewhere we missed on our quick surveillance of our chosen perimeter. All these reasons and a dozen others for the tank being there came to mind within a millisecond of seeing it. But I wasn't in the slightest bit worried about Phil's decision, up until the point Phil wanted me to go with him.

"Sean, go firm" He said "I'll take a closer look"

And without a change of breath, he looked at me and said:

"Right young un, come with me."

Instantly the words "Fuck off you maniac, lets just call it in and go round it," Came flooding to the forefront of my mind, but they were replaced by:

"No probs Phil, where do you want me?"

I only ever questioned Phil in private and always as a matter of conversation not direct confrontation. My career, after a rocky start was going really well, to well for some people. There's a fine line at the age I was, between being confident and promising and a lippy little fucker. They both could get you attention. One would get you another course lots of smiles and a pat on the back. The other would most certainly lead to a bloody good hiding. So I adopted the attitude:

Ears and eyes open, mouth shut.

Phil and I approached the sleeping mass of armour, not really giving the landmine threat the respect it deserved. We had a Royal Engineer in our section, he came to us from 9Sqn RE a few months earlier, he was the only new edition to our team but he was a good guy, most of 9 Sqn were, I could feel him cringing and grimacing with anticipation in a safe position behind us.

I couldn't see him but I pictured him with his fingers in his ears and eyes tightly shut like the Wild 'E' Coyote just about to try an Acme bomb contraption on the Road Runner.

Phil looked at me and said: "What are you fuckin grinning at"

"I'll tell you later "I said

"Stop that shit "He replied "It freaks me out when you do that, makes me think you know something I don't"

That certainly wasn't the case. I had a habit of nervous humour that manifested itself in the form of a fuckin great big grin and Phil knew it, so did the other guys, but those who didn't know me thought I was some kind of war loving psychopath who loved it when the shit hit the fan. That wasn't the case either. But when the guy with experience next to you is grinning like some fairytale cat at a time you think your gonna die, who could blame them?

On our approach I looked meticulously for damage, but nothing not even small arms fire damage, maybe it just ran out of fuel and the crew bummed a lift with another tank.

Now standing at the foot of the tank Phil climbed up and did a brief booby trap check.

I could only assume his confidence went hand in hand with his experience. The main hatch was already open and Phil climbed in.

After a few seconds I heard: "Are you coming or what?"

Once again my immediate role had changed, I was now going from close support and look out, to fellow Kamikaze.

Climbing inside, I was surprised to see a lot of controls had metal plates above them, written not only in Russian and some Arabic dialect but also in English. I concluded that it made them easier to re-sell should the respective Arab nation find themselves with an abundance of military hardware, if there is such a thing. They could sell them on to some uneducated up and coming indigenous African. Who with his ten words of English and his stone age conception of modern warfare could genocide his rival tribe in short order?

There was more room than I thought as well but that was probably because it was just me and Phil in it. I made myself at home by sitting in what I thought was the gunner's seat. Phil clambered around behind me looking for Intel, maps, notes and orders, that sort of thing. I kept myself busy by pissin about with the controls like a kid in an arcade.

"Sound effects as well eh" Phil said.

Just off to my left was a neat green wooden box about 14/14inches and about 6inches deep, it weighed easily fifteen kilos, as I found out trying to lift it. With Phil still shuffling about behind me on his own mission I pulled the box onto my lap for closer inspection of its contents, maybe it contained the Intel Phil was looking for. The lid seemed pinned as opposed to nailed down and came off with ease.

As it did there was a very loud and prominent metallic "Click" that echoed off the inside of the Turret. Phil and I froze.

The silence seemed to go on and on, the stillness of the moment long and tense. Then for the first time Phil and I were thinking alike, he said it, and I was thinking it.
"Don't fuckin move" he said slowly and calmly
He moved with his usual confidence to a position in front of me where he could see better. I'd lifted the lid a good five, six inches off the box and within a few seconds Phil could see all he needed.
"What is it?" I asked
The immediate reply came as short lived relief.
"It's an Anti Tank mine mate" Phil said
The "Anti Tank mine" bit was good news, all we'd have to do is put it down and get out. It was the "Mate" bit that caused the concern.
Phil was always relaxed about names and Rank out of Senior Rank earshot. He let even the new lads call him Phil and he always referred to us by our given nick names. I'd only ever heard him call Taff Jones mate before and that was just before he took him to the OC to be told his Father had died.

Rhetorically I said "So I can put it down then"
"Not yet" He said "Give me a chance to get out of here first, no point us both getting it"
Fuck! I thought, he's gonna leave me here the man I trusted with my life was gonna fuckin leave me. With that, I looked up to see him grinning at me with his perfect row of white teeth.
"Wanker" I said "Don't do that you make me think you know something I don't"

"I do" He said "But it's not enough. I know it's a landmine but im fucked if I know what the two wires, fixed to the lid do"

"I'll take your best guess Phil just get it off my fuckin lap" I said now more worried than ever.

"You've got thirty pounds of armour piercing explosive sat on your bollocks and you'll take my best guess", was the reply through a giggle.

With that, a joke about three Falklands Vets came to mind and my grin returned. It's an old joke and a shit one but everybody knows it, so I just quoted the punch line to Phil. And for the moments that followed Phil and I laughed like two kids in class after one had farted.

Once we'd calmed down and realized the box and lid were still in the position our conscious minds had left them, Phil set about lifting the box and lid so I could get out from under it.

Very carefully I handed the box to Phil who was now standing right in front of me. Right above me was the open hatch. Once again the atmosphere was tense and silent. I don't think either of us was even breathing. I gently released my now cramping grip and let Phil take the weight of my potential castrator. He slowly, without lifting the mine any higher stepped back. As the tank busting ordinance cleared my knees Phil turned slowly at the waist as if moving his feet would set the device off and with tenderness of an eye surgeon, set it down in almost the exact spot I'd lifted it from moments earlier, then he gently bought the lid to rest, eased his fingers from the green Armageddon and said quite casually:

"There we are"

Without a thank you, a well-done or an I owe you one and without even looking up, I shot out of that death trap like a bar of soap shooting out your hand in the bath.

Fuck, I was gone! Like shit off a wet stick. Faster than a chicken in a concentration camp, with the speed of a thousand startled gazelles. Put it as you will, but I was fuckin fast and I was fuckin gone.

For the next ten seconds I was the fasted thing alive. The speed in which I left the would be coffin sparked the rest of the Section into following me at similar speeds, I can't say for sure how far away we were but when we came to rest and looked back,

Billy shouted "Phil, are you ok mate?"

With that Sean said "Shut up ya cunt, he's not gonna hear you from here"

After long seconds we made our way back and while trying to find another lung in my arse cheeks I explained briefly what had happened. On our approach we saw Phil climbing out. Calmly he closed the hatch, jumped off the tank and made his way over to us.

"Right "He said "Let's set up an ambush on the tank and see what happens during today"

Nothing more was said about the ordeal until later that day when we were laying out in the Ambush and Phil said:

"Fuck you're fast, but at least you left it till I put it down".

We waited all that day and well into the night. As the savage heat of the desert sun gave way to the freezing cold of the exposed night we called our position and situation in, and were thankfully pulled out within the hour. Nothing came of our ambush and the mystery of the abandoned T-64 and why it was there was never solved, and so was open to all manner of conspiracy theory. My favourite was the one with the aliens in it. No matter how level headed you think a group of guys are, never underestimate the power of the X files.

Phil always reckoned they saw us coming and ran off. I remember Sean pointing out to him that they, with a fully armed tank had the upper hand. But Phil just smiled at him and said:

"Never underestimate the international fear of the British Airborne Warrior.

Three Falklands Vets

After the Falklands War, the M.O.D get together to decide how to compensate the victims of the Argentine landmines.
After much discussion and debate, mainly about how to short change the nations finest, and keep all compensation within a certain sum, a solution is reached and a test group found.
Called to Whitehall London, are three victims, an Engineer, a Royal Marine, and a Paratrooper.
Lined up in front of an M.O.D medical board, the three men are told, that they will be played out £1000 for every inch between their injury, and their testicles.
With that the Engineer with a missing foot, is called forward, the master surgeon takes a measurement of 30inches from ankle to testicle, and the panel acknowledge, to the M.O.D's grimace a payout of £30000.
Then the Royal Marine, with his leg gone from the knee is called upon, again the master surgeon takes a measurement, this time of 14inches from knee to testicle, and to the M.O.D's delight acknowledges a payout of £14000.
Conspiring in a corner, one minister says to the other with a smile:
"This ones gonna be a peanuts payout, more money for us to squander"
As the Paratrooper is called forward with no leg at all, the master surgeon finds the stump 8 inches from his groin, but upon close inspection can't find the Paratrooper's testicles.
"Is this some kind of joke?" the surgeon yells. As the ministers approach for a closer look,
"No mate" The Paratrooper says "My Bollocks are on the minefield at Goose Green!"

BADM317

She was my first love. JFK had a blue two litre Ford Sierra and he let me drive it. BADM317 was not the registration number, it was just the only way I could remember it. Not having any insurance of my own I had to remember all JFK's details in case I was pulled over. The pair of us would take it in turns to drive to Hereford, but like so many other things in our relationship it turned into a competition. Before the Swindon Gloucester bypass I could go from Aldershot to Hereford in two hours fifty minutes. JFK could take twenty minutes off my time even in the rain. We could even go the full distance without being overtaken. That car had power.

All the time he had that wonderful car it had one continuous problem, the start motor. So it goes without saying if I travelled alone, I had to park on a hill to jump start the thing when I needed to go anywhere.

Hereford has a multi-storey car park a stone throw from the Newmarket pub, our local at the time, so it was the smart place to park. I'd park our blue bullet on the parking space opposite the down ramp and as long as I timed it just right, I could get the car started before the turning to go down to the next level.

BADM317 was not just a car. She was a place to sleep and a place to eat. JFK had a "No Chicks in the car" policy. He was married at the time and didn't want to have to explain any evidence that might be left behind after any CQB with a local chick.

We liked to keep her clean too. I nearly lost my "Eat in the car" rights one night after an incident with a Kebab, a Coke and ten pints of Guinness. The car stank for weeks and B his wife was reminding him about it every time she got in, she even reminded him of it when she wasn't in the car. Funny really, he got the same earache after a similar incident at his house, two days after he'd had new carpets fitted, but that involved ten pints of Guinness a Coke and a pot noodle.

But as always JFK fought my corner and I got away with a promise to be more careful in the future.

One weekend we drove to Hereford and parked up as normal in the multi-story. Then like so many other great weekends we hit the town hard. The Newmarket was always a good start. It was our local and saved any chance of us being barred. We drank in there early then went off to debauch the rest of the town and our own good names.

The Golden Fleece was my favourite place to eat, the owner at the time was an Aussy and he made the meanest Beef and Cheese sandwiches. From there we'd venture onto the Crystal rooms or sticky carpets as it was nick named, why they put carpets in a shit pit like that was beyond me, from there we'd wander the rest of the town.

For some God forsaken reason, after Norma Genes night club we'd always end up in Manhattans, don't get me wrong I've had some of the best nights of my life in that place, and before the steroid boys took over the doors, it had some of the best doormen in the country. I even had one of my finest man moments in that club.

A mate of mine, unbeknown to him at the time was hitting on the DJ's wife, though why he was hitting on a woman who was seven months pregnant was well off my level of understanding anyway. I was on the dance floor perfecting the squaddie two-step about a yard away from him and his would be date, when he taps me on the shoulder and says.

"You ready for this mate?"

I didn't have a clue what he was on about, but I agreed anyway.

"Yes mate, ready for what?"

With that, all became apparent. Big R and I were surrounded by young lads, I say young lads they were younger than me, the eldest probably no more than twenty five. I didn't know what Big R had been up to and it didn't matter, but I rightly assumed it had something to do with the fact he had his arm round a drunken pregnant bird.

"Better to take a good beating with a friend, than watch him take one. Even if he deserves it."

I looked at the lad to my front. He stood hard as nails puffing his chest out with mates just as eager on either side of him. He looked me up and down and spat on the floor in front of me.
"What you fuckin lookin at cunt?" He yelled.
The music was loud and I could barely make what he said, then there was a gap in the music and the room quietened down.
"When this goes off young un" I said to him "I'm only interested in you"
He was still all full of balls, and verbally fucked me off, but I could see panic in him and he was looking for an out. His whole thought process had changed. As far as he knew I wasn't going to fight him and his mates. I was going straight for him. His mates took half a step back.

Then it went off. I never would have actually laid into the young lad in front of me. It would have been like beating up the school weakling, but he didn't know this. I just grabbed him and pulled him towards me. His bottle had crawled out the door moments before. His legs stayed where they were and he dropped onto his knees in front of me. A glancing blow from his mate to my left unbalanced him and he fell over the feet of the guy on his knees in front of me. Then the fool on my right, half-heartedly threw a punch with a second class stamp on it and addressed to Scotland I think, but he then fell over the head of the guy that fell over the feet of the first guy.
Now there was three guys lying at my feet and I hadn't thrown a single shot.

The doormen jumped in as they do and in the true tradition of the place no one got thrown out, we just got separated and warned. They were old school doormen back then. They were happy for people to fall out as long as you knocked it on the head when they said so. If you didn't they'd sort you out themselves and if you could and wanted to stay after that, they were happy to let you do so, as long as you behaved and didn't become a problem for anyone else. It was, and is bit of a shit hole Manhattans, but it was a great place to get drunk and let your hair down.

About an hour after the event, the three stooges approached me at the bar, to apologise of all things. I happily accepted and let them buy me a drink.

"You're fuckin well hard" One of the lads said "You dropped all three of us with one punch"

Even though that's not what happened, I was happy for that adaptation of events. In the end it was another great night out in Hereford.

At the end of the night, as usual I had to eat, and on the way back to the multi-story, and a nice warm sleeping bag, I stopped at the Chinese to pick up my usual, chicken curry, plain chow main and a coke. Food in hand I wondered back to the car.

When I got there I sat in the passenger seat with the door open and feasted. I couldn't have been more pissed off, when half trying to eat and half trying to get in my doss bag, I dropped my chow main. Fortunately for JFK's ears, not in the car, but just outside the door.

I finished the curry, took a scoop of chow main off the floor and sank the Coke. Then I chucked the wrappers on the floor next to the crime of my spilled food, shut the door and wriggled into my maggot.

Stripped down to my skiddies and pissin about trying to get comfortable. I got the hand break tangled in the sleeping bag and let it off.

I caught it in no time but the problem was the car had moved forward about three feet. Not a problem anywhere else, but in a multi-storey car park it put me in the path of any traffic that might come along early in the morning.

No problem I thought, if I time it right I can roll the car down the ramp and into the parking space opposite me on the next floor down, then sort it out in the morning. So pissed as I was I got in the drivers seat and rolled the car down the ramp, stopping about half way to better judge the distance.

Then I fucked it. The car rolled down the ramp and slowly up into the target car parking space opposite, but I put the break on two foot short of the asking price.

This left the arse end now sticking out almost as far as the front was on the upper level.

I got out the motor in my skiddies scratching my balls and my head for an answer to the problem.

I took my shoes and the jack out the car and used them to chock the wheels, then I let the hand break off and pushed the two ton beauty in my underpants, kicking the shoe's and jack under the tires and chocking as I went. After a half hour of this palaver I got the car in the space, not exactly where I wanted it, but close enough. Then I sat for a while to let the sweat dry a bit, before climbing back in the sack.

The next morning I was rudely woken up by a security guard, two in fact, the female guard stood behind the fat bloke. I didn't see her at first. He tapped on the window next to me. I wish he'd just banged it, the tapping was pissin me right off. I wound the window down,

"What's up?" I said

"Before you leave here make sure you clean your mess up" Said the guard.

I looked on the floor outside the car,

"What mess?" I quizzed

"That mess up there" The guard replied, pointing to the parking space on the next level.

"Fuck all to do with me" I said with cocky confidence.

Then without saying a word the security guard pointed to a CCTV camera on the ceiling right in front of the car and another one off to the side of it. The female security guard blushed and the fat one said:

"Best nights entertainment in twenty years mate"

I was caught red handed and I too afford a blush and agreed to clean up the mess. I got up straight way and put things right, then had to go into their office and ask for a push, I could tell the fat man wasn't gonna help so I reminded him about his nights entertainment and with a laugh he changed his mind.

I always expected to see that footage on: "You've been framed," and did my best to keep it to myself, but unfortunately for me the female Security Guard was the girlfriend of one of our lads, that night in the Pub I got to relive the whole experience again.

Using that car was a privilege that gave me a lease of life I'd never known and it was given to me by my best friend, apart from that night I never sat in her drivers seat after a drink, and I never bumped her, for a long time she was my escape. I loved that car and all she bought, and I will always have a soft spot in my heart for my time with her.

Support all your friends, in all their ventures

My friend Jim.

The Orphans

In hindsight I should have stayed away, but I always loved bikes and the rebel way of life that appeals to all youngsters. The Orphans was a small but passionate family orientated motor cycle club with ideas bigger than itself. The original Orphans were all Airborne and were referred to as Aldershot or Airborne Orphans.

The family bike club was founded by Bill, myself, Phil C and Woody. Bill talked the part and he looked the part, big moustache bald head, stocky build and tattoos all over, you could even say he looked mean but the truth was he was far from it. He wasn't a hardman in any respect but he was a great bloke. He wasn't a comedian. He never told jokes, not well anyway, but he could always make you laugh. He could find humour in anything and had a feel good factor about him. You always felt good when he was about. I was always quite a serious person till I met him, but being around him I learned to find the funny side of things, and more importantly learnt to laugh at my own mistakes and not treat them like the end of the world.

After I eventually got my bike licence, he talked me into buying this banged up old black Indian Enfield 350cc. Fuck this thing was hard work. I got it from Two Wheels in North Camp, a small town just north of Aldershot from an old guy called Mick Hunter, another nice guy. What this bloke didn't know about bikes wasn't worth knowing.

On the day I bought my new ride, I rode it out Mick's workshop turned right and within 40 yards was pulled over by the local plod and asked to produce tax and insurance. None of which I had. Once again motor bikes were at the centre of my troubles. I was banged to rights again and ended up losing my licence. The penalty was 6points and a £250 fine, which isn't too bad, except I already had 6points taken off for other minor offences like speeding, again on bikes. So I lost my licence for 6 months.

At the time I was a bit vexed and pissed off but Bill had a way of making it seem ok, his whole outlook on life was different, it was a refreshing break from my day job (The British Army). I used the Orphans as a little bit of escapism and somewhere to go and hang out after work.

As the Orphans, we did the usual bike club thing, we had parties went to bike rallies, hung round as friends and wore "Colours". Our patches, our Ensign, the thing that would distinguish us from other bike clubs. I enjoyed them but I never took them too seriously. It was a self promoted ideal with no real value, but they did separate us from other bike clubs, so they did served their purpose.

We were all at that time in the Army and I wore my BBC (Blue badge of courage) with uncompromising pride. They were my Colours, a distinction I really did have to work for. Bill never quite understood that being a Craphat. There was never any doubt about the size of the chip on Bills shoulder, but I still thought him a good bloke.

The Orphans bike club was founded by four of us initially. We each of us held office and before long our numbers grew. A year before the Orphans came together we did the West of England bike show in Shepton Mallet, All the other guys got dolled up like bikers but I wore the same as always, jeans Dbs (desert boots, also known as dessys) and a maroon top.

Phil C said to me at the bar:

"Why are you dressed like that?"

"Look around you Phil" I said "The whole room is full of guys flying their colours and these are mine mate"

"Clever Bastard" he replied and with that took off his wet proofs, and was dressed identical to me or any other paratrooper in Aldershot.

Phil C was so Airborne his bedding smelt like the sky. We loved the Airborne Brotherhood. Again, something Bill never really understood. He always sort to wear Colours of his own making. He wasn't Airborne, he was a Driver at a Hat Unit and missed the promotion ladder a few times, judging by his nine years served and only one stripe. He'd lost all ambition in the Army and just used it as a nine to five job. That's why he was so relaxed and care free. It was great to be around him but unlike some, I never wanted to be him.

Mick, his best mate was Airborne serving with 3 Para, but he'd recently been bust down to private and Court Marshalled, so his faith in the Army was running thin to say the least.

But at nineteen I was very much enjoying the Airborne Brotherhood way of life. The bike club was just bit of a hobby.

There was a time when Bill and I were very close, to a point I was at his house every day and eventually rented a room from him. I think the fact we were so close blinded him to my lack off passion and commitment to his cause. I was having a great time with the Orphans but it was always on my terms.

After later spending time with the Outlaws the best description I can give the Orphans is; we were a social club, with a wannabe bike club problem.

* * *

We did socialize lots and partied lots and with that came women. No problem for me I was single but all the clubs other higher ranks were married and that's when things started to go wrong, for the club anyway.

Over the time with the Orphans I'd become a friend to the clubs families which played a big part in all aspects of the club. At the time I was even lodging with Bill his wife and 2 kids.

The Regiment I was serving with at the time shipped me off to Cyprus for 3 weeks and when I got back my seemingly good social life was ripped out from under me.

Bill had left his wife for a newer younger bird, Mick had moved out and in with his new girlfriend and I was left still living in Bill's house listening to both families breaking their hearts for nearly a month.

I tried to contact Bill and Mick, but with no luck and every night had to go home and watch an 8 year old boy, Bills son, suffer for reasons I couldn't explain, and he, poor bugger could never understand. I've always regretted not being able to help him more but I was very young and didn't know were to start.

Then one day out the blue Bill turned up at my Unit. I didn't know whether to smack him or hug him but as it was we shook hands and embraced. It was good to see him. Somehow during his absence a contempt for him had manifested in my mind, but upon seeing him, all that went away. We were friends and that was the only reason I supported his family. In a vain hope things would go back to normal, surely that had to stand for something. So one would think!

What I should have done is stayed on talking terms with everyone and walked away, moved out of Bill's house, resigned the colours I felt sceptical about in the first place and gone back to my Unit but Bill talked me round saying things would be fine. It was his life and I've always supported my friends so I went along with him.

That weekend we partied again, this time at Mick's new girlfriend's house, she'd had problems with her ex and I'd been asked by Mick to secure the house some weeks earlier, so I knew where abouts in Farnham I had to go.

As soon as I arrived I knew there was something wrong, apart from the fact I didn't know anyone there, the members of the club that should have been there, the Vice President and Sgt at Arms, weren't there. All this would spell shit for me over the next few hours.

The other thing that was instantly apparent was, apart from a few, all the other guests were women, friends of Bill and Mick's new girlfriends.

Before that point the wives had influence on the decisions of the club, but now the women were running it and with Bill and Mick both fuck struck they could mould the club anyway they wanted and as I still had contact with all the families, I was never gonna be allowed in that mould.

Deliberately ignoring all this I got myself a beer and enjoyed the night. At about nine o'clock I was pissing about with one of the few other guys at the do and popped a side view mirror off one of the girl's cars and handed it to her. She was vain as fuck and God knows why, you'd need to drink her pretty if you were gonna talk to her and I don't think the male human body can consume enough alcohol to make you want to fuck it. Every five minutes she was back out to the car checking her make up, so I thought I'd save her the walk and hand her the side mirror of her car.

The whole party had a laugh about it and no damage was done the mirror just popped back in. but she was Mick's new girlfriend's best mate. In hindsight though it wouldn't have made a difference, it was an excuse and that's all the new girlfriends needed.

Almost instantly Bill and Mick were bitching at me about conduct and etiquette within the club, I just fucked them both off, Mick was a big lad and a lot older than me, but I'd seen him for what he was even before I went to Cyprus I liked him a lot, but he never bothered me and Bill couldn't punch his way out of a school playground, so I knew if worst came to worst I'd get home that night and one of them wouldn't.

But why should I have to think like that? We were friends, weren't we?

The reason was a simple one, the pair of them were fuck struck. It happens when you leave your childhood sweetheart for a younger benefits bird whose fucked and sucked her way through life giving you things you never had before.

During the row that followed Bill asked me for my colours, I'd felt that one coming and wasn't surprised. It wasn't a big deal either, so I gave them to him, as I did Mick snatched them off him and disappeared. A few minutes later Mick turned back up having cut the colours in half, I didn't quite see the point to that but I'm sure it had something to do with disgrace and club honour. Not a subject these two could really solidly argue.

With that pissed as I was, pissed as we all were, I went to get on my bike and in doing so dropped the fucker and with no chance of help from Bill and Mick to pick it up, I just thought, bollocks I'll get it later and walked home.

* * *

That was pretty much the end for the Orphans as a whole. I don't think Bill realized it was the families that held the club together not him. Others went the same way I did, set up at parties then fucked off and others took the initiative and just left. Only Phil went on to bigger things within the MC 1% world.

Often when I think about it I can't help but laugh, the event itself was funny looking back at it. It's a shame though they were good guys and it was a good time, there were just too many other agenda's and not enough commitment to keep it that way.
Bill went off to live in Wales shortly after the Orphans fell apart. He set up another club there. We nicked named them the Lemmings, because two or three of them had had bike accidents in the same place. Last time I spoke to him he'd adopted a Welsh Accent, another sign of his massive insecurity. He swears blind now that he's Welsh but I know he's from Aylesbury England. He never was happy with who he was. Shame, Sean Williams (Bill) was a good guy.

I realized during that time I never needed patches to be an Orphan. I was born in Aldershot and served my country from Aldershot and with no family there, I truly am an Orphan. An Aldershot Airborne Orphan.

<pre>
     One Englishman---------A Poet
    Two Englishmen----------A Club
   Three Englishmen----------An Empire
</pre>

Herman Goring

Good Idea Brigade

I was sent to the School of Military Transport in the north of England to get my driving licence.

I thought I'd come back with a car licence but the Army only did duel licences at the time. So I got my HGV two at the same time.

Leconsfield also houses raw recruits fresh out of basic training and sent up there to learn their trade. I shared a truck with two of them and a split arse from some Unit in Germany. The recruits all had tasks to complete when they weren't driving so had to stay on the Barracks, but as we were seen as experienced soldiers we were allowed to do our own thing when the driving was finished for the day.

The local pub was called the Valiant Soldier; this was quickly dubbed the "Violent Squaddie" by the troops stationed there and as it was the only pub in the area with any tolerance for soldiers, this is where I drank. As I was the only Paratrooper on the camp I was in no hurry to make Craphat friends and I've always been happy with my own company, so I drank alone.

I'd passed my driving test and just had to do the Combat phase and I had two days off before that began.

In my short time there I'd banged heads with the RP sergeant a few times. The problem was he tried to treat me like a recruit and I didn't like it. I found out later that he had failed P-company, and that's where the real problem was. I was what he couldn't be, Airborne.

On my day off, after a quick ten mile run, I went into town for a few pints. I always prefer to drink during the day when I can. It's quieter and more relaxing. Nights are always a bit busy for me. When I got to the Violent Squaddie it was empty, and Pete the barman challenged me to a friendly game of pool. As we finished the game the splitarse who shared my truck came in with a group of mates. I went down to get another pint and as I was ordering, Donna the Split, offered to get it in her round, then she invited me over to her mob to drink with them. It was an afternoon with a difference. They drank like men, swore like men and farted like men and I tried to keep up.

I asked Donna what their plans were for the rest of the day. She said they were gonna have a few in the pub then go for a curry, then back to their block with a couple of crates to finish the party. Then unexpectedly she invited me to join them.

The female accommodation is strictly off limits to men and their block sits right behind the Guardroom in Camp. They all agreed they'd just smuggle me in, but I had a better plan. I left the girls for a while and popped over the road to a Charity shop for some supplies. I got back ten minutes later and sat down to a fresh pint with a Tesco carrier bag hiding the tools for my cunning plan. Donna asked what was in the bag. I told her, and then I told her my plan. She laughed, gave me ten out of ten for initiative, then bet me a score I wouldn't do it.

The day went on, at the Indian the girls bet who could eat the hottest dish, Col Chapman and I played similar games in the Shot. But at that time I stuck with the Chicken madras. I'd never drunk with female soldiers before. It was an eye opener, they were as bad as we were. I was out drunk and out eaten that day and even though the competition was on, I couldn't bring myself to let out loud burps and farts in front of women.

After a good drink and a great feed, we all went to the local off licence for a carry out then back to the Barracks. Donna grinned at me still betting I wouldn't go through with my master plan, but with twenty quid at stake, on my wage I was well up for it.

At the gate, my ever growing pain in the arse the RP Sergeant called me over to him. I was about to walk over when Donna stopped me and wrote 8654 on the palm of my hand in eye liner.

"Room 3" She said "That's where we'll be"

"With you soon" I replied.

Then, Tesco bag under arm, I continued over to my patiently waiting Nemesis who was surrounded by the on going Guard and the girls went back to their block.

"Why didn't you show the Guard your ID card?" He said.

"Because I know him" I replied

"What's that got to do with a Part One Standing Order?" He said, with the right arse.

"What Standing Order?" I enquired

"To show your ID card anytime you're asked to by the Guard" He said

"He didn't ask to see it," He was getting wound up now, I went on "Surely you must know that recognition is the best form of identification"

The guys stood around him started laughing. I could see he felt humiliated and a bit lost for words. I felt for him, I'd seen his type quite a few times the envy of the Maroon Machine is wide spread. When Rank also requires knowledge and is no longer taken at face value guys like this always come short. He motioned with his head signalling me to move on. In silence I left and went back to the block.

It was dark outside and I'd had loads of beer by now. My plan was bound to work. In the privacy of my room I emptied the contents of the Tesco carrier bag on the bed. I'd bought some red sandals a down to the ankle blue summer dress a shawl and a straw hat. Then put them on.

The fit was a bit snug, but in the dark I could get away with it. I looked at the code Donna had written on the palm of my hand, all I had left was 654. The first digit had rubbed off and for the life of me I couldn't remember it. No matter I confidently thought, it'll take at most nine attempts to get in. Then pulling the shawl cross my shoulders I made my way over to the female accommodation.

It was the only block that had lights covering all sides of it. But that's what the disguise was for. I reached the door attracting no attention and if that first number had been 1, 2, or 3 I'd have been home and dry, but on the forth attempt I was lit up by the Dragons eye torch carried by the roaming patrols that walked the Camp.

"Are you OK there sweetheart?" A young male voice said.

I nodded keeping my back to them and still trying the door. But the guard couldn't have seen me nod.

"I said are you OK?" He called again "If you've forgotten the code I can get it for you from the Guardroom."

And with that he started radioing the Guardroom that was only twenty meters away. Bless him, he was only trying to help but I could have done without it. I was stuck for options. I couldn't run in what I wearing, it was far to snug for that. I had to get in the block, I kept trying the door. I got to 6.

"The Sarg is coming now, to let you in" said the Guard.

Fuck, that was the last thing I needed. I took a step back into the light. The RP Sergeant was ten feet away. He looked right at me and for the second time that evening I'd made him speechless. For long seconds we stared at each other and then he broke the silence.

"You'd better come with me" He said

I was bang to rights. No point putting up any kind of resistance. He walked to my side and we both walked back to the guardroom.

"Cell one" He said to his 2ic, who escorted me there, "You can stay there till morning, then you're up in front of the CSM.

He looked at me with a victorious smile and a childish smugness.

"You'll do twenty eight days inside for this" He said still grinning.

I entered the cell and got my head down. I slept like a baby.

The next morning the RP sergeant woke me up personally. Not out of pride in his work but to dig at me again and assure me I was gonna do time for what I'd done. Then he went on to say he would ask I did the time at that nick and if he got his way he would make my life hell.

"Can I go and get changed before I see the CSM?" I said.

Still wearing my blue dress and sandals.

"Not a fuckin chance" He replied.

I couldn't help but laugh. He didn't see the funny side at all, but that's all I could see. He was hoping to humiliate me. But he would have to try a lot harder than that, my character had been built by the best. I'd done a lot more embarrassing things than march through a Camp in a dress. At least I had clothes on this time.

Marching to the Admin block I turned every head on the Camp and when the CSM turned up, he saw the funny side too. As did the other Officers and Staff. In the CSM's office the RP Sergeant tried to make a bigger deal of it than it was. But like the CSM pointed out. I wasn't "Inside" the female accommodation and the Standing Order didn't cover intent.
The CSM could have nailed me to the wall but he didn't. He knew the RP had a chip on his shoulder and been out to get me for whatever he could and the CSM wasn't gonna crucify me for it. Instead he advised me to give the RP Sergeant a wide birth for my remaining time there.

I finished the course a week later and went back to Aldershot and the normality of Battalion life. When I got back to my own bed space the lads had laid a blue dress out on my bed, I wore it out that night on the piss for a laugh.

* * *

With my ability to pick a wrong un, I spent the early years of my Army career wondering if I'd ever get laid. I never had any trouble talking to women. I just pretended I was someone else. A Helicopter Pilot, a Civil Servant working for the Prime Minister and on a few beers I could get really extreme. I told one girl I was a Cruise Missile Pilot. When she asked me what that involved I told her my job was to fly Cruise Missiles to strategic locations in the Soviet Union, then I would fly back first class and the Russian's would send the missile back in the post when they were sure it was safe.
That's not the best either. I've been an eye model for Avon, a nude art model for the local university and an under water wood welder for British Telecom. It's all bullshit of course but the fun as an eighteen nineteen year old trooper was trying to sell it.

On a night out in Oxford, Stu and I told these two birds we were on the British Hockey Team that won at the Olympics, might sound extreme but if that team stood in front of you amongst fifty other men, could you point them out? It seemed to impress them no end and it looked like we might get a bit.

Stu and I had planned to catch the last train back to London and go clubbing there till we could get a train back to the shot. But one of the girls suggested we stay at hers for the night. Excellent we thought not only would we save money but things were looking better on the scoring front to.

As the night rolled on Stu had bit of a problem with some bloke at the bar we were in. Not being one to take any shit, Stu smacked him and when an eighteen stone prop forward hits you full on the jaw generally you get knocked out and this bloke did. He hit the ground like a sack of spanners, the whole place erupted. Doormen going one way and us going the other. I thought we'd blown it with the birds, but to my surprise the two girls met us outside.

We decided to go to the nearest off licence and go back to this bird's house and continue our evening there. On the short walk back to hers Stu asked if she had a boyfriend. I knew the bird I was with didn't, I asked early in the night I found that if I got the important stuff out the way early I spent less on drinks I'd never get back. Sounds a bit tight I know but a Private Soldiers wage is too. I only wished Stu had done the same.

"He's on a Rugby Tour" She said "and won't be back till tomorrow"
"That's cutting it a bit fine" I said to Stu
"We'll leave first thing" He replied "It'll be fine.

Not comforted in any way by Stu's calm James Bond approach, I went along anyway. For the rest of the walk I made small talk with the girl I was with and Stu did his animal impression and poured and dribbled all over his.

She lived in a third floor flat ten minutes from the off licence. As we walked in the front door the toilet was immediately to our right and the small window looked out the side of the block. The front room was up the corridor and to the left and the kitchen was straight ahead. Fuck knows where the bedrooms were, we weren't there that long.

We were stood in the kitchen with a beer talking and setting the mood when a loud bang on the door stopped us all in our tracks. It was her old man. Not only had he come back early but he'd bought the whole Rugby team round for a celebration. Stu's bird started to panic and mine went into a frenzy and hid somewhere. It was the last I saw of her. Twenty quid in the off licence, fifteen quid in the bar and not so much as a flash of leg.

We hid in the toilet, well we squeezed into the toilet and she let them in. Already he was losing his patients. This guy was not going to wait to be let into his own house. No sooner had she let the pissed up rabble in the door than she started to fuck things up proper.

"You can't use the toilet" She said.

With that, the reply neither of us wanted to hear.

"Why"

Then someone tried the door.

We could hear loads of them out there and a second after the door wouldn't open a voice followed heavy fists saying

"Who's in there?"

"No one" I said, with that Stu and I burst out laughing.

The door was not going to hold for long, the little brass latch had done well to hold the first bang and if it hadn't been for the lack of run up it might have gone in on that first attempt. Stu held the door, and I started to climb out the window, it was small and it was gonna be a squeeze for the big guy. I lowered myself out and took the leap. I cracked my ankle off the window sill below. But I survived the fall ok. Within seconds Stu followed me out. It was like watching a giant super man, (agile fat bastard.) We pulled ourselves together and legged it. We'd missed the last train back to London and spent the night freezing our arses off on the Station Platform laughing about the nights events.

* * *

When I wasn't backing the wrong horse or chasing the wrong dog, my sense of humour was acting as contraception. I'm not a great looking guy but I can pick holes in anything, "she's to fat, to thin, look at the size of her feet, what happened to your hair?" If I was ever gonna have a girlfriend I was gonna have to lower my standards. Mind you to look at my Ex wife you'd think I'd just thrown them out the window along with my dignity.

At the start of every LPBG Exercise the whole Brigade assembles at Cirencester. The world's largest bedroom is there. It's an aircraft hanger stacked wall to wall with bunk beds and if any man thought the guardroom stank after a night of twenty guys farting and belching, it has nothing on the humidity in that hanger after fifteen hundred men had been at it for three days.

Its an ideal place to assemble that many troops. That and it's within striking distance of RAF Lyham and RAF Brize Norton.

One afternoon Big Sid got a few of us together to go out for a pint. We got a cab into the local town and had a wander round. The day went on and the beer flowed well and about nine o'clock made our way to a small nightclub.

Within minutes Big Sid gate crashed a table of girls by the door. They received us well, and were quick to join in with our night and the humour that went with it. The night went on and the girl I was sat next to made good conversation, probably because she was driving and not drinking.

I thought I was just doing my drunken squaddie bit. But the girl I was talking to found me quite charming. The guys left about eleven to get a take away and start the walk back the Camp. I stayed for another because the girl I was talking to said she'd drop me off.

On the drive back she suggested we pull in at a picnic area just up the road from the Barracks and continue our chat in the coolness of the summer night. That's not exactly what I had in mind when she suggested that but its pretty close.

We got out the car and went and sat on one of the tables. Looking through slowly clearing beer goggles, I started to notice odd things I hadn't earlier, like the modified steering wheel in the car and the slight limp on my new girlfriend. I must have been concentrating to hard and showing it. You know when you know you're staring but you can't stop. That's how hard I was concentrating.

"I've got a false leg" She said

"I did wonder" I replied

"Does it bother you?" She said lowering her head.

"No, does it fuck," I answered "Give us a look, I never seen one before"

She shied away to start with but I made satire of it and in no time she felt comfortable talking about it and showing it to me. She was quite a good looking girl. A bit shorter then me, slim at the waist and big busted with long hair.

"You're a cross between Robo Cop and Pamela Anderson" I said

She laughed it off and pulled me in for a kiss. I discreetly avoided the kiss and turned it into a cuddle. I couldn't get that leg out of my head. I put my hand on the top of her thigh and found myself playing with it.

"Does it come off?" I said

With that she leaned back onto the picnic table, hitched her skirt up and simply popped it off.

"It's held on by light pressure" She said, handing it to me.

I stood there holding it like King Arthur did Excalibur or Luke Skywalker did a light sabre, as she explained how it worked, but I couldn't really hear her the Devil on my shoulder was telling me what a great trophy this would make for the Unit rest room.

Then it happened. I was in full flight running back to the Barracks with stolen NASA technology in hand. I could hear my new ex girlfriend yelling at me but I kept running, too scared to witness her hopping back to her car to try and run me down.

I got back to the block in short time and put the prosthetic limb under my bed and got my head down.

The next day the whole Brigade was called out onto the disused runway on the Camp. A Police car pulled up and out of the car got two local Police and a woman, a limping woman. They were met by the CO and the RSM.

"Has this got anything to do with that thing you were clunking around last night?" Sid said to me.

"Very possibly" I said back.

After walking the world's longest line up for over half an hour she got to our Platoon. She saw me out the corner of her eye and walked straight to me.

"Ok, my little sprint champ can I have the baton back please" She said with half a smile.

I looked at her, I thought she'd be really pissed off, but she seemed ok with it. The RSM sent me off to retrieve my trophy and meet them at the Guardroom. I doubled away and the Brigade was dismissed behind me.

I was back at the Guardroom leg in hand in no time. I knew I was in the shit, no point making it deeper by dragging my heels. In shame I handed her the leg then took a step back and stood to Attention. I was in the presents of half the Brigades bigwigs.

"Ill be seeing you soon" She said, then turned and walked away.

I didn't know what she meant, but I soon found out. Despite all the red faces very little was said about the whole thing. When asked I put it down to Good Idea Brigade. They fucked me off to my Unit and the LPBG went on as planned and we jumped in that afternoon.

Three weeks later the exercise ended. When we got back to the lines I was called in in front of the new OC. My punishment had been suggested by my almost new girlfriend and agreed to by my superiors. In exchange for running off with the £35,000 robotic appendage, I was to go and work with her for two weekends and then take her out to dinner and apologise. How she pulled that off I'll never know.

That next weekend I drove up to Gloucester to meet her at her place of work. She worked in a school for the physically handicapped kids. It was a place the kids could go at weekends to do sporting activities they wouldn't normally be able to do.

It was an inspiring weekend, climbing being my thing I helped out on the climbing wall for the most part. I worked with kids that had no hands, arms even legs missing. But nothing stopped these kids giving it their all. I was genuinely moved by the hard work these kids put in and I found myself counting my blessings.

On the Sunday night I took her out to dinner, if you can call KFC dinner. I apologised and I meant it. I tried to point out that I wasn't being heartless, it just seemed like the thing to do. I balls'd up my explanation the more I spoke the more heartless I sounded, so I stopped talking, she said she understood. Her character was as strong as any I've ever encountered.

I've been back to the school several times to help out over the years, and Debbie and her new husband John remain good friends of mine to this day.

* * *

Not all attempts to get me leg over went so well as to just fail. As a young trooper I chatted a bird up at the bar in the Shot (as you do) and after a good nights drinking went home with her. Well some of the way anyway. She lived in a village just outside Aldershot, we got a cab out to hers and on the way stopped at the local village pub for last knockings.

The atmosphere was not good. Civvies hate Squaddies, especially when they go out with local chicks. So we made the decision not to stay. On the short up hill walk back to her house, like so many times before I engaged my mouth before my brain.

"You'll be fucked when you get to the top of this slope, big girl like you" I said.

With that she said:

"You'll never know you cheeky fucker, now fuck off"

I took that as my queue to leave and did without a second thought. "Silly bastard" I thought.

I made my way back through the village to a bus stop on the far side hoping for a late night bus. A few minutes later a cab pulled up, rolled its window down and the cabbie said:

"Taxi for Jones"

"Yep! That's me" I answered without hesitation.

Then from nowhere a guy put his hand on my shoulder pulled me backwards and said:

"Fuck off, chancing squaddie cunt I'm Jones"

Not thinking any further than the aggressive hand on my shoulder and the "Squaddie Cunt" comment, I turned and smacked the guy with a wild left hook. He never went down but he went back nicely giving me more time and room to fight him.

The cabbie shut the passenger door and took off at a great rate of knots and the civie and I stepped into each other for the next few minutes.

It was nothing more than a drunken brawl, I got a few good shots in and took a few good shots. Then I lost my balance and as my hand gripped the curb my opponent stamped on it breaking three of my fingers. This raised the fight to a whole new level. I regained my footing and lifted the guy into the air dropping him hard and headfirst into the floor, then I stamped on his head a few times and he went limp.

I stopped my attack straight away, he was still, but he was breathing. The pub only a few doors down was now emptying out. I chose not to stay for the lynching party that could gather in a moments notice and ran the five miles back to the block, nursing my broken fingers all the way.

Later that night at about three in the morning I was woken up by the Military and civie Police.

"Are you Private Bla Bla" said one of the civie coppers.

"Yes mate" I replied "What's up?"

"Were you in a fight at a bus stop in Tongham earlier this evening?" He went on.

"Shit" I thought here we go, the spineless wankers complained now I'm in all sorts of trouble.

"Yes Sir I was" I said, It was always good forum to change from mate to Sir when the shit was flying.

"In that case" He said "I'm arresting for the Murder of Mr John Jones"

As the words left the lips of the copper my head started spinning, I felt sick and faint I couldn't believe what he was saying.

I was taken to Aldershot Police Station and advised by the CSM not to say anything until my Brief arrived, but I was panicking and couldn't seem to keep my mouth shut. I answered every question they asked. When the Brief finally arrived he quickly informed me I hadn't done myself any favours in talking.

I was in a cell for the rest of the night and most of the next day. I played the fight in my head over and over, did I really hit him that hard? I was sure he was breathing when I left him. I could see the end of my career coming out of this and a life time spent behind bars. Good job there was a toilet in the cell I couldn't stop throwing up.

After several hours I was taken in for another interview, one of the arresting officers had spotted "Inconsistencies" between my statement and the crime scene. The body of John Jones was found about fifty metres up from the bus stop and I had stated that the fight never left the bus stop. Their big question now was how did the body travel so far? A question I had no answer to. After spending the rest of the day and a very sleepless night in the cell, they let me go.

The post mortem revealed John Jones had been hit from behind by a car. The Coroner's report suggested that after our drunken punch up, Jones had recovered and started walking the same path I ran. He too was from Aldershot. Then he'd become a victim of a Hit and Run.

As much as the Police pressed for a Man slaughter charge against me they couldn't make it stick. The coroner's verdict was "Death by Misadventure" the driver was never found. In less than six hours my life had gone from;

Nearly getting me leg over, to nearly spending my life in jail. For years after I maintained the Magical ability to get myself blown out at the last minute. I've also since, then never hit anyone with a drink inside me.

"There is no limit, to the amount of trouble your dick can get you into

Mark Plausin

Northern Ireland

Before any Soldier can patrol the Streets or Rural Provinces of Northern Ireland he has to spend time at NIURTS. The Northern Ireland Urban Rural Tactical Training School. It's an All Arms school run by specialist elements from a number of Infantry Regiments and caters for each Regiment's individual needs. Northern Ireland has been a vital training ground for British troops since the seventies. Many people are of the opinion that one reason the peace talks were successful there was because Iraq was available for the use of Urban Training. After the occupation (I won't use the term liberation,) of it in 2003 by the W Bush Administrations Coalition, it became the obvious choice now that Bosnia had calmed down. It also turned out to be a well timed and shrewd political move for Tony Blair and a lucky one for Paramilitary leaders.

It's a fact that the Irish have gained the sympathy of the white world over the last thirty years, every man and his dog celebrates St Patrick's and will swear by his non existent Irish ancestors that he has green blood. It's almost become a fashion.

But the only people today that care about the Arab world is the Arab world. So for now the United Kingdom is relatively quiet and the new enemy the new face of terror has a colour. One can only hope the true patriots of Great Britain don't forget it hasn't always been this way.

* * *

Training at the school was very intense but relaxed a very professional environment. The school has a purpose built town, nick named "Tin City", used to exercise Patrol Techniques. How to exit a secure area, How to cover open areas, How to cordon off an area, and the best bit,

Riot Control. The class is divided in two. One side plays "Angry Paddy," with bricks bottles and petrol bombs and the other side puts into practice the Riot Control Tactics taught earlier that day. Having petrol bombs thrown at you and being bricked by an angry mob really is an adrenaline filled endeavour even in a controlled environment. However, throwing the petrol bombs and bricks and generally reeking havoc really does bring out your inner thug. The riot training phase is controlled aggression at its height, that's not to say with all that fire and brick dust it's a casualty free event.

The classroom is equally as taxing. There's a lot to take in and the training differs greatly from that of the Brecon Infantry School and The Depot and Training Regiment at Browning Barracks. It leans more to the policing element of military training as opposed to open Warfare. Powers of Arrest, and Stop and Search procedures the searching of vehicles, people and premises, are a few of the subjects covered. It was also the first time I bumped into the bullshit world of "PC" Political Correctness. The art of not upsetting the person who is deliberately using your own Laws to their advantage, making it easier for them to fuck you over while you smile sweetly. (I'll step off the soap box here)

The most controversial subject was the "Shoot to Kill" policy. We questioned different interpretations for hours, but it always came down to the same thing. If you as the man on the ground made a judgment call that took a life, everyone had to agree with that call, even the heads of shed that wouldn't have been there at the time. Because if you didn't have that unanimous support, you were going down.

The most popular case is probably that of Lee Clegg. I know I'm not the only one who thinks he was nothing more than a political scape goat.

Since Northern Ireland I've worked in countries where killing a man who's a direct danger to you halved the paperwork, if the other guy couldn't give an interpretation of events, then the man standing is taken at his word. Only in the UK does the dead guy get such a hearing.

The Staff at NIURTS do an outstanding job. By the time the course ended I was well educated and well prepared for whatever Northern Ireland had to offer. All I needed now was experience and that was guaranteed.

* * *

Palace Barracks is on a hillside in Hollywood Belfast, and that's where we based ourselves from. There were no surprises. It had a NAAFI a civie café and all the things you'd find on a British Army Camp anywhere around the world. It even had a very busy helicopter pad.

One night I came out the bar to find three guys trying to jump start a gazelle by pushing it across the pad. I believe they spent the next three months patrolling a cell in Colchester.

A Company started working out of Musgrave Park Hospital (MPH). None of us was allowed anything to do with hospital itself or the staff; any attempts to go wenching would be quickly followed by a twenty eight day stretch. So our bit was sort of stuck on the side of the Hospital grounds. It was here we all shaved our heads and prepped our kit ready for the real work.

Using MPH as a base of operations we travelled to Woodburn Police station and occasionally out to White Rock, it was from there we would patrol the volatile streets of the infamous West Belfast.

We patrolled in sections of six called Brick's. Four satellite bricks would patrol round one primary brick and on that team there was an RUC copper going about his business. The RUC are a very strict and disciplined Police force made up of both Protestants and Catholics alike. They dress a lot like the German Poltzi it's a distinct bottle green and they don't take any shit whatsoever. The older guys in the Company took me under their wing until I knew the ropes for myself, ever pressing to be an asset and not a burden I learned fast.

Each Brick has a female searcher. Ours was Caroline W, she was a great girl with a great sense of humour and she needed it to work with us lot. She was from the RAOC and attached to the RMP's and on loan to us, there was another searcher but she was an RMP and had her head stuck up her arse all the time thinking she was better than anyone else.

Para Reg, do things a little different in Northern Ireland and the locals don't tend to fuck about with us to the degree they do with the Hats, probably because we go out better prepared.

One of Paddy's more ruthless tactics is to lace a telegraph pole with explosives and time it so as when the female searcher walks passed it one of their scroats smacks the girl in the face and runs off. This makes the rest of the Brick surround the female victim and the semtex laced street lamp goes off and the IED gets everyone.

Our "Actions On" for such an incident is to go to ground, call the female searcher to a safe area and call the location in for the EOD to deal with. Thus keeping the patrol going and not letting Paddy call the shots.

Caroline's nose had been broken twice in such incidents. She never got an ounce of sympathy on either occasion. That said, we had respect for that bird she was bit of a Stalwart, she told me one afternoon, she loved working with the Parachute Regiment, she felt safe.

* * *

The hate for the British Soldier is deeply seeded in Northern Ireland. Children as young as four and five shout profanity such as, "You fuckin Brit cunt ya" and "Brit Bastard" from school playgrounds and tower block balconies and shockingly they can name every part of the SA80 rifle from the magazine to the gas parts and tell you what it does.

There were even several incidents of parents filling water pistols with battery acid and sending there kids out to squirt us, (Little Bastards) two days later we'd be in the QM's swapping kit, the kids had no hope, they hated us, its all they knew.

I always kept a pocket full of Mojo's. A simple two for a penny sweet, then if we got caught up in a cordon or held up for any great length of time, I'd give one to the nearest kid. He'd tell his mates and in no time I'd be surrounded by kids. No IRA sniper in his right mind would take that shot. They used the kids to attack, we used the kids to defend. I got the tip from a mate of mine in 3 Para. My guys loved it, it showed initiative and it work well to the Hearts and Minds side of things.

The kids knew everything that was going on. What cars were strange to the estate and what roads not to go down that day, they were a great source of: "On Sight Intel"

I had to play it carefully though and ration it right, because as soon as the sweet supply ended the abuse started up again. Little fuckers were only as loyal as the sweet supply.

The Honey Trap is another favourite of Paddy's. The traps been used since the dawn of time all round the world and plays directly on mans biggest enemy, "his dick" The idea is that a young usually good looking girl rubs her leg up some horny squaddie, chats him up a bit shows him a bit o leg and maybe strokes his thigh then she takes him home after he's had a few beers, and half way to falling in lust, she'll even get the cab fare, finally when they get back to hers and when his guard has been completely taken over by his hard on, the trap is sprung. To his ignorant horror his new girlfriend has lead him drunk and half naked into a room with her brother and ten of his mates and the hiding of a lifetime ensues.

Even the oldest tricks if well set up will get you, and it's a shame. But being tricked with a hard on is shameful. It's not a good position to find yourself in.

I always found the women a bit awkward to deal with in the beginning. A middle age woman spat in my face one day and called me a "Baby Killer" then kicked me in the shin. Another threw a cat at me from a first floor window (The cat ran off unharmed.) calling me a "Dirty pig fuckin Brit shit".

The women of the province all seemed to be barking mad. A man just wouldn't act like that and if he had done, I'd have just smacked him in the mouth, and have him arrested. But you just can't do that to a woman. No matter how deranged she might be. Maybe they play on that, I could never work it out, how does a mother go home and kiss her children after throwing used tampons at a passing soldier whilst calling him a "Baby killing arse sucking ignorant cunt"? It was beyond me, but I had to suck it up, we all did, and treat it as a very unique form of Character Building. A friend of mine Midland Mick once told me:

"Every man should have an Ex wife, if only to teach him restraint".

Back then Northern Ireland was a place of constant protest. The artwork on the walls was tremendous, how the fuck they did it lord only knows. I wonder if the owner of the house they painted on got a say in it and did it raise or destroy the value of the house.

The Bobby Sands memorial is bit of an exception. It's a red artless waist of space compared to some of the pieces and it's on the edge of a fast field. I recon the owner of the house put it there to stop kids kicking footballs of his wall. Hypocrisy is everywhere.

* * *

On my first tour of Northern Ireland, Southy one of the lads bet me it would rain that day. The sun was out and it was a nice day so I took the bet. That afternoon it rained, not a lot but it did rain. This went on for three days. Each day started as a bright summer's day, but each day at some point it rained. We had no access at that point to a TV or a radio so I asked him how he knew it would rain.

"They don't call it the Emerald Isle for nothing" He said "There's a ninety-six percent chance of rain everyday"

He went on to point out, it normally takes about two months to work that out and he thought he'd cash in on the new lad. It was a harmless 50p a day bet and money I was quick to get back with the same bet on the next new lad.

During that tour at MPH, Caroline had a birthday, as usual on request the Fat Splashers (Army Catering Corps) whipped up the mother of all birthday cakes. You just couldn't buy a cake like it. Everyone pulls the piss out of the ACC, the standing joke being "The Army Catering Course is the hardest course in the British Army, the punch line being; No fucker ever passed it". But in over ten years I never had a bad meal or a request they wouldn't cater for.

We put together the Birthday surprise at the end of the days Patrols just after the days debrief. I was put forward as the Birthday surprise stripper. I cut the back off some old combat trousers and filled a water bottle pouch with shaving foam and used my Para Smock to hide my naked chest. Then on the word of command from the Platoon Commander, and with the all the lads singing Happy Birthday and clapping, I did my bit.

I walked from the back of the room to the front where the Platoon Sergeant had sat Caroline on a chair facing the guys, as I walked I took off my smock the Lads clapping and now singing the stripper tune, as I got to Caroline bear chested I stopped and pulled the combat trousers off, the room roared at Caroline's response. I was stood in my boots with nothing more than a webbing belt and water bottle pouch covering my manhood. To finish the performance I sat across Caroline and tactfully rubbed shaving foam into her hair.

It was all over in a few minutes, after which we all shared out the cake. She was a good sport Caroline and unlike many in her field worth making the day memorable to her.

***

Any tour of Northern Ireland before the Cease Fire was an adrenaline filled experience. It was a time of great personal and professional development for me. It was during my first tour I first saw myself as a man among men. The need for the teams to have full confidence in each other was a necessity as it is in all areas of conflict. The guys in my Platoon even though a lot older would hang on anything I said, as I would to them, they relied on my training and their guidance as much as I relied on their experience and once again I felt part of a solid team of professionals, part of a family.

Even now some twenty years on, for security reasons not a lot can't be written (by me anyway) about other certain other events that happened in my time there. But its fair to say that a lot of the War there was as clandestine as it was high media profile. The IRA was the most advanced and well financed Para Military Organisation in the world back then, and I could never understand why, when asked by Prime Minister John Major, Bill Clinton wouldn't make American funding of their cause "Illegal," and yet when partitioned by the War Monger George W Bush the British Government gave their full support to his old mans lost war in Iraq.

Some have said that, all the Para Military Organisations in Ulster got off lightly. They signed up for peace at the right time, because the "Campaign Against Terror Packed" between the UK and the USA could have given the British Special Forces and its Intelligence Community complete autonomy to wipe them out and Intelligence does exist to do that. Adams and McGuiness could very well be dressed in those all too familiar orange suits in Guantanamo today had they dragged the peace talks on for much longer.

As a soldier I don't get a say in the politics or the policies we do as we are told, that's what they pay us and train us to do. But it is hard to live in such a hateful environment and not show and feel hate yourself. A War against militia, especially on your home soil is not like open Warfare. With our laws as they stand, with one you cant touch them and distrust malice and even hate manifests over time, with the latter you can engage them under well thought out and stringent Rules of Engagement, its also done with respect for your enemy. There are some heavy and very powerful emotions a soldier deals with and I don't believe that the public and politicians of Great Britain appreciate it's a lasting burden to many young Soldiers.

TACT: THE ART OF MAKING A POINT, WITHOUT MAKING AN ENEMY.

The Low Level Parachute Trials

Sat in the rest room on the morning of a very normal day in 1993, our Admin Sergeant Smudge comes in and like any other morning took the nominal role. But unlike any other morning he was calling us all by our nick names or first names.

Smudge to me at the time was bit of an arsehole, he found it easy to shout the odds and hand out bullshit tasks. Him and I never saw eye to eye but I never really give a shit, he was the boss. I just did as I was told knowing whatever I did wouldn't be right and I would go home at night with another handful of extras he would forget about, which to many of us just made him a bigger wanker. He would go out of his way on a daily basis to belittle some of the younger troopers and must have hated the Sergeants Mess because he was constantly in our block throwing his weight around.

Basically he was a bully and would do anything to look competent in front of his peers. However, when he wanted something you could always feel him crawling up your arse and that usually started with the use of your nick name or first name.

After taking the Nominal Role he sat in the rest room with us and started chatting like we were all best mates, which would never be the case, a day without seeing this dick was always a good day. After about 10 minutes of him bullshiting the reason arose.

"Who wants to go to America?"

A few of the newer guys shot their hands up. "Silly bastards" I said to JFK under my breath.

* * *

It was a lame game, but it does make for great humour in the Guardroom if you get the chance to do it. If a shitty job needs doing the Guard Commander will ask the guys something like: "Who's got a motor bike licence"

Or "Who hasn't been duty driver"

Of course, instantly you think I qualify for that job and it sounds like a good un. So you shoot your hand up, but when you get to where you're going, all you did was volunteer to make the tea, polish brass or clean the shit house. So with this in mind, all those who'd been in longer than 5 minutes kept their hands down.

* * *

"I need more than two" He said "I need eight"

I looked at JFK and he looked at me and said "What shitty job takes eight?"

"Fuck knows" Said Jimmy C

"It's not a shitty job" Smudge went on "Who wants two weeks in the States?" Then he looked at me and said "How about it?"

Now it had to be a set up. Everyone knew it had to be a set up. This twat hadn't had a good thing to say to me since we met, now I was being offered a two week holiday. With that our Colour Sergeant stuck his head round the corner and said to Smudge:

"You got that eight for San Diego yet?"

"Working on it" Smudge replied.

Our Colour was a great bloke and the glue that held our Platoon together. A hard fucker from the East end of London, but you never met a fairer man, he had the respect of all of us, and he put the credibility into Smudges offer. (We later found out that at the time he stuck his head round and spoke to smudge, he thought Smudge had explained the job.) So when Smudge repeated his offer all hands went up, Smudge would never admit it but that really pissed him off. Even though he had at least twenty hands, Smudge still put me down in his final eight.

"So when does this dream job start? JFK asked

"You need to be ready to go by lunchtime" He said "So you eight, fuck off get ready and back down here in two hours"

So off we went. Back to the block to pack. We needed normal working dress, Civvies and full LPBG gear.

It was only on the way back to the lines, Jim C said:

"What are we gonna be doing in the States?"

We all looked at each other blankly. With the fact that it could have been a wind up and wasn't, and the excitement of a trip to the USA, none of us thought to ask. So no one had an answer let alone an idea of what was to come.

As we walked back through the Lines the others guys met us, not with envy but with more of a: "Rather you than me" attitude and apart from a few "Good luck guys" and a few "Airborne all the way lads" no one really had anything to say.

We walked into the Unit Office which the Colour and Smudge shared.

"You all ready to go then lads" Smudge said with a sarcastic sneer.

"We're ready Sarg, but for what?" Jim C asked the question.

With that the Colour looked up. "You didn't tell them?" the question was directed at Smudge.

"Tell us what" Said Taff

"You're off to the States to test the new LOW LEVEL Parachute" Smudge said

"Low level parachute" Said Jimmy C "We jump at eight hundred feet now, with an operational height of six fifty, how fuckin low do they wanna go?"

The question seemed directed at anyone, but no one had any concrete answers.

"All your questions will be answered when you get there" Said Smudge positively.

Our concerns over this dear devil mission were short lived. After the initial shock of the task at hand, the trials became the Airborne thing to do and we considered ourselves lucky to be chosen.

* * *

By 1500 that afternoon we were at Lynham waiting for a DC10 to take us to San Diego. After a long flight and a short cold stop off in Calgary Canada, we landed in Dullas Military Airbase, where it was hot as hell. The shit part was the next part of the journey. A three hour coach drive to El Centro, which was three hours east into the Californian Desert and three hours away from the San Diego Beaches, bars and thongs we were looking forward to.

When we got to the El Centro Base, we were all amazed, it was like a Butlins holiday camp. They put us all in the same block. It had two man rooms, a TV lounge the President would have been happy with, and a vending machine room where you could get anything from a Burger to a new pair of shoes. The only problem was the air conditioning didn't work, but they solved that by saying it would be fixed the next day.

Predictably, that night we hit the Base night club. We had to show our ID on the way in and anyone under twenty one had to wear an orange bracelet. The idea being you couldn't drink. But as the legal age in the UK is eighteen the Yanks compromised and let those under age drink beer only.

The next day the job began. We would do two jumps a day, one early morning and one mid afternoon. Everyman was weighed and his container loaded up to the parachutes maximum weight limit. The bigger guys jumped with small loads, those of us of the smaller verity jumped with heavy and large loads.

It was still stupidly hot, 40 degrees plus, and I couldn't drink enough. Water and Gatorade were in abundance and we needed it. Getting on the plane, standing up and lobbin was the easy bit. It was carrying in excess of 160lbs of parachute, reserve and kit off the DZ, which was no more than a vast stretch of desert, used as an Artillery Range when we weren't landing on it, that was the big obstacle.

The new chute was great. The old one took a good three seconds to deploy fully. This one was open the second you left the plane. It looked more like a spaceship when it was deployed all very futuristic, but the best bit had to be the new harness, it fitted better in all the right places, I never felt like I was going to lose a testicle with the new harness. The old one left me wandering if I would ever have kids on more than one occasion. The work was hot and hard in parts, but we all rose very quickly to the challenge. We'd worked with the American Rangers in the past and saw them as a complete waste of space, we weren't gonna leave behind that impression of us for the Yanks

A few days into the tour and we were back in the Base Club. The Aircon had gone in the block again and it was uncomfortable to sit around and watch TV and our two man rooms got stuffy quickly. So we sought the sanctuary of the air conditioned Base Club early.

Without even thinking about it, we put our drinks on a tall table in the middle of the bar. This instantly pissed off the pilots who normally used it. We knew they were pilots, they told everyone, again and again and again. In true American style they got the arse and tried to move us on and in true Airborne style, we fucked them off. This put no end of tension in the air. Things could have gone bad at any moment, the whole bar could have erupted and we could have all ended up in the clink, but instead it went the other way and we ended up in a drinking duel.

I'd had it after an hour and went back to sweat it out in the block. The block was hot. Even with the windows open, there was no breeze at all. I jumped into a cold shower and lay on top of my bed in my skiddies and dozed off.

I was woken up at three in the morning by JKF falling all round the room trying to get his shoes off.

"I beat um" He said "I was the last one to leave mate, I beat um, Airborne"

He was pissed as a cricket. I got up and got him a glass of water, then threw him on his bed and stripped him down to his boxers and left him to sleep it off, if he could, we were up in a couple of hours to get ready for the morning lob, I wondered if he'd make it.

I jumped back on my bed and drifted off again. Then I was woken up by my locker doors being opened.

"What you doing mate?" I said

"I need a piss" came the reply.

"Not in there you don't" I said leaping off my bed.

JFK was hammered, he didn't know where he was. He was naked when I got to him, and struggling to stand. I grabbed him round the waist and turned him towards a metal bin in the corner of the room. He pissed up the door, the wall, the carpet and eventually dribbled in the bin. It was all I could do to hold him up let alone aim him at the same time.

Then the lights came on and Taff stuck his head round the door to wake us up, only to see me in my pants supporting a very naked JFK up from behind.

"Ill come back in a minute" He said, in a cool docile Welsh accent.

Taff had come in to wake us up for the morning jump. Everyone was up and getting ready and JFK was still lying on his pit pissed out of his head. I got ready myself. Then started to dress JFK, Taff came in again.

"Fuckin ell" He said "What time did he get in?"

"Around three" I replied

"Jesus" Said Taff "he was necking double JD's when I left at eleven"

Taff, good as gold leapt into action and help me dress our legless friend. At this point I was making it up as I was going along and then Taff asked the question:

"What we gonna do?"

"Get him ready and hope he sobers up before we push him out the plane" I said.

From that moment on, that was the plan. Getting JFK dressed was easy, even getting on the bus wasn't too hard for three of us. When we got to the hanger to DFC, we just lay him down by the parachutes and let him sleep while I fitted his chute for him. It was early lots of guys slept once they'd kitted up, so he wasn't attracting attention.

When the time came to get on the plane, I stood behind him and Taff in front, JFK was walking on his own by now but he still needed a lot of help with direction.

On the plane he could sleep again, we'd be in the air for about half an hour before he needed to do anything. He slept like the dead. Then same as every jump that week after a short flight it was "Stand up fit equipment" followed by "Action Stations". The jump was imminent and my best mate was still pissed as a lord.

It was too late to do anything about it now. JFK had to jump. Refusal to jump was a career stopper, but so was being too pissed to jump.

The time came and as we stepped down the C130 to the side door, I kept saying to JFK:

"Release your container, don't forget to release your container."

To land with it could break every bone from his arse down.

As we got to the door I thought the dispatcher would stop him, so I didn't wait, the second Taff went out in front of JFK I bailed both of us out.

On the way down I prayed my Brother in Arms would release his container. If he didn't it could snap both his legs not that he'd feel it in his state. As soon as I landed, I collapsed my chute, and ran over to his position. He had realised his kit and just in time. His drop rope hadn't even fully uncoiled. Out of the fifteen foot of rope he still had a good six foot still wound up.

I went back to my own gear and finished strapping it to myself. Then with Taff's help again, rigged JFK up with his gear and started the long hot tab off the DZ.

We got back to block before nine, the aircon was working again and I lay JFK on his bed and turned it on full then I left him to sleep and went for something to eat.

I didn't bother trying to wake him for lunch, I just bought him a sandwich back from the Mess, it was another hour or so he could sleep. When I did wake him at two in the afternoon, Taff and I both stood by his bed wandering what to expect. He woke up bright as a button, no hangover, nothing. (Jammy Bastard)

"What's the time?" He said

"Its two o'clock mate time for the afternoon lob" I replied

Then to the surprise of Taff and me, JFK said:

"What happened to the morning lob, was it cancelled?"

He remembered nothing, and had to hear it from half the Platoon before he'd believe it. The jump is on his card, but he still to this day has no recollection of that morning.

* * *

We got some R&R after a week and the Americans saw fit to give us six seater vans and fuel cards, along with a brief about not buying guns. Then we got three days off. JFK and I took our van and headed for the beaches of San Diego. We got there in just over three hours and parked up the van, then hit the town. It was a great first day out. A couple of hours on the beach, followed by a few beers and dinner, then we hit the Hippopotamus night club. It was fantastic. As soon as the locals heard our accents and established we weren't Australian, we were treated like celebrities.

Toward the end of the night a girl approached me and asked me if I'd dance with her. They're very forward like that American chicks. The music had slowed down and thankfully the line dancing, that endless boring always the same line dancing had stopped. So I agreed to the dance. Walking onto the dance floor with her I took her in my arms and began to rock from side to side.

"What do you do?" She said.

"I'm with British Special Forces" I replied, pushing my chest out. "You can tell you're mates you've danced with a British Paratrooper"

"Wow" She said "and you can tell you're friends, you're going home with a Californian Blonde"

Like I said, "Forward", but even with a night of deniable drunken passion on a plate, I managed to blow it.

"Not likely" I said leaning back to look at her.

"Why" She said "Do you have a Base curfew?"

"No, I just don't fuck fat birds" I answered.

Needless to say the dance ended there. She truly was a Californian blonde. All four foot and ninety kilos of her. I was being polite, an English Gentleman when I accepted the dance, it was gonna be hard enough to live that down. But going back to her place would haunt me forever. After my indiscretion not a trooper in the room was tapping off that night.

Engage brain, before opening mouth

* * *

We left the Club at five the next morning, JFK and I walked the beaches in an effort to sober up a bit. At six a restaurant called Dakotas opened with the offer;

ALL YOU CAN EAT FOR $10.

So we popped in. I knew we'd end up in trouble, the two of us were still half pissed and absolutely starving. America's a nation of grotesque, obese, lazy fat fuckers and when I read the menu I could see why. What I was about to eat on my day off these people ate daily. We started with the pancakes and moved onto the eggs. I'd never seen so many different kinds of eggs and I aimed to try them all. Then I had some kind of rice dish and JFK had the cereal and we both drank coffee like it was the only fluid left on the planet.

At half ten the management came over to our table in the form of a great big fat bald guy with egg yolk running down the front of his shirt and asked us to leave. We questioned his decision, pointing out two things, first the advert in the window and second, we had cleared every plate, no waste at all. But our argument fell on deaf ears the manager wanted us out.

Without further argument we up and left. On the way out JFK saw my Californian blonde bomber and pointed her out to me. My polite wave and smile was met with a fast passionate middle finger. I got the feeling she was a regular and had something to do with us being given the boot but I saw no gain in pushing the issue

Other highlights of the tour had to be, Taff's amazing head to toe sun burn and a fight between a guy from 216 Signals and a young Para Reg lad. Ten out of ten for effort had to go to the Reg lad, but that's the only points he'd score. The lad from 216 kicked him fuckin silly. As most fights it was over something daft, but it was caught on camera and was passed round the next day for all to see.

The trails were a great success and the new Parachute was approved on time and in the appropriate manner. It's bit of an honour to have been one of the few selected men that tried and tested the equipment that would be used by the Finest Fighting Force in the world. Equipment it would rely on for the foreseeable future. In a way we were like Infantry Test Pilots, testing new technologies, rising to the challenge of untried and tested risk, we really did;

Pave the way, so others could follow.

Mrs Turnbull

I answered the Phone one day in the Unit Admin Office I was there trying to get a leave pass and the Chief Clark ran out on some errand for the RSM (arse lickin idiot). If the Chief Clark knew I'd answered his phone the lanky fucker would have killed me. I picked the phone up and answered with all the tact of a mischievous trooper:

"War Office, Wonna Fight?" I said

A woman giggling on the end of the phone threw me a bit. I was expecting another Battalion Department to answer so I could mug them off, leaving the Chief to pick up the shit.

I spoke for several moments with a woman called Mrs Turnbull, she was a poet and she wrote a lot of things for Airborne Forces. Her father she said was a paratrooper during the World War 2, ignorantly I said I'd never read her stuff, but I'd never read anybodies stuff, fuckin poetry, who reads poetry, poetries for girls and gay Romans, but being polite and not wanting to get into to much bother, when she offered too send me some of her work I did my best to sound interested and gave her my name and address.

A week later an envelope arrived for me. I was shocked. No one ever wrote to me not even my folks. The A4 envelope was from Mrs Turnbull, in it she had sent me some of her classic poems and some of her newer work, I was sincerely grateful by the fact she'd sent them. Every soldier no matter what he'll tell you loves mail and when I read the words this beautifully eloquent woman had written, I was moved.

I never got the opportunity to tell Mrs Turnbull how much I appreciated what she sent me, I have hung the poem "Silver Wings" on a wall of everywhere I've ever lived. I can only hope someone who reads this might pass it on.

THANK YOU MRS TURNBULL, LOVE TO YOU AND
ALL YOURS, FROM ME AND ALL MINE.

Silver Wings

I never would have learned so much if you hadn't taken time,
To show me part of history, this heritage which is mine,
You took me to the ranville now quiet and serene,
No outward signs of conflict of battles there had been,
Just neat white rows of headstones where so many are at rest,
Who fought and died together having given of their best,

But what becomes of heroes once the wars are won?
When all the guns are silent and a new life has begun
What happens to these soldiers who've suffered all the pain?
Have sacrificed their lives for us and freed the world again
We remember very briefly the high price that was paid,
On that special Sunday when poppy wreaths are laid,

We soon forget their valiant deeds and push them from our minds
Show them almost no respect and treat them less than kind
How many times we turned away and didn't want to hear
The marvellous tales they have to tell so vivid and so clear.

They freed the cities of the world, where the devil cast his spell and
earned their battle honours as they followed him through hell
But the victories demand a toll and someone has to pay
Often it's the silver wings upon the red beret.

In memory of all airborne forces,
The parachute regiment
To celebrate their 50th anniversary

By lilian Turnbull

Brevet Militaire
de Parachutiste

My French issue wings number 570853

In the spring of 1993 our Squadron along with other elements of the Brigade was given the opportunity to go to France and do their Special Forces Selection course in order to receive our French Wings. At the time the abbreviation for their Specialist Forces was CRAP, but with the European Armies working so close together they were looking hard to change that. We laughed like adolescent children during their briefings as they spoke of their Crap Troops abroad and their Crap Troops in Europe.

It was an exchange tour, a Company of us for a Company of them the idea being we would slide seamlessly into each others shoes. (Not a fuckin prayer)

We flew from Lynham to Bordeaux and after a short bus ride arrived at "Camp Du Souse" home of the French Regiment 1RCP, Regiment Chasseur De Parachutist. The accommodation was bog standard but immaculate it was a bit embarrassing to know that our counterparts would be staying in our block back in the UK. Accommodation that had been built in the early seventies and had never been upgraded. Even though "Military" and "Comfort" are not two words said together in French, their living standard in Barracks superseded ours.

Their Barracks was immaculate. The lawns like billiard tables and the roads looked freshly swept, their Guard was as smart as any British Guardsman and evidence of proud tradition and Battle Honours was everywhere.

The whole Squadron was looking forward to working with the French Para's, their reputation for being tough, fit and professional was well known. A few of our guys had worked with the French Foreign Legion in the past, some said they were a waste of time others said they knew what they were about. The Legion's reputation stemmed largely from the North African Campaigns of the WW2. But unfortunately it's done very little since then. Even the CO of 1RCP General Urwald said that in his time commanding 2 REP of the Legion in Corsica their Parachute Regiment, he found the British soldier to be the best and the worst he'd worked with and was very interested in our actions and reactions over the coming weeks.

The French Foreign Legion is now largely made up of Serbs and Croats looking for French Citizenship, the perk that comes with the five year sentence but knowing the ineptitude of that lot under fire it can't be doing the professional ability of the Legion any good whatsoever.

1RCP was seventy percent French Regular and the rest conscript but the best of the conscripts, so our expectations of the Unit were high.

The French jump from two thousand feet and we jump from eight hundred. But before we could do that we had to put time in at the working end. The first thing they had us doing was Tabbing.

One of their PTI's took us on a six kilometre Tab around an old runway. The first issue here was no one knew exactly when it started. It was more like a stroll with a girlfriend. It took ten minutes to walk to the start line and when there instead of announcing the beginning of the Tab the PTI just kept walking. The bimble to the start line was no quicker than the Tab itself. The hardest part was ignoring the boredom of the endless unused runway and the surrounding grass.

It took an hour to do the Six Kilometres and the PTI was fucked at the end of it. We just bimbled along behind him talking amongst ourselves. It was not the kind of over land punishment I was use to and certainly not the "March or Die" pace we were all expecting.

The next task was a confidence course they had set up in a forest behind the Barracks. It was a series of ropes hanging in the trees. It consisted of rope ladders and bridges about twenty to thirty feet off the floor. One of their PTI's demonstrated how the course was to be done and how the safety harnesses attached at each new point. When he finished he asked who wanted a harness. Every one of us turned them down.

What the French Elite didn't know was, the night before we'd all come in off the piss and climbed around on the lame excuse for an obstacle course just for a laugh.

We all went over it once because we had to, but it definitely lacked challenge. It wasn't hard to see how embarrassed our French Instructors were.

Largely due to the fact the French had nothing to challenge us physically, they gave us an introduction to some of their hardware. It was impressive. Anti aircraft guns strapped to landrovers and quad bikes with heavy machine guns mounted on them. Their indoor CQB Range was the highlight. A corridor about thirty metres long and ten metres wide and when activated it adopted one of a series of programs through cinematic imagery. The programs went from Urban to Jungle warfare and it was long enough to get some good momentum going. As state of the art as it was we all still managed to exceed the expectations of the French Instructors. I'm sure it's a great training tool for the French Elite but it was more like a high risk arcade game to us.

The day on the range was an eye opener. The French weapon of choice is the FAMAS. A beautiful weapon perfect for Jungle and Urban Conflict. Thirty round, 5.56 magazine, iron site and a handy single round, three round or fully automatic capability.

Using this shockingly easy to use weapon, we put it though the normal paces. We fired it in the prone, kneeling, sitting and standing positions, but the nice surprise was the French also fire from the hip, standing at thirty metres we got to let rip from the hip. I'd never done that before then and it gave an edge to the day that made the whole range day memorable. I'd fired and used a hundred weapons up to that point, but none from the hip. At last as small as it was they had something to offer.

The Jumps course offered no surprises. The French jump from two thousand feet and the British Military jump from eight hundred, so when we lobbed I felt like I was up there all day. This led to a few of us pissing around, Air stealing each other trying to get down quicker.

* * *

Air stealing. A military parachute floats on one ton of air. (Work that out,) and directly above the chute the air is to thin to support another parachute. So when one parachute glides over the top of another, the bottom chute steals the air from the top chute and it collapses, shooting the top chute under the bottom chute, allowing it to re-inflate. Hence the term, AIR STEAL.

* * *

The only problem with this kind of mischief is the top chute then becomes the bottom chute and steals the air from the top canopy and so on. If you're not very careful the whole antic becomes a game of Airborne roulette. The prize being you didn't hit the ground without your chute open. But all that aside it added a bit of excitement to the descent.

At the end of each descent the C130 would climb to greater heights and the French PJI's would freefall. On the last day screams from the sky hooked our attention, one of the PJI's parachutes failed to open, as he fell his fearful blood curdling screams could be heard right across the DZ. Fortunately at about a thousand feet his reserve deployed and he landed hard but safely. He walked off the DZ helped by two of his comrades crying and sobbing like a five year old girl that had lost her doll but I'm sure us laughing at him didn't make him feel any better. Where we were from any jump you walk away from is a good un.

The most disturbing part of the tour was the Bar just outside the camp, aptly named "Bar de Parachutist". It was a typical off post shit hole with bad beer and endless opening times, the real disturbing bit though, was hanging up behind the bar were four washing lines with for want of a better term, old pants hanging off them. Not knickers, pants. Hundreds of old ripped and soiled skiddies some with dust a centimetre thick on them.

The rest of the establishment followed suit. The bar stools were just thick cut tree trunks the tables were sheets of plywood on old beer barrels and the stage had a wire cage round it and a Risk Assessment on the entrance, if the words "You're on your own in here" in French constitutes a Risk Assessment. The place stank of stale beer and fags and the women that frequented the place blended right in. It was a perfect place for us to drink in.

At the end of the tour we had a pass off parade. The time we would be awarded our French Wings. The French have a smart and proud Army. They sing when they march, not like the Yanks who sing profanity and ego in their cadence but in the perfect mix of tones you expect from a Welsh choir. It's a sincere and sombre tone and the tempo meets the steps. It sent a chill down my spine. I asked a friend of mine from 1RCP Frederic Kraits what the lyrics meant, he told me how they spoke of death and how she knows no bias, she takes the young the old the worthy and the sinister and all we can do is meet her with dignity and honour.

The meaning was deep and it was moving to watch.

I left qualified to don the wings of a French paratrooper proudly on my right breast and the invite to return and serve with French Special Forces as we all did. The French Army is not the "MARCH OR DIE" force of criminals and asylum seekers it once was but they are however, still a proud and highly motivated body of men. I have lived and served in France since 1993 and loved every minute of it. The French have managed to maintain their culture even through the invasion of legal and illegal immigrants. A lot of Britons don't like the French for their ways but I think they envy their patriotism and wish our Governments had the same spine.

When we returned to England the pass rate of the French Parachute Unit was a direct reflection of their level of training at Camp Du Souse. Many had failed the tasks set them by our Instruction team and many simply refused to partake at all. The idea of refusing was a new one on me I didn't even realise we had a choice. We didn't and don't of course but the French Army works differently.

I was mortified to find out, some of the Frogs had even refused to jump from the balloon cage. This is a cardinal sin in our Brigade. After the "Green Light Warning Order" is read you are absolutely one hundred percent going out that door, to refuse would end any career one might have. In my time with British Airborne Forces I only ever heard of one guy refusing to jump, he worked with the Logistical Battalion and was moved out of his pad and posted out before the days end.

It was a great experience to work with the French but as when our Unit worked with American Rangers it just left me knowing I was a part of the finest Military Machine in the world.

It Seemed Like The Thing To Do At The Time Sir!

Every now and then a shit job comes up at Unit level and someone has to do it. It wasn't always our Section that got it. It just felt like that. Phil, our Section Commander and a few of his mates had been caught in the cook house making egg banjos at two in the morning a week before. Instead of throwing the book at him the SSM warned him he would get the next shitty detail. No one minded the shitty job alternatives our SSM was a great bloke if you fucked up he always tried to keep it in house and deal with it himself. It was probably because of his background but it could have been his physical presence. Whatever it was the powers to be were happy to let him do things his way.

The detail that came up was "Wine Pourers" at an Officers Mess do. The job was simply to pour red and white wine for a dinner being put on for the General. The big boss, the head of shed, the boss' boss' boss' boss. So it was kind of a big deal.

The night came and as usual the job description had changed, not only were we to pour the wine at dinner but now we had to pass out drinks in the cocktail lounge. So wearing Barrack dress trousers, number two's shirt and best boots we walked round with trays handing out Bucks fizz. A mixture of sparkling white wine and orange juice. I'd never had it before and I loved it. For every glass I put on my tray I drank one. We all helped ourselves all night it made the evening quite relaxing.

As the evening went on and the fizz flowed the eight of us got more and more clumsy and had to slow things right down, I even had to stop drinking at one point I was that shit faced.

When dinner was called the Officers went to sit and we went into the kitchen to get ready for the wine pouring. I was in the kitchen less than two minutes when one of the chefs poured fish soup all down my best shirt and trousers and nearly scalded me. I'm not quite sure who was in whose way but there's a good chance it was me.

I stripped down and tried to get some cold water on the burns. With no Bucks fizz about I started on the red wine. Again, we were all having a glass so no problem. The only thing was everyone else was working, I was just sat in the kitchen naked supping posh red plonk. Naked because I was going "Commando". It was common place back then, Army pay sucked, I had jocks for work only, back then it was Commando outside office hours.

Time went on and the wine flowed. Then Phil came and sat next to me about an hour into service. I was rat arsed.

"You might as well go home mate" he said. "you can't do anything here, we'll meet you back at the block."

"Na mate" I replied "I'll stay and get a lift back with you guys"

It was a good two miles back to block and I didn't fancy the walk in my best boots. I'd still have blisters a month later.

"Take my mountain bike" Said the Chef "I'll catch a lift with this lot when we're done"

Great idea I thought.

But I completely underestimated how pissed I was, so did Phil and the Chef. I put my beret on, got on the mountain bike and rode straight through the double doors in front of me, straight into the dinning room.

Peddling gently I looked to my left and saw all the Officers dinning in a Horse shoe formation, all facing in, all facing me. The room went silent, I could just about make out my OC and the grin on my Platoon Commanders face.

"Good night Sir" I said.

And threw up my best salute held it for two then looked forward and carried on out the doors into the compound. I don't even remember getting back to the block. The next thing recall I was being woken up by my Platoon Sergeant and the SSM.

"Up you get Silly Bollocks" Said the SSM "Someone wants to see you"

"Morning Sir" I replied, dragging my arse out of bed.

I couldn't remember much about the night before but I knew it must be bad to bring the Sarg and the SSM to my bedside on a Saturday morning.

They gave me time for a record quick shower before marching me down to the lines. When we got there we went straight to the OC's office. In there was the OC the CO my Platoon Commander and two Officers I didn't recognise.

The SSM marched me in and brought me to a halt, then announced me by Rank and Name. I was struggling to remember exactly what I was there for until I looked on the desk in front of me and saw my clothes. SHIT. Through my massive hangover it came flooding back.

"Well" Said the CO.

"Yer, Sorry about that Sir" What else could I say.

"What possessed you to make that exit?" said the OC.

"It seemed like the thing to do at the time Sir" I had no other answer.

They all smiled but did their best to hide it. My Platoon Commander was doing a lousy job he stood there with a great big grin on his face.

Then the OC said, "Right Sergeant Major we have a lot to do this morning so we'll leave this for you to deal with"

"Right you are Sir" said the SSM.

With that I gathered my clothes and was marched out. The SSM then informed me I was on his shitty job list. Humbly I concurred and with that he let me go about my weekend.

* * *

The pursuit of shock humour never ended. Neither did its ability to backfire. Sandhurst Royal Military Academy has one of the better assault courses and it ends with a death slide over a lake.

For whatever reason we ended up taking part in an open day there. To start with the day's events were divided between our Platoon. Some would do the Tab, some would do the Assault Course and JFK and I quickly volunteered for the Death Slide followed by a River Crossing.

JFK came up with the idea that we should do the river crossing in ladies underwear and float across the lake on inflatable crocodiles. It was the kind of prank we were famous for and it would be good for a laugh at the end of a hot boring day rubbing shoulders with potential Rodney's.

JFK chose to wear a basque and lace hot pants. I went with a thong, hold up stockings and a red bra. The idea was to wear them under our combats and expose our wood be fetish to the Civilian on lookers during the day's finale.

But when we got there some do gooding Rupert changed the way things were to be done at the last minute. Now we would all do the Tab the Assault Course the Death Slide and the River Crossing. Our prank was about to backfire because some Rupert wanted to impress a few Civvies with the prowess and serious professionalism that was British Airborne Forces. Our backfire would be his quick shock.

The Tab, would have been as easy as any other had it not been for the thong rubbing me to within an inch away from an eating disorder and a bra that rubbed my nipples almost clean off. JFK was in similar discomfort. How the Hell did women wear this crap on a dance floor all night?

After the Tab, the Assault Course. By now I was missing skin I didn't know I had, my stockings had become little more than cheese wire and had my balls hung a little lower I might have lost them.

The death slide came as bit of a relief all I did was hang and slide. At the bottom JFK was already blowing up his croc I joined him and the crowd's cheering turned it into a race. We finished at the same time and started to undress for the crossing. It was then JFK saw the Brigadier out the corner of his eye. He tried to tip me off but I didn't get his hints and I couldn't wait to get my kit off and get into the cool water and sooth myself inflicted wounds.

In seconds I was stood naked apart from what was left of the frillies I donned under my combats. JFK not wanting to see me go it alone stripped down in quick time. We both looked like American prison rape victims. I'm not sure what the crowd found more daunting two Paratroopers in ladies knickers or the injuries we sustained wearing them.

The water soothed my burning parts and the applause from the crowd turned the crossing into the worlds slowest swimming race, JFK and I finished tied got out the other side and sloped off to get into something more comfortable. Saying that a barbwire corset would have been more comfortable.

Our antics were taken in good humour by our hosts and the day I'm told was a success.

***

A blessing of being a young soldier is the licence to fuck about a bit and not have it taken too seriously. I was sent to Colchester for an Instructors course. A good four hours from the Shot I didn't know anyone. Another guy on the course Taff was in the same boat, he came from one of those deeply inbred Welsh Units where they always referred to each other as Thomas 254 and Thomas 617 or Jones 259 they had so many Thomas's Jones's and Evans's they had to put their last three on the end to tell them apart (the film Zulu was well researched).

As the outsiders it didn't take long for us to find each other and get on. On the first night after the course introduction we hit the city of Colchester for a night out. Despite all the nice clean bars and well organised clubs in Colly we found a small underground shit hole to drink in called Fagin's Den. Same old story different town.

The course was a month long. It covered Methods of Instruction, Advanced weapons training and Navigation, Infantry Tactics, Military Law and Duties of an NCO. The instructors were the best that particular Unit had. As all British Military Instructors these men knew their jobs inside and out and could teach each point with flawless precision.

During the course we had to take lessons and were marked on our approach and abilities, one of my final exams was to teach, the stripping, assembling and normal daily cleaning of the LSW or Light Support Weapon. The OC, CSM and two of the course instructors would be my judging panel.

As with all lessons you have to start with an opening statement. It had become bit of a friendly competition as to who could come up with the best one as this was the only part of the instruction that wasn't word for word out of an Army pamphlet. My opening statement for this lesson was:

"Gentlemen, You are taught from your first day in the Army that, Cleanliness is next to Godliness, I am about to teach you that, Cleanliness will keep you as far away from God as possible".

The CSM loved it as did the other two course Instructors, the Bible Bashing OC on the other hand didn't get it and was a little pissed off to say the least. At the end of the lesson I left the class and turned to the panel for criticism. The OC asked me to explain my opening statement, I pointed out that what I meant was if your weapon was clean it wouldn't suffer stoppages and so keep working and if your rifles working you had a little less chance of meeting you maker under fire. He still didn't get it and referred to the statement as little blasphemous. At the time I could help but feel this guy is in the wrong line of work.

At the end of the course they held a cocktail party. It was a "Scale A parade," that meant attendance was compulsory. It's a good job they pointed that out too, cos Taff and I had other plans. We all knew about the event from the beginning of the course and pressure had been on from day one to, "Bring your significant other". Taff was even importing his wife from deepest darkest Wales just for the night. I on the other hand didn't have a bird in the Shot and anything I could have blagged in my short time in Colly wouldn't have been worth bringing. Phil my Section Commander said he could sort a bird out for me for the night but I declined, I'd known him too long I'd have ended up with a multicoloured six foot dwarf with one leg and balls. So I did the next best thing, I bought a date.

She cost me less than ten quid and the guy behind the counter said she would go all night. I took my date back to the block, took her out the box and blew her up. She was curvaceous with life like hair and bright red lip stick. Well that's what it said on the box, in reality I got a tenna's worth. I stuck a dress on her that I got from a second hand shop and she was ready to go.

She was the perfect date and completely unique at the party, she didn't speak she didn't drink and I didn't have to defend her honour everytime one of the guys stuck something in her. The OR's wives and girlfriends saw the funny side, the Senior Ranks wives and girlfriends saw the funny side, even the CSM and his wife saw the funny side but the OC wife, she had the same sence of humour her husband did at my final instruction exam. The heat coming off her glare was almost enough to melt my date. But to my surprise when the OC came back from wherever he was and one of the course Instructors introduced him to my new bird, he burst out laughing.

I couldn't work him out, a sentence with God not being worshipped was blasphemy but a well dressed blow up doll with more holes than a shot gun victim at a Military cocktail party was humour. I didn't take the doll to piss him off but he was the only resistance I was expecting and looking at his miss's he was definitely spending the night on the couch.

The next day at the Pass Off parade during the inspection he humorously reflected on the evening. I took a lot away from that course, one thing being that even the sternest faced person has a sense of humour.

***

There is no greater humour than that of the British soldier. We have a need to let off a bit of steam and not take things too seriously. It's a defensive mechanism in a soldier. Some would say we lack empathy, others see us as nothing more than thugs. For the most part no one gets hurt in our scatty moments. A street may lose a sign post or a building site a road cone, a pub may even lose a table and a police car a light. The safe argument is to revert to cost and replacement. But in the grand scale of things its harmless fun and for the most part it's the Tax Man that gets the bill not the individual. But like the "Character Building" exercises imposed on the new guys some civilians see it as extreme.

The British civilian should cut the British soldier some slack. Who are you to judge our behaviour in the comfort of our homeland? If you're not prepared to go through what we go through at home in training and abroad, you're in no real position to judge us.

YOU CAN TALK THE TALK,
BUT CAN YOU WALK THE WALK

Dallas, (Full metal jacket)

Take Note

THE FEAR OF JUMPING FROM A C130 IN THE MIDDLE OF THE NIGHT,

CARRYING 27lbs OF MAIN CHUTE, 14lbs OF RESERVE, WITH A 120lbs OF EQUIPMENT AND LIVE AMMUNITION STRAPPED TO YOUR LEG.

ONLY TO LAND ON A FREEZING, WET, DZ IN A FARAWAY LAND. WITH FOOD FOR FIVE DAYS AND NO REPLEN FOR TEN.

TAB FORTY MILES THROUGH MOUNTAIN, DESERT, JUNGLE OR ICE,

BATTLE AND DEFEAT A NUMERICALLY SUPERIOR FORCE,
THEN DIG IN AND WAIT FOR THE COUNTER ATTACK.

IS EASILY OVERCOME, BY NOT BEING QUALIFIED TO DO SO.

The Brotherhood

When you leave one Unit for another it's traditional to have a leaving do and leaving the Maroon Machine for 22 was no different. It started as a few quiet pints in the Unit bar and went pear shaped from there. The bar quickly filled up with the guys and a few well known Aldershot dogs (not a very flattering term for a loose Aldershot girl, but there's plenty of em, enough to give em a nick name anyway), and in no time at all I was in the middle of party tricks and drinking games.

Back then I had three party tricks;
The first one was simple; I did the splits between two bar stools. Two guys I could trust would hold the two stools I was standing on and pull them out slowly until I was in the full splits position. It got more winces than laughs and the other guys loved to have a go.
The second was to secure a crate of beer to my knob with a rope, then stand on two bar chairs and swing the crate back and forth. Once again it got more winces than laughs and not too many of the guys fancied a shot at that title.
But my favourite has to be my ability to put one hundred and sixty three, (that's my record,) one penny coins in my foreskin and seal it with a bulldog clip. It got plenty of laughs and amazed looks and absolutely no contenders for the title whatsoever.

But my party tricks could barely make the top ten.
Ritchie P would staple bar mats to his forehead then his foreskin to the bar.
Phil P could swallow a pool ball and would hurry to do so because Billy Mac could fit a pool ball in his foreskin and Phil never liked the idea of possibly sharing a ball. The list went on.
It was always a great time party trick madness. There was always a new challenge and always an abundance of new self maiming ideas and no shortage of guys to give them a go. The guys from the Jackass

movies and the Dirty Sanchez boys are fifteen years late and tame by comparison.

Odd. If the nations finest are seen blowing off a little creative steam, society see them as insane or being bullied into shameful tasks. But if a couple of Yank Hillbillies or a group of Murtha Tydfil Commandos do it, it's an instant reality show.

As the night went on it slowed down and the party tricks and drinking games gave way to funny anecdotes and war stories and by one in the morning the room had divided quietly into conversational groups. I'd had a great night and I'd had far too much to drink. As I looked around the room I could see some of the finest men I'd ever met. I never got on with all of them but they were good soldiers all. I'd made some good mates and some good acquaintances at this Unit. I'd also learned a lifetime of lessons to take with me. Some the hard way, others the easy way. All I carry with me to this day.

**

The next day I woke up on a hard cold surface with an itchy brown blanket pulled around my very naked body. With only a toilet and the metal sink for company I realized instantly I was in a police cell.

The last thing I could remember was standing talking with Billy C, Beni B and JFK, I remember us talking about Eager Beavers and ordering more Rum. There it was! The answer and the problem. Rum. I love it. With coke and ice, I love it. But it fuckin hates me. If there was ever a time on the piss I got into trouble it was because I'd been drinking Rum. That's why I don't drink it.

Two things had me astonished at this point. The first was my lack of a hangover. I had at least eight pints of Guinness and fuck knows how many rum and cokes. My head should be pounding and my guts doing tumbles, yet I had no evidence of a hangover. So if nothing else the day had started well.

The second was the daunting fact that the large reinforced steel blue door that secured the cell was open.

I stood up and moved my head from side to side just to see if the lack of hangover was too good to be true, to my delight there was still no sign of the morning after ailment. Then I made my way over to the stainless steel wall heater that doubled as a mirror for that morning face off every man has. It was hard to make out in the scratch warped metal heater but it looked like I had I thick red line painted down the centre of my face.

I licked my finger and tried to rub the mark off starting on the top of my forehead. Only to find out that it wasn't a paint or pen mark at all but an indent.

About one centimetre wide and a good two mill deep running from the middle of my forehead down passed the left side of my nose, just missing my mouth and ending on my jaw line. I ran my finger all the way down it and as I looked down at my finger for the first time realised that the strange mark run all the way down the middle of my chest and stomach and under the right side of my balls.

I was feeling a bit uncomfortable to say the least. I'd woken up in strange circumstances before but this was bordering on the twilight zone. I even reached round to scratch my arse. Just in case.

I pulled the blanket tight around my shoulders and walked so as to hide my modesty, then made my way out the cell and down the cold corridor to the custody desk. It wasn't my first time in Aldershot nick and like a good eighty percent of troopers knew my way round that bit of the station. As I made the short walk to the custody desk I was shitting myself. The last thing I needed at this point in my career was a charge for fuckin about on the piss. I'd left all that shit behind a long time ago and didn't need to start at a new Unit by banging the boards.

I poked my head round the corner to see the Custody Sergeant. A large spectacled, middle age man standing on his own going through some paperwork.

"Morning Sarg" I said

The large uniformed man turned to towards me and smiled warmly. Instantly I felt some relief.

"How's the head?" The Sergeant said in a clear confident voice.

"Fine, considering" I replied "How much trouble am I in Sarg?"

That being my only concern.

"None" He said with a smile "None whatsoever"

"Really" The surprise on my voice was obvious.

"Really" he repeated. "You are by far the politest man we've ever had in the drunk tank."

There was no tension in the room and the Sarg made for easy conversation, which was good for me, I had a few questions that needed answering.

"Can I get my clothes back sarg?" I thought that would be the best start.

"We found you that way" He said "The only thing you had on was your socks and tucked inside your left one was your ID card, sign here and you can have it back." He turned a piece of paper round on the desk and pushed it towards me.

"How come the cell door was left open" I quizzed as I signed for my Army ID card.

"We had to put you on drunk watch mate, you we're legless last night, so we checked you every fifteen minutes as a safety precaution." He went on "You were waking up on the last check so I thought I'd get the paperwork started"

All the time he spoke the large friendly sergeant had a smile and as I asked about the thick deep mark running down the middle of my body the smile turned to an uncontrollable laughter and the Sergeant struggled to give any coherent answer. He drew a hanky from his trouser pocket to wipe the tears from his eyes and started to compose himself, but as he did two Constables came in through a door behind the desk, the younger one pointing at me saying:

"Look Sarg! Tarzans awake"

With that all three of them burst into a fit of red faced laughter. I stood for a moment giving them time to pull themselves together, pulling the blanket tighter around me. The other Constable was a woman and all of a sudden my nudity became a small issue. As I looked at the custody board behind the desk I noticed my name had beside it in brackets: (TARZAN).

"What the fuck had I done" I thought.

After a minute or two the Sarg calmed down enough to explain.

The station had had a call. Not a 999 call he was quick to add at about 0300 that morning from a concerned citizen. At first the citizen thought a large dog was trying to jump his back fence possibly to get at his cats and with that in mind chose to ignore the noise. But after half an hour he changed his mind and sort to see the dog off. But on reaching his back fence armed only with a torch was quite surprised to see an unconscious naked man straddled over his six foot garden fence.

Once again the now sweating red faced Sergeant needed time to compose himself.

The citizen then phoned the police who arrived ten minutes later. The two constables behind the desk were the first at the scene. But were by no means the last. It took a total of six coppers two chairs and twenty-five minutes to get me off the fence unharmed. A patient endeavour I'm grateful for.

The Sarg gave me one of those, one size fits all, white forensic bodysuits to wear home but not an offer of a lift as I was hoping. After a bit more paper work and a few more laughs at my well deserved expense, I was escorted out the station via the café where I met the other members of the Tarzan rescue team. Then after a quick coffee and more friendly ridicule I was on my way.

* * *

The following day I made two stops. The first was back to my old Unit on a mission to fill in the gaps of what I remembered to be a great night and it was by all accounts. Each of us drank like ten men, gave 100% to our party pieces and told our favourite stories and according to the bar staff when I left I was fully clothed and in relatively good shape. So what the hell happened in the mile and half from the bar to where I was found, God only knows.

The other stop was to the good citizen I had disturbed that night. Mr Archie Thomas. As he opened his door to me he leaned back into his house and called his wife:

"Margaret, Tarzans back, and this time he's at the door"

Margaret appeared instantly as if she was stood behind the door when her husband opened it.

"Stop teasing and show him in" She said

I hadn't expected this at all. I had come to give a humble sincere apology and hang my head in shame for the inconvenience I had caused. Instead my presence was met with warmth and humour. Mr Thomas turned into the front room beckoning me in as he went. As I followed him into their cosy living room I saw pictures of my host on the walls, stood proudly with his Unit. He too was a Paratrooper in the Regiments pioneering time of World War Two.

"Tea" Margaret offered

"Yes please" I replied still a bit overwhelmed.

"I nearly didn't recognise you with your clothes on" Said Margaret, with a great big smile.

"I am so sorry" I said bowing my head to hide my blush.

"No need, no need at all" Mr Thomas said

I explained the events of the evening. Trying to give them some kind of justification. Both Mr and Mrs Thomas listened intently smiling all the way through my attempts at apology.

After a while the conversation turned to Mr Thomas's career in WW2. He didn't speak long and didn't give any real details but I felt very humble in his presence.

With a cup of tea and a handful of homemade biscuits inside me the three of us went outside, all with a fresh brew to visit the crime scene. We stood for a good twenty minutes as they took me blow by blow though an event I had no recollection of and they giggled and laughed the whole way through the story.

I asked Mr Thomas if he was worried at any point about the fact a naked man was trying to get in his garden.

"All my worries went away the second I saw your Airborne Tattoo" he said. "That's why I rang the station and not 999 so you wouldn't get into trouble."

My heart sank.

"Like will always find like" He said "Troopers will always find Troopers and when they do, no matter how, the Airborne Brotherhood should stand together"

Once again I was humbled by the words of this ageing Warrior.

I left about an hour later after more tea and biscuits, but never forgot the words and deeds of Mr and Mrs Thomas. We stayed in contact through Christmas cards and letters and anytime I was in Aldershot they'd always invite me round for tea. On a few occasions I'd take a friend, one of the other guys and they would take great delight in telling them how we'd first met. The story changed a little every time but only to add more humour. They were a beautiful couple, true sole mates. A rare solid example of True Love.

The last time I saw them both was on a Remembrance Sunday. I picked them up and took them to the Church. Then back to lines to meet up with some of the other Old and Bold Veterans as we affectionately called them. Then after a good day with old friends I took them home.

Archie died in the December of that year of nothing more than old age and a well lived life. Margaret died three weeks later. They said of old age when I enquired but I felt it more likely she died of a broken heart.

Extreme Sports

Every now and again in your life you meet a man you would trust with the lives of your children only having met him the day before. A person so charismatic that when he speaks you find yourself hanging on every word end in whose presence you just know things are gonna be ok and things are gonna go your way.

Col Chapman is one of those men. I first met Col in his office at 22 when running an errand for JFK. Col's not a big man, to be fair he's very unassuming. Quiet but very clearly spoken and fanatical about his personal fitness. Army Rugby Army Tug'o'War, keen runner, keen boxer, great soldier and a lover of white water kayaking and that's why we met.

* * *

As a young soldier I was always looking for the next thrill. Dave T, Mickey P and I went to Mexico to do BASE (Bridge, Antenna, Span, Earth) jumping when the craze first started in the early nineties. We hooked up with a couple of Yanks that did it for kicks and quickly found what we were looking for.

We jumped a thousand feet off a cliff edge and down into a ravine that was no more than two hundred metres across. It was pure adrenaline. The view was great and the rush kept me pumped all day. I only jumped once the first day but got two in a day for the following three days.

The walk back after each jump was a two mile tab, mostly uphill through hot humid jungle then onto loose rock and blazing sun. We ran it the first couple of times but half way through the second day we turned it into a steady walk. BASE jumping was a major rush but it got old quickly so I looked for other ways to entertain myself.

Bungee jumping was next, a short lived hard on that at the time was illegal in Great Britain so we went to Corsica and France to do it. Jumping from the bridges was the bigger rush, jumping from a crane had no real adrenaline value at all. Even when we found a place in Cyprus that dunked your head in the water it was a short lived thrill. Sure your arse was tested at the top but on a score of one to ten, ten being the highest, bungee jumping scored a very lame two.

The problem with the adrenaline fixes I was finding was they were over too quickly. The build up was good, the execution was great but it was always over too soon. I was looking for something to hold the rush and give me time to question my ability and address that question.

My quest to find my physical and mental limit was starting to get me into trouble.

A few of us went to London on the piss. We got to Waterloo at half nine one Saturday morning and as we walked across Waterloo bridge we stopped to look over the side, when Taff said:

"Imagine jumping from here"

As he finished his sentence I jumped over the side, turned in the air and gave my mates the bird. The water was fuckin freezing and for a very brief moment I felt my arse stick in the thick black mud, but at no point did I feel in any danger. The current was fast and I'd got under the bridge and out the other side at surprising speed. My mates had run across the road and stood waving at me and laughing.

Before I gone fifty metres a police launch pulled me out. Once they'd established I wasn't attempting suicide and wasn't pissed they let me go on my way. They took my details and all hell was to pay when my OC found out, but that's another story.

River and Shale running. The event pushed the adrenaline but when it was over it was over. Jumping from one moving vehicle to another on exercise, mountain biking at night, Europe's scariest amusement park rides, pot holing, hand gliding, nothing quenched the thirst.

I needed to find something that would hold the rush long enough to make it a challenge.

Then I found the rock. Rock climbing became a large part of my life for a long time. I'd travel all around the UK and Europe with like minded friends and climb whatever we could find. For the first year I stuck to the book and only did registered climbs that always had strange names like: "Don't drive when you're dead," and "Dead dogs don't lie" some climbs sounded more like race horses.

But after a while and after rising to the heights of extreme climbing (E1 and so on), the need to seek assents slightly off the cards became a personal necessity.

I religiously free climbed. I couldn't afford all the fancy kit on my wages so I bought a good pair of climbing shoes and a chalk bag. I could have progressed a lot quicker with all the gear but I couldn't afford it. The difference between free and rope climbing is: "the safety net factor". Ropes and harnesses allow the climber to push the limits safely, my budget gave me no such luxury. Every time I pushed the limits or wanted to extend my personal standards my knowledge, fitness and audacity had to do the work. For a long time the rock and I were good friends. It was one of two sports that would give me all I was looking for.

* * *

JFK had lost a throw line (it's a rope in a bag used to rescue paddlers that come out of their kayaks in rapids or fast moving water) on an Adventure Training exercise and was looking to replace it by any means. Apparently, he'd made that all time great balls up of not securing one end when he threw the other end in and in turn threw the whole thing in the river. Leaving some poor volunteer to get washed a hundred meters down stream, only to be volunteered again to wade around in the rapids and try and find the lost item as he was the only wet one and no one else was keen on splashing around in a Scottish river in November.

All adventure training equipment is signed out the stores and the person who signs for it is directly accountable for its return or replacement. Our RQMS or store man at the time was a right wanker. He had this unshakable belief that stores were for storing till the end of time, getting anything even a simple kit exchange was a nightmare and he loved to bill you for anything he could and if it was a star item you lost he would have you banging the boards in no short order. So JFK was keen to source another throw line.

On the same exercise I'd done the rock climbing, that was the time in my life when the Rock and I were very frequent adversaries (Oh how I loved the rock). It was the sport that held the rush. I could climb for hours and the adrenaline would flow the whole time. Each second challenges everything you know about yourself. If I pushed the boat out and climbed beyond my ability the rush would last all day. I used to climb with a mate of mine Dave T, he was hell of a lot better than me that's why I liked climbing with him, he would have me doing things I wouldn't have seen myself. He pushed my limits further every time we climbed. We use to meet up at Guilford University some weekends to use their indoor climbing wall. Other times we'd travel to the coast and put a good weekend's rock running in.

When I told him what I'd been up to for the last two weeks he told me about a mate of his Andy who was at 22, he'd not long done a similar adventure training exercise at the same place. As we talked the name Col Chapman and kayaking came up a few times in the conversation. So when JFK asked if I could get a throw line or knew anyone that could, I said I'd give a mate of mine a call.

I rang Dave T and asked if it was possible to get hold of this bloke Col Chapman through his mate Andy. If he was the kayaking mad man his mate Andy had spoken about he was bound to have one or at least know where I could get one.

Dave was quick to come back with info on how to reach Col and I handed it to JFK without giving it much more thought. The next day JFK comes to me and says:

"Can you do me a favour? Go to 22 and grab a throw line off this guy Col Chapman I need it today"

JFK had it all ready for me, a Landrover, directions the whole nine yards, and it never occurred to me why.

"Why the urgency mate" I said "And why aren't you going?"

Not that it mattered JFK was my direct boss at the time and I enjoyed working for him, but he loved to get out and this was a great excuse.

"I got shit loads on" He said "but I need it today and I'll cover for you"

"No worries" I said "leave it with me." And with that I drove off.

After a bit of breakfast and a few wrong turns I arrived at 22 lines just before lunch. The first thing that struck me was the civilian security, we did all our own staging on at Montgomery Lines. To see a civie doing it seemed a bit odd. I said to the Guard:

"I've come to see Col Chapman do you know him"

"Who doesn't" Was the sarcastic reply.

"Typical fuckin civie" I thought,

"Ok then Smart Arse! Where does he work and how do I find him?" I said.

Not impressed with the "Smart Arse" comment he quickly became more difficult and vague, I would blame it on him being a power tripin civie, but truth be known if some arsehole approached me on stag with an attitude I'd have fucked him around a bit to. It helps to pass the time.

After a search of the landy and a trip to the guardroom for a visitors pass, I finally get directions and an escort to Col's Office. It was at this point I realized that Col Chapman must be a bit more important than a Corporal in the Training Wing which I just assumed he was. I couldn't have been more right. Col Chapman was the RSM, the Regimental Sergeant Major, the Top Dog.

Now I knew for sure that JFK needed a throw line and I knew he wanted one that day, I also knew that if I could borrow a throw line without a signature JFK would never replace it. I love the man but kit admin is not his strength. He borrowed a pair of climbing boots off me once. I got back two different size boots and two different makes. Oh! And no laces.

Now it was easy to reason with a training wing corporal. I could say I'd lost it and replace it later with the interest being a few beers. But if you borrowed anything from an RSM of any Regiment he was getting the same item back on time, serviceable and cleaner than when you borrowed it, if that was possible.

So from the second I found out he was the RSM, my strategy went from, get a throw line today at all costs, to ask the RSM nicely where I could buy a throw line, him being a kayakist he might know, and get the fuck out of there.

My escort took me to the door of the RSM's Office and left me. He was a busy man, I found myself in a queue and I stood in the corridor at ease and waited my turn.

After about fifteen minutes it was my turn.

"Come in" Said Col

I came to attention and smartly marched myself in coming to an equally smart hold on the end of his desk.

"Morning Sir" I said

"Good Morning young man" He said "Very smartly done, now who are you? and what can I do for you?" He said in a very calming voice

"Sir, I'm looking for a throw line" I answered standing rigidly to attention, wincing inside having only answered one of his two questions.

"Ok" Said Col "take a seat"

I thought he was joking, "Take a seat". Taking a seat in an RSM's office for a Private Soldier was like being allowed to dunk your biscuit in the Prime Minister's morning tea. But he wasn't joking so I sat.

For the next twenty minutes we talked about throw lines and at one point the RSM offered to lend me his. I politely declined knowing if I gave it to JFK he'd never see it again. I thanked the RSM for his time and his advice and as smartly as I marched in I marched out. That was the first time I met Col Chapman.

* * *

Four months later I'd made it to 22 myself. The civie security were still difficult wankers and Col was still the RSM. He made a point of meeting all the new guys to the Unit personally. Surprisingly he remembered me. Another gift of Col's was, he never forgot anyone he met and he always had time for everyone he met. Col had in front of him the letter I'd written and sent to him a week earlier introducing myself. It was quite an informal greeting and I was seen with Stu another new arrival. Stu was a massive Scotsman from Stirling. All six foot four of him played prop for his Regiment and he always reminded me of the honey monster. Col took the time to tell us what was expected of us, then pointed us in the direction of our new Squadrons.

When I got there things were amazingly relaxed. It was all first name terms and informal Orders. It was a far cry from the disciplined structure of Airborne Forces and took a lot of getting use to.

* * *

Every year Col took a contingent from 22 and its attached Units to the Ardeche gorge in France for adventure training. The training being white water kayaking. I'm not even sure how it came about but my name was on his list of candidates. When he approached me I was a bit reluctant, why the hell would anyone want to spend time after work hours with the RSM. Sure work for the man but socialize with him! I'd have felt more comfortable having Prince Charles watch me win a pissing contest.

That aside I agreed, who was I to turn down the most powerful man in the Regiment?

After weeks of careful planning the exercise was a go. We drove to the Ardeche in two mini buses. One pulling the boats the other pulling a trailer full of kit. Three guys in one bus four in the other. The drive was long but broken up by plenty of breaks and a cross channel ferry crossing. The French roads side service stations are some of the best I've ever stopped at, they're like small shopping malls and the one Franc massage chairs quickly became a big hit. Each road had a toll gate that effectively kept congestion to a minimum, in over five hundred miles I don't think we witnessed a single traffic jam.

The main road ended about eighty odd kilometres from our destination Valon Pon Arc. The smooth French highway gave way to an old narrow twisting road that hugged the contours of the gorge. It was slow going but the views are among the more spectacular in the world to drive though. It was through Col I learned to appreciate my surroundings and not just fight in them.

We arrived at our campsite late in the afternoon and in no time at all we had camp set up. Tents up, fire going and brew on, all happy.

Wasting no time, that evening "The Boss" gave the first lecture, "Equipment to be used and carried". We called Col, Boss at that time, we were in a civilian environment and calling the RSM "Sir" as we would any other time was a little out of place.

Col took us through all the kit we'd use and need over the next two weeks. Making sure we all knew who had what and how to use it. The man had a way of putting things so you'd never forget. Everyone tired from the journey we all crashed early that night after a couple of hours sat round the fire with a few beers reflecting on Col's lecture and looking forward to what was to come.

The next day we all got up early, bright eyed and bushy tailed dying to get started. By nine o'clock that first day we were stood by our boats next to the waters edge.

The Kayak. Bow, Stern, Cockpit, Gunnels, Rocker and all important Inherent Buoyancy. Or long yellow boat for the layman. With that, a paddle, helmet, splash deck and life preserver. We were set. How hard could it be? After a swim test I would find out.

Neal C (or Onion) was Col's Assistant Instructor for the exercise, When I first met him I couldn't work him out and to be honest I didn't really like him but I was wrong, after a while he turned out to be a really good guy and him and his wife Jo became friends of mine. He gave a demonstration on how to get in and out of the Kayak. Then demonstrated the Capsize Drill. This would be our first lesson. Onion paddled out, turned to face us, put his paddle out to one side and capsized the boat. To do this he had to rock the Kayak from side to side and overbalance to tip the boat. After giving hand signals for a T-rescue that never came, he calmly popped his spray deck and leaned his body forward out of the Kayak, then he came to the surface and yelled:

"CAPSIZE".

Looked simple enough and once again all I could think was how hard could it be?

"Right" Col said "get in your boats keeping the sterns on the bank"

I got in no probs! A bit of a squeeze but on the whole it felt pretty safe. Then Col got us one by one to float out and do the capsize drill. I pushed my boat off the bank and with paddle in hand started to move out into the open water.

The second that boat left the security of the bank and was floating in the water my arse cheeks tightened. The Kayak felt about as stable as a rock stars marriage. I was only in four inches of water and I felt tremendously out of my depth. I gingerly made my way out to Col. Its easily the longest five metre journey of my life, I'd climbed a hundred and twenty feet of E2 rock face and felt less in trouble. I was so pathetic Col got hold of the front of my boat and turned it for me. Once in position I put my paddle to one side, took a deep breath and rocked the Kayak till it went over.

Being stuck in a boat upside down in cold water, no matter how much safety kit you've got on, is not a natural position to be in and I was well outside my comfort zone. There were no hand signals from me. I shot out that boat like shit off a stick. The last time I did something that fast it was to leave Phil in a Tank with a tripped anti tank mine. I wasn't elegant or right in my method as Col pointed out. But I felt safer knowing one thing was for sure. I could get out that boat and fast.

The rest of the day covered the T-rescue and the basic strokes. Col used a frizzbi game to help us refine our techniques. Its fair to say I spent most of that day upside down and pulling my boat to the shore and emptying it out. Definitely the harder way to spend the day.

That nights lecture covered reading the river, names of waves, what they did and how they would affect the boat, all this aimed at keeping us out of trouble and in the boat upright. The rest of the lecture covered hazards of the river and safe areas along with other general river knowledge, once again done with Col's calm hypnotic teaching method, if he'd taught me at school I'd be a professor now, I've never forgotten a thing the man ever told me.

Later that night we sat round the fire with a few beers and exchanged war stories. Col never said a lot he was more of a listener. He'd sit with his mug of tea and smile to himself as we told each other how good we were. He was always the last to eat and the first to sleep.

The rest of the week was spent perfecting our new skills and on occasion Col would give us the option to throw ourselves down a small slalom course not too far from where we were training. Col's instruction bought us all along quickly and by the end of the week I could stay upright through all the basic strokes, breaking in and out of moving water and even in small rapids. Everything was coming together nicely.

After the first week Col took us on our first short expedition. Less than twenty kilometres from the mill pond we did our training at to the campsite. Three sets of grade three rapids and the Arc itself would challenge us on the one day event.

The first set of rapids was by far the biggest challenge of the week. Directly translated its name is "The three teeth", and it earned its name. From the very top, it sucked me in chewed me up rolled me over and shit me out the other end. Half way down I capsized. My head hit the floor the front of the boat the back of the boat and when I eventually got out the boat my head nearly went up my own arse. I felt like I was in a washing machine on the spin cycle. I took in a good breath of water and scrapped my thigh and banged my arse off every rock on the way down I had no control whatsoever.

At the bottom a French kayaker had pulled my boat to the side and found my paddle. I made my way to the side of the river thanking the man in my best drowning French. Beaten up, cut and bruised I joined the two lads that went before me. They'd also come a cropper half way down.

From that moment on I've loved white water kayaking.

That day was a long one and that wasn't the last hiding I got that day or that week. That night back at the campsite I was a bit pissed off with myself for constantly capsizing the kayak. Col pointed out that there was a path of least resistance in most rapids and that my constant rolling over was me not taking it. I was challenging myself and that's exactly what he wanted to see.

Some of the group never got wet and I think that pissed Col off. Not because they were great paddlers on the contrary, but because they wouldn't push themselves and sat comfortably on the flowing route. I didn't see the point of that for me the idea was to push the limits while I had the expertise available to help me out if I fucked things up too badly.

Col pushed our individual ability to the very limits. When the water came over my boat and I'd mistook up from down and left from right I'd listen intently for the calm rolling words of advice from Col and as long as I listened things often went my way, if it didn't go my way it was because I wasn't quick enough.

Some nights we'd pop out to local restaurants, the rule being to order our meals in French. Valon Pon Arc is a wonderful French village and the square comes to life at night. The close streets hold the cool of the evening and the locals drink wine, read the local rag and chat amongst themselves. The cobbled streets and the colourful shutters on the windows are the trade marks of small town France. If you close your eyes and think of a quaint French village you'd probably picture Valon.

In total I did eight tours in ten years of the Ardeche with Colin and loved every one of them. Each trip had its own special adventure, its own group of characters and the mini bus was bumped on every trip. Col and I became very close friends over the following fourteen years, he is a man whose council I could trust and whose company I enjoyed, he has three wonderful kids and its been a pleasure to watch them grow. Col and I lost contact for a while because of my work commitments, he married in that time and when we got together again to catch up he spoke of Claire his new wife with the very same spark and tenderness he did when he spoke of his children. Col and I returned to the Ardeche as civilians and enjoyed the calm French social life as much as the water.

Kayaking white water is a sport born to hold your adrenaline levels high for as long as you're physical and mental ability can handle it. I'm not a great paddler by any means and I must confess the sport for me is not the same without Colin around to push my ability, but I love the water and the excitement of not knowing how its gonna go and having to rely constantly on the standard of my tuition to safely enjoy violent raging white water.

IF YOU'RE NOT GETTING WET, YOU'RE NOT TRYING

Onion.

RIP
COLIN JOHN CHAPMAN
1954-2009
FATHERS
SOLDIERS, FRIENDS
ALWAYS

Judo

For as long as I can remember I've had to fight. I fought with my brothers and for them. On the streets of every new estate we moved to and in every new school we were cursed with. Every time we moved the street, estate or school hard man wanted to know if he was keeping his title and never being one to back away I'd be obliged to find out. I took as many titles as I took good hidings but that's life.

Having younger brothers that were bigger than me by my tenth birthday meant I needed to be able to hit hard and fast. They were good boys and never gave me much call to "whack em". They learned fast that it was easier to do as I asked them, than to go ten rounds.

Having a violent drunk father like mine, I learned to duck and move quickly, to read the room and use it to my instant advantage all using peripheral vision. If I took my eyes off the old man for half a second he saw that as great disrespect and would lash harder and the beating would last longer. In a sick twisted way it was all good preparation to combat sports.

Despite the disapproving and condescending comments from the old man, I joined Aldershot Boxing Club and competed with some success in my teen years, taking junior titles in Hampshire and fighting in the ABA's under fifteens reaching the regional semi finals and for a while managed it without the old mans hindrance. Which wasn't that hard at the time as he was never really around and when he was he never paid any attention to us boys anyway. Aldershot Boxing club is a stones throw from the football ground. Di Evans was the coach. He'd tell me on a daily basis:

"Son you got no style, no finesse and no grace, but young un, you got an iron jaw and you can hit boy"

I was one of the smaller lads at the club but Di use to say I boxed like an aging heavy weight that's not a compliment either. He was a pugilistic perfectionist. I remember one of the mums came in one afternoon when I was talking to Di and she asked why he never made any of us kid wear head guards

"I teach Boxing here" he said "not fighting."

And he was right, to appreciate his words you have to have both fought in the street and in the ring. Boxing is an art form. He was a lovely old guy and a good mentor in those early days.

Then as I got older I studied Ju Jitsu, with equal success taking my Dan grade in five years. The training was completely different from that of Boxing as was the sport. As traditional as the sport is I stuck to the combative side. I struggled in the early days because of my lack of finesse and co-ordination but hard training and good coaching from the world's best put that right in no time. Brazilian Ju Jitsu is as unforgiving as any sport I've ever done. Every aspect of the fight game must be explored and trained. I knew when I started BJJ that I could bang, but after hearing the words of Renzo Gracie I would have to revise my whole fight game, he simply said:

"If you can't grapple you can't fight"

After that the grapple and ground game became a passion of mine. I studied techniques from all round the world. I even worked the techniques that didn't work for me. I believe you don't have to be able to do every technique perfectly but if you know it exists you can avoid it or set them up with it.

But it's thanks to Sergeant Major Paul Colman that I found Judo.
Paul, or Sir as I called him then, approached me on a Tuesday morning asking if I was.
"Fighting Fit"
"Absolutely Sir" I replied with great enthusiasm.
"Good" He said "There's a Judo competition at the weekend and I've put your name down for the team"
"I've never done Judo before Sir" I queried

"Not to worry" He said "I'll be taking the training every night this week"

"Ok Sir I'll see you there then" I said

Not quite sure what I'd let myself in for I went happily along to the first training session.

I can honestly say it was the hardest single PT session I'd ever had and I loved it. From my very first Judo lesson I was hooked. All we really did was grip and move. Paul taught us just one hold down and one throw and already I was in love with this sport. At this point it wasn't a far cry from BJJ. I had a few rough edges that needed ironing out though.

One point scoring objective of Judo is to hold your opponent down for thirty seconds and every time I found myself being held down I'd sink my teeth into the arm or chest of my lesser aggressive opponent in order to regain the upper hand or I'd push my fingers up my opponents arse so they'd close their legs making it easier to turn them over. Which believe it or not is considered unsporting and illegal in the sport of Judo. As is striking with the head, poking in the eyes and grabbing by the balls. So I had to work on my personal discipline but that came as I got better at the techniques of the sport.

With the Army novice championships less than a week away the team that Paul had chosen trained twice a day. Sticking with the one throw, one hold down, and constant practice of controlling the opponent via grips.

The British Army Novice Championships was held in Fox Gym at the Army School of Physical Education. It was a big day for the Unit. Having fought in front of crowds before I found myself being the one to give advice, not on Judo techniques but on nerves and competition preparation. I'd competed a lot before for Boxing, Ju Jitsu and Gymnastics. So I was no stranger to atmosphere and competition pressure. But as this was a novice event it was a knee shaking first for some of the others. So I spent most of the day saying:

"That's normal, you'll be fine, take deep breaths" And "Just remember, control is key"

I won my first fight and lost my second and third but all my fights went the distance. The team overall did well, we came fifth out of twenty-two teams. The day was a long nerve racking one and I was pleased that our Commanding Officer and his wife had taken the time to come and see us fight. At the end of the day a PTI John M was taking names of people who wanted to do Army Squad Training. Straight away I was bang up for it and with the CO there I could find out then if it was OK with him. As soon as he gave me the nod I put my name on the list.

After that day I went full out to find and train Judo. It took about a month to sort out but I ended up doing four and five classes a week. Monday night at Frimley, it was run and taken by Ritchie Dove a lovely man with lots of patients. It was a technique night mainly with Randori (Free Practice) at the end.

Wednesday, was either Camberley or Guildford depending on where I was during the day. Camberley was run by Mark and Burny Earl at the time. It also had a lot of full time Judo players there from the British team. So I was guaranteed a good session. Mark works everyone hard as you'd expect from a National Coach. But he worked himself hard to. In the time I trained there, there wasn't a single session I didn't see him on the mat with the rest of the Squad. I even had the opportunity to fight him myself a few times but not with a lot of success. Each session was a massive learning curve for me. I always enjoyed his lessons.

Guildford was more of a club level club and more light randori than anything else. I used it as a place to try out anything and everything I'd learned from any other club.

Thursday, I went up to High Wycombe for their club night and on Friday the Unit Team got together for a conditioning and technique night followed by a full on Randori session as only testosterone filled soldiers can have.

Judo became a passion. I fought every competition I could find and went to every grading I qualified for. I made great friends through the sport, fought them and fought with them. Ritchie Dove from Frimely put a team together every year to fight the Kent open and the South England Team events. I was honoured when he asked if I'd fight for him and his club; "Osaka Dojo". That year under the instruction of Ritchie I took one Gold medal, three Silver and three Bronze in different national and international competitions around the country. I trained every spare minute I had and travelled hundreds of miles, just to fight.

In just two years I had my 1st kyu or top brown. Just one away from 1st Dan, Black

Belt. At the same time this was happening, I'd left Airborne Forces and the British Army.

It didn't slow my training down when I was in the country. If anything I did more. I was married at the time to a woman I couldn't stand, but we all make one big mistake in our lives that follows us round like a lost dog for the rest of it, I used any excuse to get out the house and Judo was as good a reason as any.

I worked a lot abroad when I left the Army but when in the UK I was training six sometimes seven times a week with one goal, my 1st Dan. It was never too far from thoughts.

On Wednesday nights at this time I was training in Bushy North Watford at the Bourne hall DoJo. The head guy there was Chris Knox 5th Dan and he truly is a Judo Guru. He knows this sport inside out and is a technical wizard. After getting to know Chris a little better we started training a few nights a week together at clubs all round London.

One night we went to train with an old friend of his Percy, a WW2 veteran who was captured during the war and set up a DoJo in his prison camp using cardboard for mats. The pictures on his walls amazed me.

It was at this club I first met Chris in Randori. Shortly before I'd met him he'd undergone an operation on a torn bicep and was keeping his Randori to a minimum, the opportunity to fight him hadn't arisen till now. I'd like to say I took it easy on Chris but i didn't get the chance his technique and timing were far far superior to mine. Everything I did he had an answer for, its one of the more enjoyable hidings I've ever had.

Chris's coaching and direction over the following six months put me in a position to go for my Dan Grade. I'd travelled around the country fighting every grading and competition I could find. Fighting for the hundred points I needed for the grade. I had seventy points and Chris offered to take me to a Dan grading in Southampton. I jumped at the chance.

When we got there I was paired off with other fighters for the day. My fights came quickly and I won both my fights by Ippon (ten points). This taking my total to ninety.

Then to my surprise because I'd won both fights by Ippon I was offered a line up. This I hadn't expected.

A line up is when you fight three other fighters simultaneously. If I beat them all by Ippon (ten points) then I would have won my Dan grade. Or I could wait until the next grading or competition, score Ippon in one fight bringing my tally to one hundred and qualify that way.

I took the line up. The first fight was a guy my size wearing British flags. This would make him a very experienced fighter. I was so wound up by the time the fight came I ripped him out the ground and finished him in under a few seconds.

The second fight was potentially my spoiler, he was a big fat guy that used his weight to pull his opponents down and lie on them. This was his tactic during my fight with him too, what pissed me off more was that fact he wasn't bothered about winning he just didn't want me to succeed. The second time he dragged me to the ground I didn't fight it, I went down to the floor with him and let the fat bulking mass strangle me, once he was fully committed to the strangle I turned him over into an arm lock and he tapped out. My win.

The third guy was a lot bigger than me and about ten years older, I won that match through pure aggression and audacity. He simply couldn't control me, conditioning won the day. A long fifteen minutes later I'd qualified for my 1st Dan Black Belt. Chris had worked my technical game hard. Between that and the fact I wanted it more than they did the reward was mine.

Although I had the points I still needed to complete the theory side of the BJA's requirements, in order to wear the coveted Black belt. A week later Chris took me to Bedford to see another old friend of his Robin who took me through the theory test. After passing that it was mine, a BJA 1st Dan.

Chris is a great mentor, and a good friend.

As soon as I got my licence back from the British Judo Association, with the Dan grade stamp in it. I went down to Frimley to train at Ritchie Doves. Ritchie had seen and trained me in the beginning and now two years later I walked onto his mats as a Dan Grade.

When I entered the DoJo with my Black Belt wrapped proudly round my waist Ritchie smiled walked up to me and gave me a massive hug.

"Great News" He said "You more than deserve it"

After the session we spoke about Chris and how the grade came about. He was so proud of me and I am so grateful to him for his coaching and the opportunities he'd given me. My BJJ background came as a great help in my Judo accomplishment but considering Judo derives from Ju Jitsu the two sports are worlds apart.

With a Dan Grade came a whole new Judo world. I went on to fight international events at Dan Grade level such as the Kent International the Ipswich Open and the British Open. I fought in France, Germany and Ireland to name my favourites

It also gave me the opportunity to teach and referee kids at their grading's. I've also had the privilege to coach my own son and the honour to watch him grade and fight in competition. He fights like a lion. He's twice the young warrior I ever was, I'm so very proud of him.

Even now years after I made the decision to retire from competition I train at clubs wherever I am in the world. Knowing that the coaching I've received and the respect I've got for the sport and its players stands me in good stead.

As time went on and my military career took off to new levels my Martial Arts studies sat on the back burner for good while. My love for the fight game was rekindled by an out of the blue friendship with two great guys, Dave Scarborough and Mark Wooldridge of Hemel Hempstead. Both accomplished fighters in their fields, Dave in the Muay Thai world and Mark primarily in Ti Quon Do. Both fighters loved to mix the Martial Arts something I'd been doing for almost twenty years at that point. I'd mixed Judo with Karate in the UK, Arrest and Restraint with Ju Jitsu and Aikido in Northern Ireland. In Eastern Europe Wrestling and Judo with Tsambo and Boxing and Grappling in North Africa. I contested and fought all round the world in all manner of Mixed Martial Arts, with gloves without gloves for money for food and for free, only to find out I could have done it on my own doorstep.

The three of us would get together most mornings and go through techniques that covered the Standing and Ground techniques then we'd work the transition from one to the other, all the important aspects of MMA. After that we'd punch the living shit out of each other for the next hour. Then when we could we'd meet up with larger class's and do the same there. I've fought all around the world and these two men are exceptional fighters. Since meeting them I've not let a week go by when I haven't trained on at least one aspect of my fight game.

*MORE SWEAT IN TRAINING,
LESS BLOOD IN BATTLE*

Ishmael Jassat BYO

CHECHNYA

I'd left the Army and was living in a dogshit town North of Watford with a wife I couldn't stand. We got married about eighteen months before. I wed her out of pity. A shit reason I know but I was young and "It seemed like the thing to do at the time".

She and I used to climb together, she was better than me and she was a good training partner and I should have left it there. But when her husband left her for some teenager I felt sorry for her and before I knew it we were seeing more of each other than usual. I didn't see the wrong at the time, I knew it wasn't going anywhere but so what. Did it have to? She was bad news though, I'd been told this by all my close friends and told to get out while I could but at the time I didn't see the harm.

It ended up that when her and her ex husband Bill divorced she would be kicked out of her married quarter and put in a one bedroom hostel in her home town and could be there for years she said. She played on that one hard. She had two kids a boy and girl and to be fair they were great kids. She told me how hard life would be on them in a hostel, how they'd be victims of crime and peer pressure. She told me all this one night on the piss. I felt so sorry for her, she'd gone from comfortable family life to homeless, all because some Aldershot dog had rubbed her leg up her husband and he fell for her hook line and sinker. It didn't seem fair and I had no answers but I offered to do anything I could to help.

Have you ever said something and wished you hadn't?

She disappeared for a couple of days to see a friend of hers and when she came back she reminded me of my offer to help and told me her new cunning plan. She suggested we get married till she got herself sorted, then we could get the marriage annulled. Sounded simple enough and the white knight in me came out. Not a bad plan I thought and again I just didn't see the harm surely this simple plan would sort all her problems and her kids would be fine.

The Wedding

At 0800 on the Saturday we got married, I climbed out of Karen S's bed a girlfriend of mine at the time. I met her through Judo she was great fun both on and off the piss. The night before was a hectic one and I'd spilt curry sauce all down my shirt so borrowed another one from Phil P to get married in. I turned up at the registry office in Aldershot after a good breakfast with the lads at 1100. I had to borrow 50 pence off a mate of mine for the marriage licence because I was short and I had no wedding rings. To top that I had a date to meet Karen that afternoon.

As soon as it was over I went back on the piss with my mates, but I did have to bend to a meal a little later in the evening. The new bride was fuming but that's as seriously as I took the whole thing. It was done to help her and her kids. There were guys marrying immigrants for money so they could stay in the country at least I did this for free.

Staying out her way was easy in the Army, I still had my room on camp and volunteered for every Op I could. In eighteen months I saw her for less than two weeks and it seemed to suit us both down to the ground.

Because of Politics and events in my past, my ten year career with British Special Forces was all but over so I made the decision one night on duty at 22 to leave the Army. I went in the next day to inform the SSM of my decision. He sat me down and pointed out that I had no home to go to and no civilian trade I was married to a woman I obviously didn't want to be around and if I stayed in another year I could have a pension. But my mind was set, all the time the SSM was talking and playing devils advocate I was making plans. My convenient wife had used me for her gain now I would use our situation for mine.

Because I had a wife and two kids the local council would house me and I could get a sixty percent discount on a house because of the time I'd served in the Army, even though the kids weren't mine and the wedding was a sham the paper trail was perfect. Once I'd formulated a working plan and not being one to fuck about, things moved quickly. Because of the circumstances behind my decision to leave the Army I didn't have to give a years notice and after a long interview with my CO he invoked special powers and I left Her Majesties Forces three months later. It was a big step, I felt very alone.

The hardest thing about Civie Street was finding reasons not to go home. We had the happy families chat, and I tried it, it just wasn't me. I just didn't love this woman. I had things in life I wanted to do and they didn't involve her and her kids. On top of that I hated her family. Greedy, manipulating, cowardice, are all words you could use to describe anyone of them. I was only happy in her presence when I was pissed. Judo was a great escape but it was only in the evenings and good work was hard to find at the time so I found myself going from temp job to temp job.

It wasn't long before I was approached by a popular contact in the private military world Joe. I could have approached him at anytime but I waited for him to contact me. He had all the right connections and would have no trouble finding me if he had work in my field. Lucky for me he did. He had work for ten men in Eastern Europe. It was a twelve week contract for Infantry Advisers. I jumped at the chance. I met with the other guys in the Grapes pub in Hereford a week later and got a very basic brief. The job was in Chechnya.

Chechnya lies on the northern side of the Caucasus mountain range and spans between the Black Sea and the Caspian Sea. It's also the largest oil producing region in the former Soviet Union and because of this has great strategic and political importance. The Caucasus history reads like that of Afghanistan, every fucker over the last thousand years has tried to take it for themselves. The Persians in the 1400's, the Otterman Turks in the 1700's and the Tsarist Russia in the 1800's. It was even occupied by the Tamerlane Mongols and then Russian Cossacks of a while. But like Afghanistan it fought against all odds and beat the numerically superior and more technology advanced invaders.

Even with all that history the Russians in 1994 ran onto the end of another unwinnable war. After the break up of the Soviet Union in 1991 independence movements had been successful in Georgia, Armenia, and Azerbaijan, so Chechnya tried its luck.

Their leader and later our boss was Johkar Dudayev. He ran things in Chechnya without interference from Moscow for the next two years, but not well. Subsidies from Russia were stopped and Chechnya slipped into a black market economy. It ran guns like Kenyon's run marathons. With all the conflict in neighbouring countries there was no shortage of buyers or sellers, but the revenue went to the few and never catered for the Chechen population.

Dudayev could give a mean speech and the people were left feeling patriotic and proud, but still hungry. What made it worse was every time Dudayev opened his mouth he blamed the country's problems on Yeltsin and not his own lack of economic knowledge, so he wasn't making any friends in the Kremlin either.

The main reason Dudayev was given the room he was given, was all down to disruption in the Kremlin. But in 1993 Yeltsin defeated the Communist Party and a new constitution for Russia was drawn up. With the Kremlin parties all now singing from the same song sheet they now turned their attentions to what they called: "The Chechnya Issue."

In 1993 Chechnya refused to sign a unification treaty with Yeltsin's new Russia and went all out to declare independence. While the Chechens spoke and partitioned Russia used this time to put whole Armoured and Artillery Divisions on Chechnya's doorstep. They also financed and armed Dudayev's opposition, but all to no avail. In the November of 1993 Dudayev won the first National Election. His first move was to throw out all the remaining Russian parties. The separatist threat to Russia in this strategically important region was now very real.

Shortly after the elections, the opposition funded and advised by the Kremlin staged an unsuccessful armed coup. This quickly became an International embarrassment for Yeltsin who then took matters into his own hands.

Yeltsin ordered the night and day bombardment of Grozny the Chechen Capital. Hoping for a quick and decisive victory, he then ordered a full armoured attack on the city with a view to catching Dudayev in short time.

Yeltsin obviously never studied Military history. Not world history but their own. If Hitler couldn't successfully take Stalingrad with heavy armour, what in the world made Yeltsin think he could do it to Grozny?

The endless bombing started in the December, initially aiming only at Military targets. But the bombardment quickly spread to built up civilian areas. Within days it was obvious the Russian strategy was to raise the city to the ground, driving the Chechen forces out that way. But the strategy made little sense, there were more ethnic Russians in Grozny than Chechens. In just a few days civilian casualties were in there thousands.

The Russians committed to one large assault that was promptly beaten back by the Chechen forces using only RPG's, homemade anti-tank mines and the Soviet made AK47. The conscripts in their large tanks and Armoured Personnel Carriers were no match for agility and resourcefulness of the Chechen fighter in his own back yard.

The Russians retreated, their arse's toughly kicked. Then within hours they put the City under siege and mercilessly resumed their relentless bombardment, with no concern whatsoever for the growing humanitarian issue and all with one aim. To reduce the city to ashes and force the Chechen fighters into open ground.

After two months of heavy fighting and countless dead on each side. Russia managed to take control Grozny, they failed however to seal off the city and the Chechen troops disappeared like ghosts into the Caucasus mountains and settled into tactics they'd used for a thousand years against hundreds of adversaries. GUERRILLA WARFARE.

The only way to describe the events 1994 and 1995 in Chechnya is Genocide. Not just for the Chechen people but for the ethnic

Russian civilian population. The Russian Armies Units were ordered to kill indiscriminately. This was bad for troop and Russian moral all over the former Soviet Union. With what was left of Grozny in Russian control, the Red Army turned its attention to the rest of the county. Burning villages and bombing small towns to the ground. Destroying anything that resembled infrastructure. Pulling down anything the people could use. People died in their hundreds, every hour of every day. With the worlds media concentrated on the atrocities in Bosnia and the mass graves of Srebrenica, the Kremlin had free reign and very little international pressure to stop. And that's when we came in.

During the spring of 1996 it was obvious the Russian Army had spread its outdated resources too thinly. The local Commanders on the ground struggled to gain and keep control of their areas. The elements beat their equipment and the Chechen Militia beat their troops. The guerrilla tactics adopted worked well. They made small dents in the Russian war machine, but they were permanent dents. With Russian logistical supply lines under constant attack it became harder and harder for the Russians to take care of their own and their desertion rate became astounding. On more than one occasion we'd find deserters in the countryside, no weapons no food or water trying desperately to get home, they were easily coerced into giving away Intelligence on their Units in exchange for food and a lift. Slowly but surely the Chechens were taking back their country.

* * *

We landed in Gori in Georgia and travelled by road for eleven hours across the Russian boarder to Makhachkala. A city on the coast of the Caspian Sea. Even as far South as it was it had not escaped Russian attention. Although it had avoided serious bombardment it had become a Garrison for Russian troops who treated the place like a Ghetto. Drunk and undisciplined they walked the streets of this once proud City showing it little or no respect.

We spent two days there waiting for our contact to come down from Buynaksk a small town to the west of us closer to the Caucasus mountain range and the protection it would give us over the coming months.

I don't think anyone has ever been so pleased to see me. Our contact treated us like celebrities and we hadn't done anything. He was a professional actor in peace time. His repertoire boasted a few well known Shakespeare plays and a small speaking part in local TV soap opera. But he was appointed Minister of Defence when the trouble started because he had two years of conscript service under his belt and everyone else had one. So when we turned up with a minimum ten years Military experience a piece, we instantly became mentors and advisors to a Minister.

We travelled the forty miles or so to Buynksk the old fashioned way. In a cart pulled by mules.

We didn't have a lot of kit so there was plenty of room. But the journey was slow and cold, really fuckin cold. We'd been give clothes back in Makhachkala by a very helpful old woman who had to rally round everywhere using flawless discretion to get all our sizes. Not just for warmth but to blend in. There was an uncontested media black out at that time and all foreign aid turned away or shut down in Chechnya. So we couldn't pose as journalists or aid workers, we'd be arrested on sight and hopefully deported, the Gulag time didn't bear worth thinking about. So we were locals or bust and in the fire fight of our lives if caught and at that time it would have been a very short fire fight. We weren't armed yet.

It took most of the day to get to the small town and when we got there we were taken in by a local family. At first we tried to turn the offer down. If we got caught we'd only bring more suffering to the doorstep of this wonderful, simple, loving family. But they wouldn't hear of it. They saw us not as cheerleaders for their cause, but as fighting men. Fighting for them and they loved us for it.

Nothing else much happened that day. We were free to move around the town as we pleased. I was having a great time meeting the people and playing marbles with the kids. Every house I passed offered a hot drink a thumbs up and conversation I could only nod to. These people were so friendly and seemed so content despite the troubles.

That night we ate goat stew and spuds. There was loads of it and it was hot. Over supper the Minister came in. We nick named him Poppy because when he said his name that was the prominent syllable. He enjoyed his nick name. It made him feel like one of the lads. He came to tell us we'd be moving early the next day deeper into the mountains to a camp. There we'd meet Dudayev and be given arms and handed our respective Commands.

"Commands" Mick said.

Mick was the oldest of us and had taken it upon himself to be our "leader" for want of a better word. He'd done the full twenty two years in the Army, nearly all of it at Hereford. I had no issue with him taking charge none of us did. He knew his stuff that was sure. He handled us all very well. He never ordered anything to be done, he just made good suggestions. (Clever bastard) and like every time he spoke, with that single word, "Commands" he had a good point.

Poppy explained that he was of the understanding; we were sent to lead the Chechen guerrilla's in a major offensive planned for later in the year.

The room erupted like an old Roman Senate. We all had important questions and they needed addressing before we went any further and we all wanted the first answer, the room got louder. Mick piped up and silenced the room.

"We're guests in this house Gentleman" He said "We will act accordingly"

Then he turned his attentions to Poppy.

"The job description we can change, if you can raise the money" He went on "The time span is more of a problem, we're only contracted for three months some of these guys have other commitments beyond that, how long do you need us for?"

Mick was good, his silk tongue had asked every question we had in two simple sentences.

Poppy couldn't have been any more sorry for the confusion and went on to explain that he could raise more money. There was no shortage of money, the black market economy there was an opulent one. I began to feel like a real scumbag, these people had shown nothing but love, taken us in and fed us. Not only were we charging them for it but now we wanted more. Sean must have read my mind. He leaned forward and whispered in my ear:

"Don't feel bad mate, the fighting hasn't started yet"

It didn't make me feel any better, but I knew the point the he was making.

Everybody calmed down and after two hours of negotiations and discussion it worked out not all of us could stay. Six went home. It wasn't the new job it was the time span. Our three months was now five and if we met any hiccups or delays which was already on the cards having gone over the new tasks the job wouldn't be finished at the right time. Then the weather would shut the gorge and we'd be stuck in Chechnya for the winter. That took our five months to a very likely eight. A long time to be away from home for happy family men.

The guys that were going home had a weeks wait in the village before they could get back to Makhachkala and they were paid well for the time they did. I spoke to Dave T when I got back to the UK, he said they were treated like hero's for that week in the village even though they were the ones going home. He said he never felt so bad in his life and had it not been for family commitments he would have walked back up the range to where we were.

The next day as promised we were up before the sparrows, back on the mule drawn cart heading out to the great Caucasus. We travelled west though a beautiful smelling thick pine forest. In the distance Kazbek the highest point in the Caucasus. The range was magnificent. Endless miles of unspoilt snow drifts deep valleys and ice cold crystal clear springs.

The four of us, me, Sean, Jock and old Mick, engaged in all manner of squaddie humour from dirty jokes to practical pranks. We took it in turns to sit with the driver. He didn't speak English and our Russian and Chechen was all but non-existent, but it was company and he did appreciate it, occasionally he'd say something and point to a spot in the distance. Every now and again we'd jump off the back of the cart and run ahead. Sightseeing mainly but all with a view to keeping warm. It was dry, but very very cold.

We arrived at the camp late that night. It felt like we'd been travelling for days. My arse was killing me my joints didn't want to bend and every muscle in my body thirsted warmth. The games had stopped after dark and we'd sat in silence for the last five hours. It was too dangerous to get out the cart at night. Cliff edges were unstable and never far away.

We hit the ground running when we arrived, no time for rest to many things to organize. Dudayev wasn't there but we'd expected that. Instead his 2IC greeted us and gave Dudayev's apologies. There was no light allowed outside at this camp at night, it wasn't the main camp more of an out post. The 2ic took us passed an anti-aircraft position to a scrimed up wooden shack. Inside we drank welcome hot tea and ate more goat stew, no spuds this time. As we ate and warmed up the 2ic told us more about our new roles. Intent on finishing the hot welcome food the three of us were happy to let Mick take the new orders and hand tasks down to us as he saw fit. He'd done a sterling job so far, why question him now?

The 2ic left the room. While he was gone Mick explained our new Commands.

"Right Gents" He said with his usual confidence, "Basically they've got 1600 men, enough arms and ammunition to win WW3 and a handful of light vehicles, by that I mean soft top Landrovers and a few assorted four wheel drives, they want too divide all that lot between us so we can train them and lead in an offensive on somewhere later in the year."

"Fuck that's brief" Jock said.

"That's four hundred men a piece" I said "I'm not sure where I'd start Mick"

"It's not a problem" Mick said with smile "We'll train instructors and they'll train their guys. You won't even know you've got four hundred men till the big Op."

"And what about the offensive Mick? " said Jock. "Working in pairs, we're good for a Platoon attack at best. Maybe four of us together could pull off a Company strength attack but with this language barrier mate. Anything bigger is a bullshit dream."

I looked at Sean, we were both impressed by Jock's foresight. The higher ranks always thought ten steps ahead. Sean said his biggest concern before Jock spoke was making up four hundred nick names.

With so much going on I never had any major concerns. I was just hoping to come out alive. It wasn't the Russians I was worried about either. It was hypothermia and starvation that bothered me.

"It's a lot worse than that Jock" Mick said "It's an urban offensive, fighting in built up areas my friend"

FIBUA was challenging enough when comms and planning were good but with us not speaking the same lingo we'd have to be very careful not to make casualties of our own men.

"Hang on" Sean said "We've got 1600 men to take an urban area. We could take that town Makhachkala with five hundred. Where's this offensive? Manchester."

We all fell silent Sean was right. What urban area would demand the recourses we had? Then it came to me:

"They're gonna try and retake Grozny" I said

"No more guess's" Said Mick, for the first time a seriousness in his voice, "They're obviously trying to keep it secret, if it goes wrong lets not be stuck out here as the prime suspects for a leek in Intel."

Once again the old man had a very strong and valid point.

A little while later the 2ic came back in with uniforms and badges of rank for us. As we sized them all up and found the best combinations, Sean said:

"Isn't wearing this construed as spying?"

We all stopped what we were doing and looked at Sean, another valid point.

"Advisor, mercenary, soldier, spy, the battlefields are different but the objective's the same" Said Mick

"The penalties not" Said Sean "What if we get caught?"

"Don't" said Jock.

I loved the lack of sympathy in the room. It took the edge off the tension that had mounted since we arrived.

"Where'd you get that word, construed from?" I asked.

With that everyone had bit of a laugh and the tension eased a little more.

All of us dressed in our second hand but new to us uniforms, we were shown to our pits and crashed out for the night.

The next morning I woke up hungry and bursting for a piss. It was so cold during the night I thought better of getting up to go. The sun was out but not yet warming the ground and the view was fantastic. It was still cold but bearable. A smokeless fire was lit and breakfast was on the boil, goat stew again. There were small gatherings of troops all round sipping at tea and laughing. Everything seemed so normal so surreal, we were meant to be at war and yet this could have just been any training exercise in Brecon.

I looked down at the combats I was wearing, reached into the pocket and pulled out a pair of dark brown leather gloves and put them on. A young soldier walked up to me and handed me a mug of hot tea then saluted. I returned the gesture. Then for the first time it hit me. I'd gone from jobless civilian to Military advisor and now stood as a Mercenary Lieutenant Colonel in less than a week and all I'd really done was change clothes. It gave my perspective on life a whole new angle.

I felt myself change a lot over the next three months. The intense cold stopped bothering me and I learned patients and reasoning. Mick's plan to train just an instruction team for each Battalion was a good one and his constant advice and guidance was priceless. I asked when I wasn't sure but he didn't offer if I didn't ask.

We trained instructors three days a week who intern passed their teachings down the line. We kept it simple. We started with section attacks and pairs fire manoeuvre then went onto Platoon attacks.

Jock was right. It was a nightmare. It took all four of us to hold it together and at this point we were only dealing with the cream of what they had. It fast became apparent we would have to roll in the mud with the rest of them to pull the offensive off.

Once we had them working as an organised team we started on the Fib and Dib. In the past they'd fought in poorly organised but effective threes and fours. That was ok to disrupt a position for a short time but it wasn't enough to re-take a position and hold it. They'd never fought as a large single body of men and I'm surprised they didn't kill more of each other in their earlier conflicts, but they had complete faith in us and learned quickly.

Unlike privately paid African troops who have a sixty percent desertion rate under fire, I never doubted the courage of these men. I knew in my heart they would stand to the last man.

Knowing that meant my judgement had to be sound, some of these men were gonna die under my Command. I had to make sure if that was the case they didn't die needlessly, my own skills and judgment would have to be as sound as I could get it.

At night we'd join our troops in local Op's of "Hit and Hinder." We'd hit soft Russian targets. Road sentries, light vehicle patrols, small depots and logistical lines.

One night we picked on a small logistical post. It had fuel and we needed it. We needed to work silently, but it was always gonna get messy.

I moved into position so I could dispatch a gate guard in silence. He was lighting a fag against the side of the fence. My weapon of choice was a beautiful and razor sharp fixed blade knife I'd taken from a dead conscript two nights earlier. God knows where he got it from.

The unsuspecting guard had struck his lighter a good eight or ten times. Any night vision he had was long gone. The approach was easy. Then the lights in the compound dimmed making both me and the guard look into the lit area to see if there was a problem.

I thought I'd lose my opportunity and moved back. I grabbed his helmet and forced his head for back of his neck and giving my blade access to ba stantly he reached down and grabbed my left leg he tripped me putting me flat on my back.

He was stood, bent over me fighting against the hold I still had of the back of his helmet, I kicked at his left knee hoping to bring him down on top of me. I couldn't afford to let him go. His rifle still strapped to his back all he had to do was step back pull it round and shoot.

Keeping a good grip that my life now depended on I stabbed repeatedly into the neck of the Russian sentry. Aiming each time for the vocal cords and garrotted artery, at the same time still working to take the legs away from my target. After a bloody onslaught that seemed to never end the heavy man fell between my legs. I pull his head into my chest and smothered the remaining life from his body. He stopped struggling and became a dead weight giving the occasional twitch. I rolled him off with ease thanks to fifteen years of Judo and looked around to see what attention I'd mustered.

Fortunately for us only Sean, Mick and a few of our guys saw the brutal adlibbed ambush. I could feel them all holding their breath. I could taste blood and earth in my mouth and I was covered from forehead to waist in my enemy's claret and my heart was racing ten to the dozen. I didn't feel scared, I felt immortal.

The side gate now unguarded we went to work robbing the place blind. No one else was killed that night. Once inside the remaining Russian forces folded at the sight of armed aggressive Chechens. Even though our new pupils were all for executing the surrendered troops we had made it clear in all our lessons that wasn't to happen. They were to be disarmed and left to their own devices. The chances were they would desert anyway and if they didn't they would fear and respect the Chechen troops for their humanity. The mission was a great success. Not only did we get fuel but we got winter parkers and gloves as well.

Life went on like that for some time. The training went onto over more advanced areas of fighting in built up areas using sewers as routes of movement, leaving link men and most other aspects of the job. Not once did we let it slip that we thought Grozny was the target. But we trained them for that very objective.

As the training of the instructors came to an end. We engaged more and more in missions of mischief against our Russian foes. We had complete autonomy to do whatever we wanted to disrupt the Russian occupation. We lay ambushes for their patrols and logistical lines, bribed conscript for access to their armouries, then cleaned them out. Laid charges in the wells they used for water. Stole their mail. Shot the windows out their vehicles just so they'd freeze. Anything we could do to piss them off, we did. It was hairy at times but on the whole a great experience and a great chance to abuse my Military training without losing sleep over it.

In the August, the four of us and a handful of other Officers were called to a meeting at a makeshift HQ in the valleys outside Besian. There for the first time in the five months we were there we got to meet Dudayev. Through an interpreter he thanked us for our hard work to date. Then thanked us again for what we were about to do. Once again we let Mick take the orders and pass the Intel down to us.

Our theories were right, Grozny was the target the date of execution was a week away. We each of us had our own role to play. To lead our men into a designated area of the city. Take it and hold it at all costs and kill anything that spoke Russian or looked like it might.

We had no accurate maps of the city because the bombings had changed everything. No ladders or hooks and no reliable Intelligence on the whereabouts of enemy gun positions and strong holds. This mission looked very close to being over and it hadn't begun yet.

After the brief we took the long trip back to our own camp. I called up my Company and Platoon Commanders and gave them the agreed brief. We deliberately kept certain details from them like the dates and target areas, but I was sure they knew anyway.

The night missions would continue as normal so as not to tip the Russian's off to our intentions, if any of the four of us was caught the game would be up. I'd not known torture at this point in my life but I knew from courses in the British Army that talking was a matter of time, no one holds out indefinitely. So the four of us stayed in the camp for the rest of that week putting together the best plan we could in the time we had. In the end it would all boil down to the standard of training we'd given them over the last few months and our own abilities to Ad-Lib under fire.

On the 6th of August an hour before dawn it started. By 0900 we'd put nearly 1600 men on the streets of Grozny. We were like rats, down every ally in every manhole cover, down every cellar and in every attic whether it had a roof or not and not many did.

The Russian's didn't have a clue we were coming, but they knew exactly who was hitting them. They panicked in great numbers, some leaving there posts without a fight in the hope of getting out the city and to the sanctuary of their Artillery Batteries beyond the city limits.

We took fortified positions with relative ease, although not without our own casualties, by the end of that day I'd lost twenty three good men.

We took and held our designated area. The Russian troops that tried to get away were cut down from all angles in the streets without mercy. By the days end there was an estimated 12'000 Russian troops under siege in different areas of the city, hiding in the ruins waiting to be cut down by an enemy they couldn't find to fight.

The Chechens had moved back in. Once things settled we set about storming houses and other buildings, some empty, others housed pockets of Russian troops that had made small strongholds in a vain hope of rescue from a Russian counter attack.

We took them all, anyone left alive was disarmed and given the choice, die in the fight or run back to their lines. Many fearing their own Artillery ran. The unarmed troops were cut down in the streets by other Chechen Units who weren't aware they'd been released, but by then that wasn't my problem.

The Russians took time to counter, we found out later that the reports they were getting from their own were so conflicting they weren't even sure what parts of the city had been taken and what troops they had holding out, the fact was we had it all. After twenty four hours they countered with a massive armoured assault. The T-54's and the slightly later model Battle tanks the T-62's supported by BMP's and BRDM's rolled into the city. It was the perfect mistake. All the Red Armies years of warfare, they seemed to have learned nothing. We ambushed with surgical precision. A hundred million dollar tank is so easily turned into a seventy two ton road block with the help of a £200 RPG. As the troops bailed from their would be metal coffins in threes and fours we picked them off, without guilt or bad conscience.

Over the last five months I'd seen the victims of the Russian war machine and how it killed and maimed indiscriminately. I watched a mother crying over one half of her child as the other half lay ten feet away in the road, after an Artillery strike. I'd seen children crushed in the streets of small towns by the unforgiving tracks of Russian tanks and I'd looked into the eyes of a friends daughter who'd been abducted and gang rapped then left for dead by bored drunk Russian troops.
Now whether they ran fought or rolled up in a ball and cried it didn't matter. It was good killing. This wasn't a small Camp or Depot in the mountains where the "Hearts and Minds" tactics made a difference. This was the capital city, they would do anything to win and we couldn't win unless we were more committed than them. It was shit or bust.

We fought back the first counter attack, it was large but it felt half hearted, they didn't really want it. Their troops were on their way back before they arrived. They were just going through the motions to please the Generals and the Kremlin. The next day the second counter attack had little more than the first. Again they used heavy armour but we'd stalled their offensive by midday. We scattered their beaten and tired troops into the surrounding areas. They returned to scrap metal and a maze of booby traps it would take months to clear. That was Mick's idea. (Clever Bastard).

Within the week we'd fought them to a stand still. They'd been forced to withdraw their troops and armour well back from the city limits for fear of more attacks. Jock had taken his men and hit their logistic lines from their rear. The only Army being re-supplied at this point was ours, with their supplies.

For them to try and retake Grozny from us at this point would take a committed full on assault and would cost them thousands more lives and an untold amount in Military assets.

Over the next two months they half heartedly tried and tried again to break the siege. They bombed us day and night and sent in small fighting patrols that we ambushed and left dead in the street. We were dug in like ticks on a goats arse and regularly took the fight to them in their own compounds. Their troop moral was at an all time low.

After eight weeks a dodgy cease fire started. I say dodgy because we heard about it and read about it, but we were still engaging on a daily basis and it wasn't to share rations. During the equally dodgy peace talks Moscow refused Chechen independence and loosely declared Chechnya a terrorist state. That was our queue to leave. There's a fine line between Freedom Fighter and Terrorist and like it or not that line is defined by "The nearest Superpowers interpretation of your clients politics". There's also the penalty. One gets you a pat on the back, the other revokes your passport and sees to it you never work abroad again.

We made our way back to one of our outpost and after three day met up with Poppy who got us back to Makhachkala. We stayed there for two days and in that time we were treated like heroes. Everyone except the occupying Russian troops knew who we were and what we'd done for their cause. On the second night we caught up with some Georgian contacts we'd made in our time in Chechnya and they got us back into Georgia unhindered.

We stopped in T'bilisi for the night in a great hotel. Warm room, clean sheets and food that wasn't goat for the first time in seven months. It was heaven. Hard to believe our Chechen Brothers in Arms were fighting for their lives only a mountain range away. That night the four us sat down to dinner, drank shit loads of red wine and dug up every humours event of our time in Chechnya. It wasn't a time for war stories. We were caught in the bubble of escapism and happy to stay there. The tears and anger that would inevitably come could wait.

The Chechen war of 1994 to 1996 was classed as one of the bloodiest conflicts since the Second World War. It was a model example of how a highly motivated Guerrilla movement can fuck over a Military Superpower. It also questioned the worth of the Russian conscripted soldier.

The Battles for Grozny saw the death of over 6000 Russian troops and an estimated 100'000

Civilians, mostly ethnic Russians. In total I lost forty-six men in the conflict, Sean lost fifty-four, Jock lost eighty-one and Mick lost thirty-eight, mainly due to lack of communications. But for what? Fuck all, that's what. In 1999 under Vladimir Putin, Russia went back in with twice the fire power and three times the numbers. They are still there today. So is the media black out.

My soul was put on trial during the retake of Grozny. I never even dreamed I'd be a party to some of the events there. I learned in combat that strength of leadership is tested when men under your command start dieing, I learned, that compassion in conflict is a powerful tool. I also learned through test and action that I will do anything to keep me and mine safe and well. No matter who, it cost what.

I've never had a single sleepless night because of the things I did in that time. I've only ever lost sleep over the things I saw.

THE MOST COMMITTED WINS

Running Guns

With Grozny back under Chechen control and the overall pay packet not all that great. Sean and I took the opportunity to earn money another way. Sean was a single man and I was in no hurry to get back to the Dragon Queen. So when offered we took a job for Georgian Intelligence. We met a few of their operatives during the quieter times of the Chechen war. They consisted mainly of Ex KGB but were all Georgian born (bloods thicker than water). For the most part they just observed the conflict, but in an emergency they could supply ammunition and rations that and they would give us the heads up on major Soviet movement.

They'd offered the four of us work in the past but we turned it down on account we were committed to our posts for Chechnya's struggle.

The work they had for us at the time we did accept was deniability based. At that time the Georgian Government was still a puppet of the great Mother Russia but there was dissention in the ranks of Georgia's halls of power and more than one political voice wanted the Iron hand removed from their arse. Basically we did the work their Intelligence community wanted doing for the greater good of Georgia and if we got caught they could deny any part of our actions by simply blaming the Chechens and private Military interference.

Georgia had not long had its independence from Russia, and for as long as they were neighbours and Georgia's NATO and UN memberships were not confirmed, Russia was a constant threat, so any local conflict in surrounding areas stood as a good buffer zone.

Our job was to Run Guns. Guns and ammunition from Georgia into Chechnya and deliver them to the Chechen resistance. A small well trained and well equipped rebel Army living in the mountains, many of the very same troops we'd Commanded not a month earlier.

The work we did is not to be confused with Arms Dealing and Dealers. They're the big guys, the men that have political backing from somewhere round the world. They do the big deals, they source usually using Government backed Intel and purchase using other peoples silent money reserves. All we did was deliver a product safely and on time, that product just happened to be guns and across a hostile boarder.

The manifest's read medical supplies and as long as the border guards and road blockades never checked or questioned that. We'd be fine.

Even though at the time the capital was back under Chechen control the rest of the province was still semi controlled by what seemed to be randomly placed Russian Regiments. The area was split down and each province was under control of local Soviet Commanders the same way they did in Afghanistan. (Look how well that turned out for them).

Every crossroads had a roadblock as did every mountain pass. The Great Caucasus mountain range generally has three routes over the year to get anywhere. A winter route that avoids deep snow. A summer route that avoids deep snow. And a thaw route that avoids thawing deep snow. Each route was covered at some point by Russian guard posts some of which were nothing more than a barrier supported by a simple wooden hut with a stove in it. Some of these occupied by the same guys for up to six months. A real shitty job by any Military's standards.

Bribing guards became the norm, the Russian conscripts were underpaid, undersupplied and their moral was criminally low. They loved sherry, bread and Zippo lighters and if we had any left, hot coffee. Some of the time they just wanted to chat.

The runs could take anything from three days to a week. We used long wheel base landrovers, towing two trailers a piece and we took two to five tons per convoy in any one run. The routes were up to us. We liked it that way. Our cargo's had great value and not just to the Chechen underground. The Georgian Intelligence had one very stricked rule:

"Account For Your Load"

That meant your load could get there or it could come back. We could even destroy the load if the need arose, but don't fuckin lose it. At any cost don't lose the load. In the event of an ambush, blow the fuckin thing up, but don't lose it.

In that neck of the woods it could mean disaster for anyone and everyone. That quantity of untraceable weapons could arm any local separatist group planning a coup and because of the geography of the Caucasus they could pretty much find their way to anywhere. ETA in Spain would snatch them up, they could cross the water to Palestine, get to Germany and into the hands of the RAF or worst of all the cargo could find its way into Northern Ireland and be used to kill one of our own. So no matter what, we accounted for that load every second we had it and having complete autonomy of the routes made the job hell of a lot easier.

We placed charges on the insides of each trailer. Sean and I had the remote detonators for our own loads. Even if we didn't take a third landy we always took a third man, Cartuly. We called him Charlie. He was Georgian Special Forces not Intelligence, we needed him to interpret the local lingo and drive the third landy when we used it. He was a quiet man until he'd had half a bottle of Vodka and we had a thousand uses for him. He was a hard looking bastard too. Thick but short black hair, five o'clock shadow at nine in the morning, six foot four with chizzled Eastern European features and he smiled with a perfect row of white teeth.

I knew he was there to keep eyes on us and the shipments but he never played on it and never questioned our choices or decisions, he just seemed to come along for the ride and despite the small language barrier we read each other well. The three of us were an effective and close team, considering.

On one run Charlie's Landy slid down a mud bank. It was pissing down with rain and getting dark so we chose to pull in for the night and attempt recovery in the morning. The three of us huddled into the front of Sean's landy and shared thick cheese sandwiches and hot soup. It was cold wet and miserable outside and the comfort of our water tight cab was more than welcome. The three of us took it in turns to stay awake. There was not much need for an external guard in the position we were in. We'd corralled the trailers and could see the loads clearly. Then for a little extra advanced warning I set trip flairs round our perimeter. If anyone had come within fifty yards we'd have known about it and if they came up the road we could see them.

As the sun rose on the next day there wasn't a cloud in the sky. Sean woke myself and Charlie and had us both "Stand to". Charlie in an instant was in the back of the landy his arcs covered the load and with the help of a Dragonov sniper rifle he could do it with lethal precision. I slid out the passenger side door and took my position to cover the front of the vehicle. I left the door open so I could keep close verbal comms with the other two. Then Sean started the engine and took out his remote control for the charges strapped to the load. We sat for a second in silence,

"Over there" Sean said and pointed to the road.

About sixty yards away three men stood in the middle of the road in the direction we hoped to take.

"What is it?" Asked Charlie, like a true professional he wouldn't take his eyes off his arcs of fire but was keen to be updated.

"Three targets in the road" I said "How's you?"

"All clear here" He replied.

Sean got out the driver side door and pointed his AK47 at the three men in the road. We didn't have to say anything we all knew our roles. I adopted the patrol position with my rifle having established they weren't Russian Regulars, and knowing I was covered walked towards the three men all the time sighting positions to bury myself in should this encounter go tits up. My heart was racing as I approached. If they were bandits things would very bad very quickly.

Even before I reached the would be target I was smiling. The three men in the road had all served under me during the Chechen War. This didn't mean they wouldn't turn us over for our load but if they did we'd be more likely to live and at least we knew where it would go. They all smiled back which comforted me slowing my heart to more normal pace. We greeted with the traditional kiss on both cheeks and then stood talking in the road for the next ten minutes. As it turned out the load we had was for them and when we hadn't turned up the night before they were sent out to find us.

I walked back with them to Sean and Charlie's position, they were as relieved as I was that the encounter was a friendly one. Its not the fire fight or the detonation of the cargo that bothered us, it wasn't the escape and evasion that would have to follow that. It was the long cold walk back to Georgia that would follow all that lot we dreaded most.

There were twelve of them in total and in true Guerrilla warfare style they seem to come out of nowhere when the signal was given. They all came in handy dragging the bogged in landrover out the mud and back up the slope and onto the road. Once back on the road they clambered on anywhere they could (no point them walking) and took us through a safer although rougher route to our destination. When we got there we stayed the night, it was good to see the hospitality hadn't changed, we drank the local hooch, ate goat, and bragged about how good we were during the war. Mocking the Red War Machine with every word.

Each run had its own story and valuable lessons were learnt on each trip. The hardest Reds to get round were the newer guys. A man who's been freezing in the same spot for a month or two was easily influenced with simple luxuries. However, the man that just arrived the man whose boots still fitted and whose coat didn't have rips and tears in it was all jobs worth. We always kept one of us at the rear with a Dragonov sniper rifle trained on the questioning guard, if at any point we couldn't keep him from inspecting the load the Tail End Charlie's job was to slot him, giving us a valuable head start on whatever action we'd take. Depending on where the compromised road block was we would either detonate the load and run for it or kill everyone at the road block and make for our destination and the sanctuary of the mountains. Fortunately it was never necessary but we had to allow for the contingency.

It was a great job and if it came with R&R I could have made a career out of it. Sean and I loved the work and we worked well together, even when other influences came in we never let them divide us, we worked together as a single Unit that's how we stayed alive.

But all things must come to an end. We'd made a few quid and met and made Bothers in Arms that we'd never forget. But it was very rough living and the job didn't come with holiday pay. To be honest I missed a hot shower a normal bed and meat that wasn't goat and I missed a pint in a pub with friends that spoke the same language. I missed England. I also craved Chinese food, chicken curry and plain chow mein. It was time to go home.

* * *

Things in the UK had changed very little in my time away. People still moaned about the weather the Government still raped the working man and single mums were still on a free ride at the cost of millions a year to the honest working tax payer. British society was losing control of its youth, the bobby on the beat still had no control at all and the treatment of old age pensioners was still a Great British sin. So not a lot of change at all.

In fact the only change for me was, I'd become a father to a bouncing baby boy, I called him Jim after my best friend and one of the finest men I've ever met. I loved that little man from the minute I saw him. I'd been back about a week when my best friend pulled me to one side and advised me to have a paternity test done after hearing about my sons mum and an old acquaintance of mine Tony N getting together in my absence. (I know what your thinking but she's better known for her sanctimonious very loud mouth, not her class) A friend of mine Stu D worked at Cardiff hospital, he helped me to have it done quickly and on the quiet. He had a son Alistair four months older than Jim and it was the perfect excuse to meet up and have the process done privately without interference from her family,

Stu had their lab do all the tests there and then on the Friday and after a good weekend being the proud Dad I returned home with my son Jim. All was well, Jim was mine and his Mother was none the wiser. Id never been so proud and pleased, I was a DAD.

I spoke to JFK about her adultery and asked him what I should do. Killing the boyfriend would be easy. Filling him in easier, kicking her out would present its own problems because of her two kids and I had my eyes firmly on the house the council had given me. So leaving her at that time wasn't really on the cards either.

"How do you feel about it?" JFK said.

"I don't really care mate" I said "But I have to do something don't I?"

"Why?" JFK replied "You don't even like the woman and be honest if little Jimmy hadn't arrived would you be there now? Why get into trouble for someone so insignificant? Just treat the place like a hotel, as long as the boys OK what does it matter?"

He was right as usual. I wasn't going to get my arse out about it and end up doing time. From then on I used any excuse to not be around her. Judo, work, out with friends, anything I could think of. I took Jim everywhere I could. I loved his company and being with him made it easier to cope with the events that took place in Eastern Europe.

So life went on, I was getting my washing done I was getting fed life was easy, life was convenient and it gave me the time I needed to put my life together the way I wanted it. I wanted rid of her for starters, she was pure poison and I wanted to be left alone with my son and a house to call my own, she had used me to get what she wanted but it wasn't gonna be free. It would take a lot of patients on my part and a lot of tolerance, but I knew eventually I'd get my wish. All I had to do was put up with the venom of the York family and give Jims mum enough rope to fuck things up for herself.

* * *

I was sat in my garden one day watching my boy play, when Sue the younger but larger one of Jim's aunties came round with her new boyfriend, Mark Fleet. Instantly we didn't like each other. He was the confident cocky one and I was the other confident cocky one. We were too much alike to see eye to eye. That afternoon came and went and I hoped not to see him again. Sue went through boyfriends like a pig through truffles so I wasn't likely to anyway.

However I did end up meeting Mark a couple of times after that and the tension eased a little between us each time (Beer's good for that). Then one day he said he'd like to try Judo. I was training most evenings myself at the time and I was sure he was sent by Sue and my Ex to see if I was having an affair. It didn't bother me though, that wasn't my game it was her's, and she was just judging me by her low standards.

Mark came down to Fimley to train with me at Ritchie Doves place. He had no coordination no fitness level at all and zero finesse, but he could fight. He was breathing so hard after the first fight I thought his arse cheeks would turn into lungs, after the second fight he had to go out the fire door to throw up. He was bright red and looked like he'd faint at any minute but he never stopped fighting. I didn't fight Mark that night. I just coached him.

Mark and I were spending more and more time together, he trained with me three or four times a week and his Judo came on fast, more down to his own determination than my coaching. Over the following two years he went on to take two gold medals and a bronze at the National Events such as the Kent Open. What he lacked in technique he made up for in spirit. He fights like a bull, relentless and unforgiving.

At weekends we'd go out for a few pints and put the world to rights and every chance we got we trained. Over the next year I could have counted the days on one hand that I hadn't seen Mark. We'd become good friends. He had a daughter, Megan from an earlier relationship with a wonderful woman, Claire. She really is one of life's Saints. Megan's a year older than my Jim and we'd take the kids out at weekends, we even used them as an excuse to see the new Star Wars movies. It's been a pleasure to watch them grow up together.

When Mark married Sue, I was honoured to be his best man. His family and Sue's family the York's let them both down. When after a years notice they didn't show up at the Wedding. Even though it was in the Caribbean, it worked out with the year's notice they'd given they only needed to save twenty pounds a week. I wouldn't have missed it for the world. When no one else bothered to show I rang JFK. Three days later he was there in the Dominican Republic and Mark had the two witnesses he needed.

Over the last twelve years Mark Fleet has supported me through a messy divorce and a successful custody battle and is God Father to my girls. He flew 9500 miles stopping at three unstable African nations to be the Best Man at my wedding to Angela. He's escorted my son through third world countries just so I could see him. We've worked together, fought in bars together and supported each other through life's harder times. He has three girls and a son, and is the finest Father I've ever known and these just the things I can write about.

In spite of BJ he is the closest thing I have to a younger brother. He's not only the greatest guy I know, but the best friend I know of and I'm lucky and honoured to say:

HE IS MY FRIEND

Rules Of Engagement

It didn't take long for the Private Military world to get its hands on the former Yugoslavia. Between the UN and NATO the amount of resources being pulled together and used was phenomenal. camps quickly became Garrisons and small temporary towns were being built to accommodate other non military services. At first our military and security expertise was not welcome by the politicians of Europe or the UN bureaucrats, but as the use of civilian logistics became the norm and the Ground Commanders became more and more challenged with the security of their own men and equipment the need for private assistance grew.

* * *

The men in the blue helmets became all but useless as the balls of the Serbian warlords grew. The Rules of Engagement for UN Troops seemed almost undetermined even after the establishment of the continuing war crimes. No one I ever spoke to understood the policy in place, it was yet another conflict that challenged the very need and validity of a United Nations Armed Forces and this gave the warlords the licence they needed. They ran a mock on the Bosnian landscape killing raping and maiming at will like some ancient Viking Army. The Bosnian crisis was a great embarrassment to white Europe. The atrocities that went on there were supposed to have ended with the last Great War, World War Two.

In the fifty years since then the word Genocide had become largely synonymous with black and Oriental cultures courtesy of Dictators such as Pol Pot and Ide Amine to name the more popular. It was absolute power that corrupted Pol Pot and the same could be said of Amine, but since the dawn of time blacks African tribes have always off'd each other in record numbers this made easier by the western world's constant supply of arms and expertise, so its more likely that it was opportunity in his case.

The truth is the western world has so much to gain out of warring black nations and instability in Africa that when they massacre each other to within an inch of tribal extinction, all Europe and America will do is talk loud and impose bullshit sanctions with more holes in than an ambushed soft top Landrover.

It is a fact pointed out by the Canadian Commanding Officer of the UN during the Hutu

Genocide of the Tutsi in Rwanda in 1994, that no Government in the western civilised world gives a shit about black or white Africans.

The events of the Bosnian conflict escalated so fast the rest of the world failed to see it coming, by the time they did the atrocities were in full swing. Heavily rumoured in Sarajevo and Zagreb all fears were confirmed with the discovery of the shallow mass graves just outside the small town of Srebrenica on the Bosnian Serbian boarder.

One of the graves measured nearly a hundred metres long and six feet deep packed to the point of over spilling with bodies. Not a single man of fighting age among them, just half naked raped and beaten women and children frozen solid in that mountain grave. Horror like this had not been seen since the concentration camps of WW2. The last time white set out to genocide white was at the hands of Adolf Hitler.

VE Day, VJ Day, the efforts made by the armies and Governments of the world to remember the wars and their dead on November 11th each year. The money and time spent by the UN and Jewish community to track down and bring to justice war criminals from all conflicts. The worlds medias constant attempts to keep the horrors from fading. All this in hope the world wouldn't forget or repeat the crimes against our fellow man. Yet we did. At that time

I felt man had wasted his time and efforts. As a race we'd learned nothing.

Where man is given Power, Weapons and Free Reign,
Atrocity will follow!
WHY?
Because it does!

* * *

Amtrans Co was a large trucking company that won a contract with Brussels to run supplies from Hamburg and Hanover in Germany to Sarajevo Pristina and Nis in the former Yugoslavia. They carried anything from tractor parts to building supplies but as far as we knew never ammunition or weapons. Their Logistical route was straight forward. Down through Germany and Austria though Slovenia and Croatia to Split on the coast of the Adriatic Sea. From there our teams would take control of the security of the loads to their destinations.

A problem area and popular ambush site was one of the routes on the eastern flank of Sarajevo passed the small town of Gorazde. Our early recognisance of that area proved well founded when on the third day of our recon a small convoy of UN trucks was ambushed. Unable at that time to engage we called upon the relevant support for the under equipped UN troops.

From day one this hot spot was going to be a problem.

Our weapons and ammunition was supplied by another UN tender winning German company accommodated on the same secure sight as us. Their armoury was a stone throw from our sleeping accommodation and so under our watch when we were in camp.

The arguments and lack of mission appreciation started the second we drew our ammunition. The fat German civilian sausage eating fuckwit they had in place of a Quarter Master with a military background refused to give us anymore than twenty rounds per man. I pointed out to him that Twenty rounds wasn't enough to fire fight our way out of a school playground, then explained to him our job was to secure and protect cargo through some of the more hostile areas of the conflict, after which I insisted on at least two hundred rounds per man with smoke grenades flairs and side arms, but with arrogance typical of Germans, he fucked me off with some homemade bullshit excuse about as real as his twenty nine inch waist line.

At that time I was working with a small very well trained and experienced team of eight, when we got back to our billet every one of them voiced their concerns in the usual manner fitting a fighting man dealing with ineptitude. After letting them rant for a few minutes, Danny and I calmed the others down. The guys were right and none of us was going out with only twenty rounds. It was enough ammunition to make any aggressor think but it wasn't enough to keep the load or us and the drivers alive. Any hope we have of getting the Boxheads decision reversed was dashed at that point too because it was Friday, and that far back from the fighting the bulk of the camp was free to take the weekend off leaving the camp under a skeleton guard.

Danny took me off to one side and between us we came up with an option that sat right on that very thin line that divides madness and genius and our obstacle became our answer.

As the new arrivals we were obliged to be volunteered for the first available weekend duty, that just so happened to be this weekend. As Guard Commander I would have access to the whole camp and both of its armouries.

After a full brief I took over control of camp security from our French counterparts at 1800 hours. I took Johnny G with me on the 2100 hours inspections of the armouries after a visit to the Mess hall. By 2145 hours the empty Burgan's taken in by Johnny G and myself weighed almost as much as I did.

NATO ammo box's are sealed with a steel wire that feeds though a lead button then its twisted at the end, its done to exploit any tampering. But if you're gentle and careful enough the wire twists back nice and the button slides right off and replacing it is just as easy with that touch of tender loving care. We walked out of there with four hundred rounds per man Smoke Grenades Flash bangs and Parachute flares, I decided to compromise on the side arms.

I knew the German store man would have a perpetual inventory to do each day, but I knew from his fat arsed lazy way he was a receipt counter, he'd never physically check a box let alone pick one up from the back to check its contents.

For the next two month all was quiet. We ran our loads from Split to Pristina Sarajevo and Nis without hindrance. I shared a cab a few times with a middle age Scottish driver called Sam but we all called him Jock.

"Fuckin Squaddies" He'd say in a thick Scottish accent, "My fuckin Mother gives me a perfectly good fuckin name and you fuckers change it first fuckin chance you get"

Despite his light hearted protest we all still called him Jock, he was a nice guy and a refreshing break from the long silent rides with French or German drivers, he was a true Scottish patriot passionately hating all Englishmen, he wouldn't even speak to me properly until I let it slip my mother was from Glasgow. He smoked fifty fags a day drank a bottle of whisky a night and swore more than any man I've ever met.

I was pleasantly surprised at how well the convoys were supported. One freezing cold morning one of the trucks had a tyre go. The bang was enough to bring all of our team to arms. The convoy stopped and we all took our well practiced tactical positions and waited. The driver of the vehicle knew exactly what it was, established the fact and put our wits at rest in no time. Another good thing about the civilian drivers chosen for the job was their experience, they each had thousands of miles and driving hours under their belts and most of them had worked all round the world. Within an hour a UN recovery truck turned up with an armed escort and did the necessary to put the lame thirty eight ton truck back in the game.

Half way through our four month tour things took a very dramatic turn for the worst. A mile away from the hot spot we'd recce'd two months earlier and passed though at least a dozen times since, our convoy of three articulated wagons carrying long steel piping, medical supplies and rations, came under very effective enemy fire from our left flank. Everything got very loud and aggressive very quickly.

In the opening seconds of the ambush the driver in the front wagon was shot dead. The truck veered off to the right and came to a halt but managed to stay on the road. Johnny G was his immediate escort, he took a bit of shrapnel in the cheek but other than that was unharmed. He pulled the dead driver down across the seats and exited via the passenger side door and took position in front of the wagon and started giving covering fire.

The rest of the convoy stopped dead and every man jack got out took cover and returned fire. Within seconds I was calling the first fire control orders. I didn't have to worry about the other two drivers their escorts had them sorted.

The incoming fire was coming from a small cottage on the side of the hill about two hundred metres away. Not a great place to initiate an ambush from as they were about to find out. The intensity of the incoming rounds was so great it cut through the straps of the rear wagon carrying the steel piping sending it rolling off the back. Kippy and Dinger moved like startled cats to get out the way but Kippy caught one of the pipes in the hip sending him crashing into the ground. With the front covered by me and Phil C, Johnny was able to get to Kippy and administer the first aid and morphine he needed. We later found out the pipe had crushed his pelvis the extent off his injuries was severe.

I gave the order to release all the smoke we had to our front, there was no wind so it would give good cover from calculated fire. As soon as the white fog was at it thickest what was left of the section gave covering fire with remarkable accuracy given the fog and Phil C and I went left flanking.

There was a pine forest to our left, we took a route just inside the tree line until we came parallel to the cottage. It was at that point the two of us went in hard and fast. I didn't give a shit about the load I don't believe any of us did, but we had a man down and one injured giving first aid my only thought was to get my guys and the drivers out in as few pieces as possible.

Phil C and I had worked together for years and read each other well. I couldn't say for sure how many were dead before we entered the cottage but our efforts to take control of the fight in the early stages hadn't been wasted.

We took the two room cottage with relative ease. I entered through a window in the side, Phil C a half second behind me. The air in the room was thick with dust and the stale smell a cigarette smoke, they'd been held up in this house a while. The furniture in the room must have been antique and fast became worthless. We were so close to the enemy in that room our rounds went through the bodies of the men standing and ripped the furniture apart. Without losing momentum we hit the second room, most of the men alive were wounded but still armed. In my time in that place I'd seen and smelt horrors only fiction and history should know, I'd seen the aftermath of people who'd been burned alive and seen women commit suicide after being mercilessly raped and beaten by Serb militia. I had no problem killing these people, they were armed that was enough.

After an hour of mayhem the ambush was completely squashed, the support we'd called for in the initial contact report still hadn't arrived. Phil C and I confirmed and searched the dead, I was uneasy about having such a small section so far apart so we booby trapped the cottage and returned to the others using our approach route.

When we returned to the convoy Kippy was stable but in a bad way. The shock was leaving Johnny now and the pain from his facial injury was setting in. We all reloaded and secured the drivers. After securing our location and the dead driver as best we could Phil C put a brew on, ten minutes later to the amazement of the drivers we were sat drinking tea.

It took another hour for support to arrive. If it had been a flat tyre or engine trouble they'd have been there in half an hour but because we'd made a contact report they had to wait for a military team to respond first, they responded in the true United Nations style;

LATE AND AFTER THE FACT

When we got back to camp there were obvious questions the local ground Commander wanted answering, the big one being:

"How did you sustain a fire fight for that long with only twenty rounds per man?"

I didn't even try and bullshit him. He wasn't happy with my answer but as a military veteran he appreciated it. My team was allowed to finish our tour but the fat German was out of a job by the end of that day and the company he worked for came under scrutiny. The contract for our Company wasn't renewed at the end of its term. My actions seemed to set the standard and other teams wouldn't go out as lightly armed as the UN would have them. I got called in over it, but I told them I didn't give a shit if the Company lost the contract or not. I may have been wrong, there are things I should have done in the time between taking the extra ammunition and having to use it, but the way I saw it was, my actions kept my guys alive. Thirteen men died that day, one driver and twelve men that would have killed me and mine in a heart beat.

Johkar Dudayev Chechen Leader

Out with my boy

Blessed with true friends, Jed, Mike, Me, The Prince and Mark Fleet

Hunting with Giants

LPBG 1992

On patrol in Belfast, Bobby Sand Memorial in the background

Me no1 in the door on the LLPT

Out enjoying the three teeth

Team line up for the South England teams event

Alternative Agendas

The events that happened in Central America, like epic events in anyone's life should have their own book. But like Chechnya I've glanced over it because it changed me in so many ways and extended my list of personal and business contacts no end.

* * *

I met Simon in Venezuela. The company had taken a job that involved burning opium crops in an area south east of Capibara and North of the Sierra de Curupira, right on the disputed border with Brazil. Simon was working for the SIS (MI6) at the time and had been in Central America for a few years.

Our base of operations was somewhere in the South Sierra Parima region. It was a small Garrison in the middle of the jungle surrounded on two sides by a wonderful postcard mountain range. Green at the base and white with snow and glaciers at the apex.

The bulk of the Garrison was tentage surrounded by sandbags, not there so much to protect from incoming fire, more to stop them blowing away when the choppers came in and that was hourly. There were eight landing pads constantly on the go. The fuel came in by day on trucks. But only after midday as the road was closed in the morning to land light aircraft which brought people and supplies. There was an estate of tented accommodation and it had three large mess tents. One for the Venezuelan dressed Yanks. One for us the working end of this operation and one for the administration. Officers and Agency representatives.

They called it Camp San Fernando after the only place they were allowed to go on R&R when on tour here, but we called it El Dorado.

* * *

Our objective was to insert by helicopter, tab through the trees usually no more than two miles to the co-ordinates given to us a few hours earlier. lay charges and get out quick, then after a half mile or so lay snap ambushes to make sure we wern't being followed. That was also the time to reload and deal with any minor snags. Then we'd move out to an RV, again given to us hours before to be extracted.

The only resistance we ever encountered was a few passionate, poorly paid, lightly armed soldiers, which we were more than equipped to handle. For all intensive purposes we were a fighting patrol and that being the case each of us carried enough arm's, ammunition, APM's and other killing and maiming equipment to start a small uprising.

I must admit it did surprise me that the crops weren't a lot better protected, but after asking around it was pointed out to me that it was the labs that were heavily guarded not the crops.

After each operation we were extracted back to El Dorado either to wait for the next objective or stand down for a few days until a new mission window opened.

* * *

El Dorado. We gave it that nick name not because it was a city of gold but because it was unbelievable South American bullshit. It was built and run by various United States Agencies and Regiments all dressed as Venezuela regular forces, but all using US military equipment. Even a civilian with no training could work out who they were but the Yanks seemed happy with their ineffective rouse.

The US troops were there solely to run El Dorado. They had control of all communications both incoming and outgoing. Control of all logistical movement on and off the complex, be it by air or land. The Mess was run by them, camp security and the medical centre, even camp maintenance was done by them (which was good). I don't mind mucking in but if there's someone else to clean out the shit house that's great, especially in the heat of the jungle when you can't stand the smell of your own shit, let alone the crap of three hundred other men.

Apart from two interpreters and a Government liaison officer there were no Venezuelans allowed on the complex.

After ten minutes in the Mess it wasn't hard to see who the working end of this operation was. The teams doing the work were a mixture of British, French, Israeli, Pilipino and Malaysian private troops. Not a Yank anywhere on the mission side of things. Obviously to give some kind of loose but plausible deniability should things go wrong. (Plausible Deniability, would I ever get out of this Grey area?) America is like a small child in that respect, alone in a room with you and a piece of chocolate that goes missing when you turn your back. You know it was them, everyone knows it was them, but because you didn't see it happen, it wasn't them. It's typical American logic.

The Mess hall at night became a bar. Yanks are good like that too. Their not well known for their tolerance of discomfort or their jungle tactics come to think of it and that's where I met Simon. Pissed as a Vicar. He came over and introduced himself and to no real surprise he knew all our names before we said them. Nevertheless, he was the voice of doom.

"Your extractions will get later and later" He said "Don't trust them" He said "I can get you out in the morning"

He was hammered and not very confidence inspiring. We sat him down and asked him to explain. In his drunken state he babbled on about how teams had been left in the jungle and how they'd never been seen again. This sort of thing was always a minor risk with this kind of work but Simon made it out to be a regular thing. We all had a good drink that night with nothing to do the next day. But it wasn't a very relaxed night with the MI6 doom monger refusing to Fuck off.

The next day I made a point of bumping into Simon with Sean another member of our team, hoping to get Simon to elaborate on his previous nights ranting's. He pulled the two of us to one side.

"Don't stay too long guys" He said "Do a few drops if you must then go home"

"Is it that bad?" Said Sean

"Not all the time" Simon went on, "But the new pilots spook easily and their navigation over the jungle is shite to say the least"

"What do you mean new pilots?" I said. "This is supposed to be a well established operation"

Simon explained, "The pilots rotate every six to eight weeks, when they first arrive their young and fresh out of flight school their soul priority is the chopper and not so much the pick up"

"How's that fuckin work" I said

"Here they can get experience in Special Forces Operations and never lose a man, not one of theirs anyway." Simon Said

The penny dropped. The Yanks used this anti drug campaign as the perfect training ground for its own troops. We were nothing short of cannon fodder. No matter how many men they left lost or killed it wasn't on their body count. We didn't matter, we were just guns for hire.

"So what's your role in all this?" I said to Simon

"I can't really go into that" He replied "But I spend a lot of time trying to get you lads to go home and not enough time trying to find you."

Sean and I looked at Simon in total amazement, how could the company not know this and still send us in, more importantly what next?

"I can tell you this with certainty" Simon went on, "You're on your own out here. This is an expensive clandestine war between North and Central America. Britain has no part in it and will support no Briton taking part in it. Is that clear gentlemen?"

We both nodded.

* * *

Sean and I took our news back to the other guys. We all sat down and worked the "Pros and Cons". The job paid well but did it cover the risk? That said did any job we'd done over the last five years? What were the odds of being left behind? How reliable was the spook. A hundred questions came up.

Then Dinger came up with a very valid point. Why were we listening to the ramblings of a pissed up SIS operative? If he was who he said he was that made him a "Spy". The very nature of his job was to lie and cheat to achieve his own objectives. None of the British Intelligence services was any less scheming and underhanded than that of the CIA, MOSSAD, GEO or any other Intelligence Service on the planet. That's their job and they do it well. So was there any need for us to give Simons doom and gloom side of life any attention at all?

Dinger sold the point well and we all agreed to give Simon a wide birth and do what we'd come to do. We were due to drop in the next day at dawn and spent the remainder of the day prepping kit, cleaning and testing weapons and getting briefed on our new comms and ordinance. Then we hit our pits early.

The next morning we were up dressed and ready and loaded onto the choppers before sunrise. Our maps only covered a five mile area around the target. Everything had to be remembered, nothing written down. Eight of us in the bird, the noise, the downdraft, the cam cream the weapons, the excitement of fighting as part of a team. It was hard on material.

The flight lasted a good hour and a half. The sun was on the rise but it wasn't quite daylight. It was cold but the adrenaline stopped the chill getting through. We made nervous humour and went over a few "Actions On". Then the pilot called "Action Stations", a very familiar term to a British Paratrooper, with that order we prepared to De Bus.

The chopper hovered about two feet off the ground, the co-pilot gave the order to move and in the order we'd practiced a hundred times, we dispatched ourselves. Within seconds the chopper was gone. I hoped he was going the right way because I took our initial baring off his flight path, just like we use to do in the LPBG.

The extraction point was in another clearing four hundred meters to our left flank but the target was a good two miles north. The patrol to get there was meticulous and professionally done. We knew jungle well and worked it to our advantage in every step.

I'd never seen an opium crop before that first mission, I don't think any of us had. It was fuckin huge, the Yanks could have hit it with a B52 from thirty thousand feet. Probably would have cost less too.

The security was light no more than ten men in our target area, lightly armed and not very vigilant. There was no need to engage them taking their lives would achieve nothing. We lay the charges unchallenged and with silent ease. Then pulled back to a safe OP chosen by us on the way in, then we sat back and watched the fireworks. I was impressed.

The charges we were given looked like black bricks with a covered switch that simply went from "Safe" to "Armed". The cover was secured by a tight metal slide, I could just about remove it with both thumbs. Then it was a simple case of lift the cover and flick the switch. The brief we'd had on the devices had informed us that the switch was one way and once armed it couldn't be put back to safe. Each man carried one of the devices and the ordinance was to be laid fifty meters apart and we had to be at least three hundred meters away when they went off. We never worked it like that though. We had four guys laying and two guys watching in support. The comm's kit given to us was state of the art, we could talk to each other even without line of sight for anything up to half a mile and we used this to work things our way.

We'd had no live demonstration of the ordinance we carried and now I could see why. To do so would only show half the continent where El Dorado was. It levelled everything.

It truly was a firework display the Chinese Ancestry would have been proud of and we were all a bit happier that the metal slide was such hard work to get out. When the dust settled, anything not on fire was either still flying through the air or landing miles away.

It was impressive.

The first extraction was uneventful and went like clock work. We got on the chopper at the appointed time having made sure we weren't followed. Excited as we were we said little on the flight back. We didn't want the Yanks to think we were too impressed with their gadgets. For the next three weeks that's how it was. We dropped in every two or three days, a different location for each mission and Simon played the "Lord of Doom" in between time.

* * *

Then one morning we got up as usual, we got ready and briefed as usual. Then as we'd done a dozen times before, we inserted into our target location, fired the ground completing our mission and hot footed it to the RV. Then we got to the appointed RV and waited for the extraction, and nothing.

The choppers had been spot on time for every mission so far now they were an hour late. Optimistically Sean said: "The spook said they'd get later"
That eased the tension for a while, they hadn't not come they were just late.
Then they were four hours late. The daylight was slowly being replaced by the jet black jungle night. We needed to make decisions. I called the guys in.
"Lads its obvious their not coming today" I said "There's an ERV four miles from here" I pointed to an area right on the edge of the map. "But the pick up's not till 1700 tomorrow"
"We can lay up here tonight" Said Pete "Its safe enough, and make our way there at daybreak"
Everyone agreed, we had rations and kit for a tactical night out. That aside it was the only immediate option. We couldn't even be 100% sure we were in Venezuela. An hour and a half flight could be

a week's walk in the jungle, but in which direction? And asking for local help this close to the target would be suicidal. We spent the night in silence. Taking the watch in turns. No lights and no food, just water. The smell of our rations would carry for miles and could bring no end of shit our way. We stayed aware, we stayed alive.

At first light we moved and by 0900 we were in sight of the ERV. We chose to lie up and observe the new extraction point and move closer nearer to the extraction time. The day went passed surprisingly fast. I slept for most of it. Spirits were still high. This was only a delay after all. That's what the ERV was for, events such as this. There could be any number of reasons why they never came. Technical failure, poor navigation, mix up in orders the list could go on.

But at 1705 that day the list stopped, still they never came, every second after the ERV extraction time was like another hour. Phil and I made our way up to a vantage point that gave us a good 360 degree view. If there was a chopper within ten miles we'd have seen it. We gave it an hour then rejoined the team. It was getting dark again. We had to create options and make big decisions but more importantly right now we had to eat. We made the decision to go firm that night and eat cold rations and use the time to plan our next move. It was a long night, the sound of our thoughts was almost defining.

We had no clue of our exact position or the way back to El Dorado. We had twenty-four hours rations per man, emergency first aid kits and enough firepower to fight the continent. Our new mandate was to get out the area undetected, find civilisation and somehow get back to the UK.

First thing first we had to leave the area. With no great desire to scale the Andes or get lost in the Amazon we chose to go north and hopefully back into Venezuela. Whatever happened if we went north far enough we'd hit the coast and civilization.

We patrolled in silence, moving by day and resting by night. The jungle was thick and unforgiving. The ground loose underfoot making the scaling of ridges very dangerous. Dinger estimated we were covering eight maybe ten miles a day. It was slow going but we had adopted a fully tactical approach to getting out the area. Moral was still surprisingly high. At night we'd take it in turns to bitch but it always turned into a joke. We all had the same concerns and we all took them seriously but it was easier to take the piss out of them than break down with worry. After four days and nights we held parliament and addressed the more immediate issues.

All of us were carrying far too much to go on as we were. Now we'd put distance between us and our target area we needed to start doing some serious mileage and find a road or large river. It was still too early to use local help. We weren't far enough away from the target area for that. We reckoned at least two hundred miles before we contacted any locals for aid.

The bush telegraph is fast and we didn't want to bump into the Amigo whose crops we'd been flattening. We'd also drawn out the rations we had just about as far as they'd go. Water was everywhere but we had to find food and soon.

We dug a large hole and set about lightening our Burgan's I took out everything I didn't need. All the excess ammo the claymores and the spare parts and ancillaries for the comms kit we had, straight away I was twenty pounds lighter. Then I stripped my webbing down to essentials only. Ammo pouch's and water bottle pouch's. I was still carrying a good fifty pound but as we got further away I could dump more.

Food, everyone was hungry, Johnny was a jungle wizard, he would forage and find bugs and grubs the size of his thumb. Occasionally he'd find a root or pod we could eat but if he wasn't a 100% sure he left it well alone. The last thing we needed was any of us with gut rot.

We divided the day into two parts. In the morning we'd get up get our shit together and put down as much mileage as possible. We took it in turns to go point man, but everyone kept track of the bearing. The jungle was still thick but we estimated we were doing a good ten twelve miles between first light and two in the afternoon. Still slow but we were still being careful. We weren't quite Non Tac just yet.

In the afternoons we'd lay up. Johnny would take off and do his bit taking a different one of us each time to help. The rest of us would set up camp. Gather water and prep for the next day. This was the routine for the next nine days. We knew we'd been travelling in a straight line but we'd hoped to have seen some signs of life by now, but no, nothing, just dense jungle, mile after mile of thick green vegetation and the very occasional clearing.

Johnny was doing a sterling job as hunter gatherer, the life forms he found for us to eat were a great source of protein and always the topic of conversation at food time, but we needed carbs, we were burning a lot of energy on our marches that had become less and less tactical as the days went on and as we tired we covered less ground.

We'd been out now sixteen days when we came across a river running east to west. Not very deep, two foot maybe. That night I suggested we stay put for a few days. Get good rest and patch ourselves up before carrying on north. The idea got the vote and we stayed put on the river bank for the next three days. It was a good time to wash clothes and do all my other personal admin. We kept spirits high and boredom at bay with good conversation and betting on competition. We competed at everything from who could piss the furthest to racing bugs up trees and betting thousands of pounds we didn't have. Moral at this point was still very high our attitude was:

We weren't lost, we were looking for a new way home.

With us all well rested and put back together as best we could we started north again leaving the small river behind us. Straight from the off we resumed our march and rest routine.
Even though we had a few static days my feet were still in bits, my foot powder had run out a week earlier and I was losing weight at an astonishing rate, but the good news was the hunger pains wore off a couple of days earlier as did the heartburn, but I still ate everything that came my way. We all did. At this point we estimated our travel rate as less than eight miles a day. Our marches got shorter

and the rest periods got longer. At any other time this terrain and distance would have been a piece of piss, but with no food it was a challenge (I'd never use the word struggle).

Each night we'd sit down and try to create new options, but until we found some kind of civilization there wasn't much else we could do but try and find it. One night for no apparent reason the group moral seemed to take a slump and tempers seemed short, no one spoke for a good hour, I could feel the tension in the air, but before anyone could feed off it Johnny piped up and said:

"Gentlemen we are no longer looking for a new way home, our mission has change. Civilisation is lost gentlemen and we have to find and rescue her"

We all laughed, the breaking of the atmosphere in the camp made it funnier than it really was but no one cared, his few humorous words put a whole new spin on things. The jungle's a very dangerous place to lose your self control as apprehensive and worried as I was I had to hold it together. I knew the others felt the same and we all knew if one guy went down he'd be a massive burden on the others. Not just physically but more importantly to moral. After that moment we fed off each others high times and dug deep to keep our hard moments in check.

Eleven days from the river we hit a road running north east to south west. Twenty nine days into our ordeal and we find our first proof man had been here before.

To use the word "Road" is probably a bit ambitious. It was more of a dirt track that you could get a car down if you were man enough to try. Although on closer inspection of the road it was used more for carts pulled by cattle and mules.

Even though at that time I thought moral was high the road gave everyone a new lease of life. We all perked up a bit and we made two new choices that day. It was refreshing just to have that option. First we'd watch the road for a day or so to see what kind of traffic it got and how often and secondly, we'd follow the road but travel by night.

We pulled back off the road to an OP site found by Phil and Carl on a short recce. Johnny went off on his daily mission taking me with him and the others found water and set up the OP.
Although malnourished, weak and exhausted. We had no trouble slipping back into a fully tactical mode. We all off loaded more and more non essential kit to lighten our loads but Phil quite rightly insisted we maintained a fighting capacity. We cleaned our weapons everyday and kept them loaded and made ready at all times. I was carrying about four hundred rounds and one claymore as was the rest. Not really enough to engage a fighting force but more than enough to get out of shit quick. We sat in the OP for two days and saw fuck all.

At the end of the second day we decided to move. That night with Johnny on point we hit the dirt track in staggered formation and tabbed our arses off. The two days in the OP gave all our feet time to dry out and Johnny had found an abundance of fungus we could eat and carry with us as we moved. The road was a blessing underfoot at long last something firm to Tab on. Even resting every hour we estimated moving over ten miles that first night. Still slow but better. We had surpassed our two hundred mile get away zone. Now we could debate how we'd approach the locals when we encountered them. Some suggested the "Hearts and Minds" approach, others said stay away. We chose in the end to play it by ear.

Three more days of nocturnal movement saw us at a fork in the road. We stuck to our guns and took the north route. With our new route came the aroma of food cooking and by the morning we stood on a hill overlooking a small village. Out of instinct we all went to ground. We formed up off the road and quickly reached the decision to observe our new found fortune before we attempted any approach.
I thought I'd be happy to see civilization again but I wasn't I was worried. These people might work for the Cartels or have sym-

pathisers amongst them. If that was the case we could end up being tortured and killed. Or they might feed us and help us out. The concern in everyone's mind at this time was; did we have the energy and stamina to evade a hunter force if things went bad? In full heath I would put money on us any day of the week but in our present condition I just didn't know.

We divided into two teams and watched the village for the next two days. Not much went on. No vehicles came or went. Kids played on the one street it had. Women gossiped and the men didn't do much more. The village didn't have any phone lines or electricity but it had an abundance of goats and chickens and as soon as it got dark the village slept.

We came together at an agreed RV away from the village. None of us wanted contact with the villagers, we all thought we were still too close to our original target area even though we'd moved constantly for the last month, so we went round and joined the dirt track a few miles north again and resumed moving by night only.

Seeing the village hit moral hard. For the first time since we were deserted by the Americans all heads looked only at the floor. We had found the maiden called civilisation and rather than rescue her we left her alone. We all feared the dragon. It was a quiet and miserable night each man punished himself in his own way.

That night we covered good ground and the following morning could see another village in the distance. Too far to get to that night without moving during the day, but close enough to get to the following night.

The next night everyone had a new approach, we'd all regretted not asking the other villagers for help, yet we stayed away for good reason. I was concerned that it was our physical condition that would force our hand in this next village.

As much as I didn't want to be captured we needed help. Johnny's foot had gone a bit mankie, he was braving it out but for how much longer was anybody's guess. Phil had had the shits for the last three days and Carl had a very angry looking rash on his neck. He said it did hurt but I wouldn't want it.

The next night around midnight we reached the village that turned out to be a small town and once again unanimously agreed to observe before acting. The town was too big to watch from all sides as we had done with the village. So we picked one good OP and all laid up there.

As the sun came up the town came to life. It had electricity a small market place, proper shops and a host of things third world towns have, but more importantly it had phone lines.

We sat down to discuss our next move. Not all were in favour of going into the town. I however insisted two of us go in. The town wasn't big enough for us to blend in but it was big enough to lose yourself in.

I had a pair of shorts and a black t-shirt. I cleaned myself up, rolled my Jungle boots down and "presto" a backpacker not a soldier. I took Johnny who dressed pretty much the same only his T-shirt had "Fuck em all" written across the front and a big flying cock on the back. One could only hope no-one took offence.

One of our objectives was to find a medical facility. The help Johnny needed with his foot was becoming more urgent. He also spoke a little Spanish, a lot more than he let on.

We left it till the afternoon to go in. The sun on its way down and the midday heat subsiding the town got busier. The town folk were a toothless friendly bunch. We were greeted with smiles and nods and curious points as oppose to suspicion. Johnny's T-shirt made a couple of old girls blush, then they held their hands out as if to compare the phallic symbol to what they were use to. Then it was our turn to blush.

If anyone asked we told them we were backpackers and that seemed to satisfy them. Between us we had a few thousand Bolivar so money wasn't a problem. Things looked positive for the first time in a while.

For security the others had moved to a new OP that Johnny and I didn't know and we agreed to meet them at seven that evening at a location on the road we came in on. If anything went wrong and we didn't turn up the others were to bug out and put as much distance between them and the town as possible, preferably not in a northern direction. Johnny and I if caught would bluff the lost tourist thing for as long as we could and wing it from there.

The town had no set medical centre as such but it did have a chemist. I picked up some stuff for Phil's shits but they didn't really have anything for Johnny's foot that we didn't already have. For now he would have to griz it out. From there we moved on to find food. In no time at all the dry bag I'd brought with us was full of bread and apples. The bread wasn't much as bread goes but hey, it was bread. I'd have eaten hard shit at that point if it had enough nuts in it.

We took a different way back to the RV and on our route bumped into a potential life line. A bus stop. Johnny and I spotted it together. Johnny grabbed the first passer by and asked about the buses and the route. After a broken English Spanish "bit o this bit o that" conversation. Johnny turned to me.

"What did he say" I said to Johnny I was so excited I couldn't stand still.

"I don't fuckin believe it" Johnny said "The bus gets here and leaves again day after tomorrow"

"Where's it going?" I said, desperate for some kind of direction.

Johnny turned back to our new best friend and asked the question. Then after what seemed like forever he turned back to me and said:

"The bus goes to Guaina, the next big town." He replied. "Takes about nineteen hours"

I could hardly contain myself I didn't know whether to cry or laugh, but in the back of my mind I knew our new found fortune could be too good to be true. It was a quick grounding. Johnny however was loving the moment he almost skipped back to the RV.

We got back and met the others at the appointed time. Then we all made our way back to our safe harbour area and there we shared the news.

The excitement burst out of every man. We jumped up and down and hugged each other, there were even a few tears. No one seemed to care that we were fully tactical again. As things calmed down I pulled out my dry bag and the excitement filled our harbour area again. I didn't think grown men could be so happy.

After we calmed down we moved a short distance from the place of all our excitement. That night we maintained a fully tactical harbour area. We'd exposed ourselves for the first time in thirty nine days now we had to ride that wave. The next day we stayed away from the town and watched closely to see if our presence there had attracted any unwanted attention. To our great relief we hadn't. Lady luck seemed to be on our side.

Our new found luck posed its own problems. We couldn't get on the bus dressed as we were, in full jungle combats. So each of us would have to civvy ourselves up best we could. We all got rid of our boots and bought flip flops on the morning of our departure from the market, for a few cents. Those who didn't have any spare shorts cut there combats down, T-shirts weren't a problem as long as no one took offence to slogans like "Death from Above" "Kill em all, and let Allah sort them out" and "God was a Commando, he failed P-Company". That and a few cheap pairs of sunglasses and a couple of hats later and we were all set.

Another problem was we couldn't get on the bus carrying the weapons we were carrying. We all carried 9mm browning pistols as standard and we could conceal them no problem, but we still had a small arsenal of rifles, grenades and anti personal mines between us. We pulled our heads together and decided to; each of us carry a concealed sidearm and as much ammunition as we could hide. Three of us would carry rifles hidden in dry bags and the rest would load up with what was left of the med kits and rations. I felt very vulnerable. It was refreshing not to have to lug around all that dead weight, but that weight brought comfort and peace of mind.

We'd gone to a lot of trouble to fit in as lost or over eager tourists but we still had to get over the basic obstacle of; could we afford the bus fare? If we couldn't we would end up having to walk the bus route and nineteen hours on a bus could be as much as another week on foot in our condition.

After doing a bit of shopping on the market we made our way to the bus stop. We decided to stay together, the town was small and it wouldn't take the brains of an Arch Bishop to know we were together anyway. The other advantage was; if it did kick off we would be together as a fighting force and not split up. We made contingency plans for that event and prayed we'd not need them.

The bus arrived mid morning, it had no chance of an MOT pass and I was surprised it made it. There were just as many people on the roof as there were inside it. People had been slowly turning up since we arrived and by now the bus stop was packed. I wondered if we'd even get on. We got there so early we were first in the queue and no one seemed interested in pushing in but would that change when the bus arrived?

Lucky for us it didn't. Johnny did the talking. As it was we didn't have enough to travel in the bus which was the bad news. But we could, for the rest of our money and Johnny's watch, travel on the roof. If I'm honest I was glad about that. A bit of fresh air, better all round observation and an easier exit if we needed it.

Half an hour into the bus journey the lads and I were sat in a circle at the back end of the bus. Water was abundant and we still had bread and apples from our first shopping trip two days earlier. Even though we hadn't really eaten for weeks it was hard to get lots of food down, a few bites and I was full.

It was like sitting in a beer garden with my mates in the UK on a hot summer's day. We laughed and joked about events in our unfortunate ordeal. Phil falling over a hundred feet into a rock pool and walking out injury free, Carl gagging on a meal of maggots and half of them coming out his nose and the bottom of my foot coming off when my immersion foot was at its worst. Moral was at an all time high and it was so nice not to be fuckin walking. The road was nothing more than dried mud and lumps of rock, it made for a bumpy uncomfortable ride. My arse and back were killing me and I'd have traded my 9mm for a kidney belt but on the whole I didn't care, I wasn't walking.

The actual drive took eighteen hours the driver stopped every three hours or so, so people could stretch and take a piss. For some reason he kicked a young man off the bus at one stop. The driver dragged the guy off by the hair, flat handed him round the jaw and wouldn't let him back on. We kept to ourselves the driver seemed quite a friendly bloke, whatever this guy did to piss him off like that was none of our business.

We got to Guaina in the early hours of the next morning. This was not a small town this was a big town. No more than 25000 people I would say but it was a metropolis compared to what we'd seen over the last 42 days. Well armed and broke we needed once again to make options. With my pushy bartering skills that I'd perfected in Mexico I managed to get more bread, lemons and a map in trade for needles from our medical supplies and a webbing belt with pouches that hadn't fitted me in weeks. The map showed a river flowing north south a few miles east of the town something we'd have to investigate. The next bus didn't leave for a week, it was a three day trip that went to the next major town La Parague and I knew hanging round a large town with nothing to do for a week could draw unwanted attention.

The river wasn't huge but it was deep and flowing north and more boats went up it than buses went on the road. There was a very small fishing village on the riverside, when we got there a few of the guys split off and went to stare at the river, Johnny went off to see about getting a lift, and Carl and I went off to explore the tiny village. Within five minutes me and Carl were playing football with six local children. Friendly little buggers. We played for a good twenty minutes then we both crashed through shear exhaustion and sat on the side to watch.

Johnny joined us,

"Any joy with the lift?" I said.

"None," he replied "They've got the transport, we just don't have the price even with your bartering talents"

As we spoke amongst ourselves one of the kid's fathers came out and approached us. In a brief exchange with Johnny we found out he was inviting us to his place for a cool drink. As we walked to his humble wooden home Johnny was spoke with him, he turned and said:

"He likes the way you play football"

We sat in the two room house for a good half hour drinking cool water and talking through Johnny. He was translating my questions about fishing and river trade, when Carl tapped me on the elbow and motioned towards a shelf in the corner. On the shelf was a sling and two colt magazines. The type used on the FAMAS the SA80 and the M16. The same magazines we used. Our host looked round to see what Carl and I were looking at, as he did he stood up, talking.

"What's he saying?" The question was aimed at Johnny.

"He says, he knows what you're looking at"

Then the middle aged man picked up the two magazines. The atmosphere in the room changed. Still talking our host went into the next room. I asked Johnny again what he was saying. Before he could answer our host came back into the room carrying an old but clean M16.

As soon as we saw it we drew on him and instinctively took positions round the room. Our target panicked and put the rifle down, all the time talking to Johnny.

"He doesn't want any trouble" Johnny translated. "He just wanted to show it to us".

Seeing the rifle had no magazine attached I motioned for our host to pull the working parts to the rear. Once I'd established the weapon was empty we secured our Browning's and we all sat down again. I thought our host was gonna have a heart attack. He spoke to Johnny and Johnny translated.

"He says he ran out of ammunition about five years ago, he was a local Government appointed peacekeeper, that's why he's got the M16 but with the economy the way it is he cant get anymore rounds"

Not for the first time I was amazed at how far Johnny's "Little bit o Spanish" would go. I later found out he'd studied Spanish for years and even lived in Mexico for a year. Amazing some of the things you don't know about your friends.

"Ask him if he's got a boat" I said.

The answer came back, yes.

"Tell our new friend, I've got ninety rounds and a new magazine if he'll get us to La Paragua" the next large town on the map.

Our host was ecstatic at the deal and couldn't wait to help, what I was offering equated to the cost of a years salary. We'd have to keep an eye on him till we were safely on the river, but for now things seemed to be going our way again.

Later that afternoon Sammy our boat Captain and owner loaded us onto his boat, it was bit of a squeeze and the thing was gonna never break any water speed records, but like the bus we all agreed it was better than walking. The trip was a good hundred and fifty miles and would take anything up to a week. We took the provisions we could and Sammy said we could pick up more food on route. The start of the river trip was peaceful. The river flowed briskly through the same deep hostile jungle we'd walked through for the last month or so. Mile after mile there was no river bank just thick over hanging dense foliage. Damsel flies the size of my palm hovered off the top of the water, fish leapt out to catch flies and large colourful birds took off from their tree top homes. If I'd had a beer, I could have been on holiday on any tropical island in the world. At the end of the first day we pulled onto a beach. It was like a truck stop for boats, half a dozen other fishermen pulled in too. Apparently it was one of only two places we could dock for the night in that area. Even though we all sat round the same fire we kept ourselves to ourselves. Sammy had never pressed us as to what we were doing there and when one of the other fisherman asked in our defence Sammy said; he had been employed by a forest research program to take us up river.

For the next five days not much changed. We fell comfortably into a routine of fishing and boat cleaning. I didn't now it, but Carls Father was a fisherman in Exeter England and Carl turned out to be a dab hand all round on the ageing vessel. Carl took it upon himself to do some minor repairs on the boat. You'd think Sammy had won the lottery with how happy he was about that.

On the fifth night we could see the lights of La Paragua in the distance. It was here we made the decision to leave all the rifles and ammunition we had with Sammy and press on with only the 9 mils. Sammy was over the moon, we left him four times what we said we would. I got to know Sammy well over the week he was a good man and thanks to Sammy's wife we had colourful and tasteful civilian T-shits and hats. Our transformation from abandoned fighting patrol to lost British tourists was almost complete.

Early the next afternoon we arrived in La Paragua. We said our grateful goodbyes to a grateful Sammy who was now the heaviest armed civilian in the country. He gave us a handful of money that he insisted we take and wished us well.

La Paragua was larger than Guaina but still small as towns go. We found a grotty little café in the town square and with the money Sammy had left us we all sat for a welcome glass of coke with ice and a straw. This was civilization. It was paradise in a glass. I had a brain freeze after the first sip but I couldn't stop drinking. I downed it in one and ordered another round we laughed at each other as our eyes welled up from the bubble fix. It was pure delight.

We'd been sat for a good twenty minutes contemplating our next move when two local police walked up to our table and keeping a few yards distance drew their weapons and started yelling.

"Everyone put your hands on the table" Johnny said.

Knowing how trigger happy these Zorro dodgers could be we didn't fuck about, we sat very still with our hands stuck fast to the white plastic table in front of us.

Then the reason for the excitement came to light. Pete's T-shirt had ridden up when he sat down and hooked over the top of his handgun showing it to the whole fuckin café. It wasn't long before a meat wagon arrived with more support for the two very nervous local police officers.

Keeping us well covered and starting with Pete they made us stand up one by one and put our weapons on a table next to the parked meat wagon. Then after a quick search we were bundled in the back. I was the last to be called forward, when I got the table to disarm it had on it; eight 9 mil pistols, thirty magazines, eight knifes and eleven grenades, three garrotting wires a handful of plastic cuffs and a ranger anti personnel mine. This was making the local law more and more nervous and they hadn't checked our packs yet.

After a very short drive we found ourselves in the local nick and locked in a large cell. There was a lot of shouting and shoving but we all just went with it. After a while stuck quite comfortably in the old western style prison cell the local Chief of Police came in and started asking questions. We'd had a lot of time on our hands over the last fifty days and a lot of that time was spent on our cover story. The idea was at the first opportunity we'd pull into any European Embassy and say we were holiday makers who'd lost all our passports, money and credentials in a boating accident then let them take it up from there, but the fact we'd been caught with all that weaponry left a great big "You lying bastards" sticker over the holes in any cover story we had. At this point we were fucked.

The only saving grace was their English was about as fluent as my ancient Greek. So it wasn't so much ignorance we pleaded it was, "I don't understand" and for now that would have to do. They interviewed us one by one and with the frustration of the language barrier and us all playing the "No Com Pren Day" card, each interview ended up with each one of us taking bit of a whack, nothing serious just a couple of well placed flat handers and thrown back in our communal cell.

Fortunately for us we had Johnny, we never let on he knew what they were saying and as the days went on they said more and more in front of us thinking we were clueless.
Their theory in the general gist of the conversation was that we'd been hired by a local village as a security force for whatever reason. Them thinking that was better than a half dozen alternatives. It was definitely better than the truth. Johnny also picked up in their conversations that they'd sent for an interpreter from the German consol in Ciudad Guayanna a city a hundred and fifty miles to the north. For whatever daft reason they thought we were German.

Eight fuckin days in that cell sweating our arses off, the only time the air changed was when the main door opened and we got a movement of hot air. We took it in turns to use the bed and the only entertainment was cockroach racing but even that's got its limit. Then a drunk was thrown in with us on the third day. When he arrived all he wanted to do was fight us all. To start with, none of us was interested. Even though we were being fed every one of us was still massively undernourished and we were all weak as kittens. But even after we let him have the bed to sleep it off he woke up violent kicking the guys that were sat against the wall and slapping Carl who was having a piss round the back of the head. Phil looked over to me, I knew what he was thinking I got up and smacked the drunk in the throat sending him choking and retching across the floor, he calmed right down after that. He sat in the corner and didn't utter another word. The guards that saw it laughed at him. He was obviously a regular here. They let him out the next day. We never spoke a word the whole time he was in that cell. There was always a chance he was a plant. Even now our biggest fear was being picked up by the Cartels.

On the ninth day the Boxhead turned up. He was a German Spanish interpreter that spoke less English than I spoke Spanish. The local police chief went off his fuckin head. He started throwing things round the station, swinging wildly at his men and ranting at the Boxhead who stood his ground well for a pen pusher I thought. Then the Chief started pointing at us and making shooting gestures with his hands. At that point I started getting worried, the Chief had waited patiently for help with the problem of us. Now it arrived it couldn't help. I was getting the feeling he was gonna solve us himself.

Things calmed down and Johnny started quietly interpreting the heated debate between the Chief and the Boxhead,

"They've got it stuck firm I their heads we're a locally hired security force," Johnny said

"Go on" Said Sean eagerly

"It's hard," Johnny said "Their talking so fuckin fast, something about European scum and stealing work and behaving like animals, usual anti immigrant stuff "

Great I thought, just what we need a Central American bigot with power over our lives.

"I don't believe it" Johnny said turning pale

"What, what" Sean said.

"The police Chief's so pissed off he's gonna release us into the custody of the Boxhead and we have to be out the town today"

The police Chief and our new best mate the German interpreter turned and looked at us. We all sat there grinning like kids at Christmas knowing what was coming. The cat was out the bag for the first time since we were arrested. They knew we had an idea what they were on about, the Chief exploded again and stomped out the station cursing and ranting.

Johnny spoke to the interpreter, he was right we were to go with the German and be held in the German Embassy until someone decided what was to happen to us.

Two weeks later the team and I were back in the UK. My bodyweight had gone from a hundred and three kilos to sixty five. My beard grew long and thin and my eyes sat deep in their sockets. I didn't realize how bad our conditions were till we got back to the world.

We all tried to make noise about our ordeal and expose the Americans for their treachery.

How many deserted teams never made it home?

We all refused to have anything to do with the United States of America or anything American again. Although right in our protest's we were told to let it go and informed that if we trod on the wrong toes the other foot might come down to squash us. That in mind and with families to feed and bills to pay we all agreed to leave it at that.

Six months later I met Simon in the Litchfield pub in Hereford. I had the distinct feeling it wasn't a coincidence. He gave me a social and friendly debrief and offered me work in the same breath. I turned him down knowing the work would always be there if things got that bad.

A year later things were that bad and once again I was approached by Simon. This time I took the work, it paid well and I made it home within the set time frame, what more could I ask for? Simon and I remain work associates to this day, maybe even friends. I say maybe because you never know with a man in his field whether you're friends or if you're just another asset for his own agenda, but I enjoy his company anyway and he pays on time.

THE FIRMS

Some of us after leaving the Armed Forces find ourselves; "In between jobs".

I found a great job packing boxes in a warehouse, the pay was good the hours were ok and for the most part the blokes I worked with were, well, "ok" I suppose. Some had been there years. They knew nothing other than home the local bar and the warehouse. It killed me to listen to them talk at the bar. All they talked about was work and they did it with such excitement. Personally I just couldn't get a hard on about box packing products and toner. The only real entertainment was the warehouse manager Damery and his side kick Carol.

He was a 25 year old power tripping idiot (you can picture the type) all pamphlet knowledge bluff and balls, but no real man management skills to speak of and no business sense whatsoever, hence the warehouse job.

Carol, who closely resembled that witch Grot Bags off the Rod and Emu show had even less of a clue and took great pleasure in yelling at everyone pretty much all day. Reinforcing something I'd heard years before,

"People who speak harshly usually do so to cover gaps in their knowledge."

If that's true, from the way Carol spoke she didn't have a fuckin clue.

I'd been there about two weeks when she decided she'd have a go at me. I left my packing bench to take a piss and I heard Carol yelling at me to:

"Get back to that station" and "where do you think you're going"

I ignored her and carried on with what I was doing. Two minutes later on my way back from the toilet she stood in front of me like a headmistress in front of a kid that messed about in class. She was about to say something when I stopped her.

I should have said:

"Sorry about that I'll ask next time"

However the words:

"Get out my fuckin way you naggin old cow" slipped out instead.

She stood there speechless, a first so I was told later. Then she literally ran into Damery's office to give her version of events.

After lunch Damery called me into his office, he always trod very carefully around me. He'd do his usual shouting and teddy throwing with the others but he always asked me to do things and was always quite polite about it. Just as well really or I'd have knocked the fucker out. Something I ended up doing a few years later when he got a bit over familiar with me in a night club around a couple of his mates, but like him they too were full of piss and wind and they took no time at all to sort out.

In his office he was as polite as ever, even diplomatic, he was sat on the end of his desk and although invited to sit I remained standing. All was going well a lot better than I expected. Right up to the point when he wanted to give me a written warning for my behaviour. Until that point he'd done all the talking. As soon as I went to open my mouth to defend myself he held his hand up, looked at the floor and said:

"I have spoken"

What I should have done was walk out in silence and let him have his moment, he could have gone off to the bar that night and told of how he had tamed the new guy, but instead I took him round the throat with one hand, grabbed him by the balls with other and bent him backwards over his desk. Once I had his full attention I pointed out that I wasn't a fuckin school kid and wasn't going to ask permission from some power tripping fat bitch as to whether or not I could use the toilet.

Quite funny looking back, not knowing which area to try and guard he just patted his stomach rapidly with both hands breathing like a woman in labour and apologizing with every breath. I let go and calmly walked out and went back to work.

Damery wasn't seen again that day and didn't come in the next day either which left Carol in the mangers seat, she wasted no time in pulling me into the office, that little bit of power meant so much to her, (sad really) she sat in Damery's chair leaning back with her fingers interlinked across the spare tyre she carried between her tits and the other tyres that made up her frame and proceeded to lecture me on things I should know in order to get on. I had no time for that shit, so saying nothing I walked out and went back to work.

Then she yelled out after me:

"I've read your CV, there's no place for you people in civvy street"

Fuck that hit a nerve, but I wasn't going to prove her point by acting on it. All CV's were confidential that probably explained Damery's way towards me, but Carol must have had access to it at some point that morning. I carried on working then just before lunch Carol walked up behind me and said:

"I'm the person who can get you fired"

I turned and looked her up and down, then replied:

"Not for sexual harassment, no fuckers gonna fall for that"

"You'd better learn some respect" she said, and walked off.

I'd had enough of her by now and had to sort things out. I wasn't going to hit her or argue with her so I went over to invoicing on the other side of the warehouse where her boyfriend worked. I had 5 minutes with him right before lunch, then as normal they went home together to eat. I never laid a hand on him, never raised my voice, I didn't even make eye contact with him I just spoke nice and softly in his ear just for a few minutes and he got my point.

I don't know what he said to Carol that lunch time but she never spoke to me again.

The next day Damery turned up with three other bods in suits. My first thought was of the incident in his office the day before and what he might have done about it. I found out later he never mentioned it to anyone. (Fuckin right too, cheeky bastard) but as it turned out they were the company big bosses come to tell us the company had been sold and we were all redundant effective in two weeks. The job was never going to be a career for me so I declined the two extra weeks work and left that morning. I felt for the old guys that had been there so long, of course they got bit of a pay off but they still lost their jobs and their safe little routines.

So I found myself "Between Jobs".

* * *

The Police didn't want me, (not much of a surprise there) the Ambulance service wasn't recruiting and I'd failed the Fire Service selection because I spelt "Intact" wrong on the dictation test. So that pretty much left me with a cleaning or driving job in the local paper, or working for a PMC or Organized crime and guess what! Yep! No mop, steering wheel or long foreign tour for me. My path would lie for now with the latter.

I'd met Ian in the Golden Fleece Pub in Hereford a few years before, a nice feller, big jolly bald bloke would be a good description and being as there's not much room in the Fleece he was hard to miss.
Ian and his Firm ran everything from Aberystwyth to Worcester and down to Gloucester. And with contacts in London, Manchester, Glasgow and Newcastle not to mention his European connections he could supply anything from specialist car parts to cocaine in large quantities, whore's for free and confidential police information. He had dirt on everybody who was anybody and knew how to exploit it and with his interest's in the Devonshire fishing industry he did a nice side line in body disposal, but his biggest earner by far was

the loan business, any amount from £10 to £100'000 he would and could lend it.

Not a problem if you could pay it and the interest back but if you couldn't that's when we would meet. I wasn't the guy that made the weekly collections. I wasn't the guy that came round to give you a slap if you were late paying. I was the guy that supplied and executed the plan to retrieve the money if you were stupid enough to decide not to pay.

"A beaten man is done, a scared man will do anything."

Some of the people that owed Ian money had public status and career rank. Every now and again one of them would step out of line and hide behind their public office or uniform to avoid paying. Some owned large grounds and stayed at home to avoid confrontation. Dealing with this was my speciality. It was a whole different side of me and at the time it came real easy.

My first real job for Ian had nothing to do with the collection of funds though. It was a DI from Worcester nick, a career copper and quite a young guy. He had a wife two kids and a nice house with a good size mortgage know doubt. At face value it was the perfect family but the truth of it was; this guy fucked around any chance he could get. From what I could gather he never shit on his own doorstep. Instead he spent his time in Shrewsbury. He spent most weekends playing around the younger culture there and had a bit of a name for himself as a Casanova.

On this one particular occasion though he stuck his dick in the wrong dog and not only would it run its mouth off, but she would take him for everything he had. I suppose the good news was that she was good looking. Insult to injury would be to lose everything for a fat ugly bird. The bad news for him anyway was that she was seventeen had an on going love affair with Mr Cocaine and had found out where he lived, but that wasn't the best of it. Not only was she playing him for money, she was pregnant and was happy to go for DNA tests and tell little wifey everything. However, the icing on the cake had to be the fact that she was Ian's daughter's best friend and much to the detriment of many a man, women talk and daughters talk to good fathers.

Hooking him was brutally simple and a lot easier than I thought. I turned up on his door step on a Sunday, (knowing he wasn't in) posing as an Independent Surveyor. His wife answered the door and I went to work.

"Hello," I said with a smile, "The local council have sent me,"

Instantly she interrupted. Just what I needed, her attention.

"On a Sunday? if this is a con" She was rolling "If you're one of those confidence tricksters you might as well know my husband in an Inspector"

I was getting the feeling already that she could go on all day. I interrupted:

"That's not the case at all Madam" She'd bitten and I was about to reel her in, "Here's my ID, I'm an independent surveyor employed by the council to take some details of your council tax that's all. Like the man that reads your Gas meter, he'll be an Independent too. Not a direct employee of British Gas and so is at liberty to work out of office hours. Hoping to catch people at home.

"Oh, I'm so sorry" She said "I didn't mean to be so hard, but you just never know"

"Rare for someone to be so vigilant" I said "But good to see"

Then I lay the land mine.

"If you could just give this to your husband for me" I said handing her a thick brown envelope with the DI's name on it. "My contact details are there on the back"

I pointed to the name and mobile number I'd written on the back. I made sure I wrote over the glue that sealed the envelope to discourage Mrs DI from opening it first.

In the package I'd left photo's, names, addresses and dates. Things he might possibly have taken in his stride and tired to negotiate a quick deal or arrest me and have his guys help him keep it from his wife had I handed it to him. But I didn't, his wife did. She had it all day without opening it then handed him the time bomb at the dinner table as she told the story of her Sunday visitor.

I had one phone especially for him. It rang constantly for the next two days. I ignored it. On the third day about 10.00 in the morning I answered it. He was so highly strung by then he would have sold me his soul.

We never hit him for money, his bit on the side was doing a sterling job of that and part of our little deal was us keeping her off his front door. All we ever wanted was information, names and address's put to car registrations. Phone numbers given home address's forewarning on any local police operations and raids info on possible competition for the Firm that kind of thing. We were good with all intelligence, I mean we couldn't send someone round to give a guy a good hiding if our tame DI had just given us an address there would be an obvious paper or computer trail for that. So we'd sit on it and follow the guy and when opportunity knocked several weeks later we'd simply open the door and punish the guy accordingly. Our new tame DI turned out to be a great asset over the following years. Ian's held him close throughout his tainted career. As far as I know he's still on the books today.

Like I said, some owed money, some had just pissed the big guy off, and some jobs were bought or passed on, they were a favourite of mine, it wasn't so personal they didn't owe you and you didn't know them. It was pure business. You did your job, you got paid. It was perfect.
One particular moment of genius from me, although particularly brutal and immoral was with a foreign diplomat, Ian ran him a tab at one of his not so legal gambling outlets to the sum of £200'000. At the time I was surprised Ian's places hosted such cliental, but like he said:

"Vice is a business that doesn't need location or advertising, the customer will always find you, and they always pay cash"

He was a fuckin genius envied by many and feared by the rest, but every now and again somebody thought themselves beyond the reach of the big guy and this time it was this diplomat. Ian had already done the norm, sent guys round, phoned him, threatened to tell the wife, all the usual. All he did was change his numbers and employ bodyguards from his home country, this pissed Ian off no end and as sure as shit stinks, when he was that pissed off someone's life was about to take a turn on the dramatic side.

I remember clearly getting the call. I was on another job on the Blackbird Lees estate in Oxford. What a shit hole, for the most part it was nothing more than a brick pikky estate. Broken down and stripped cars everywhere, kids raking havoc and jobless adults pissing it up on every curb. For the few good folks there it must be a real hell on earth.

We had a safe house there run by a young single mum Gaynor, (nice girl) never judged us and put up with a ton of shit on a regular basis, she'd put guys up on the run, hide various packages and even helped out in a few stings we had going and she did it all with a smile bless her. I'd just left her house carrying £50'000 from a sale of 9mm pistols sold down in Kent. The dodgy bit was already done and the money left at Gaynors. I just picked it up on my way passed. Walking back to my car praying the fuckin wheels would still be on it, Ian rang.

He was trying to explain the job to me but all I got was a very angry onslaught of: "fuck, shit, cunt, mugging off, kill and bastard," so I cut him short and suggested and I mean suggested not told, that he settle down and have a drink, then I told him I'd be there in a couple of hours. With that he found a new state of calmness and in that deep relaxed voice he had that sent the hackles up on the back of my neck he said:

"I need this sorted, now"

Not one to disappoint the big guy I put foot to floor and made Hereford in just over an hour. When I got there Ian was surprisingly calm and collected, he told me the goings on and gave me the info I needed to come up with a plan to get his money back.

I followed the diplomat for nearly a month but none of the normal opportunities presented themselves at all, he was covered 24/7 by his new team both him and the wife, when she ever did leave the house which really wasn't often, I had to get the job done (I was being paid stupidly well.) Ian never asked for any updates he had put the job to me and that was that. He once said to me:

"You're a job done, do you know that"

I asked him to explain one night when we were pissed and he pointed out that I was one of three guys he had that once given a job he could guarantee it was done, I prided myself on that ever since, I'm also sure that was the point of the comment, he had a great way about him, you always knew when you were being manipulated but you always felt good about it. With all this in mind I had to find a solution.

I took the weekend off to gather my thoughts and see my son. I must have had a Quinten Tarentino moment over that weekend because by the time I got back to Hereford I had a great plan, it went against the grain a bit and if I didn't spend the rest of my life in jail it should work.

It was simple really. If I couldn't get to him or his wife I'd have to go though his kids. He had two girls that boarded at St Margaret's school in Bushy, North London and he collected them personally every Friday. I'd obtained his new mobile number from another of Ian's connections and with help from Jock one of Ian's less morally understanding guys set about my new found plan.

We waited outside the school on the very next Friday, helpfully enough the diplomat parked less than 30 feet in front of me. Jock who was at the end of the street walked to the gates, his timing was perfect the two girls stepped out just in front of him and with that he very subtly sprayed the school bag of one of the girls with petrol. Oblivious to this the girls ran to their fathers beautiful black limo and Jock walk straight on and disappeared, with that I rang the father whose car by now would stink of unleaded fuel and pointed out to him that if he didn't pay his dues that weekend the next time we'd set the kids alight, I never would have done it or let it be done but he didn't know that and sure enough that weekend one of his new found, non English speaking bodyguards dropped the money off to a young lady in a bar on the Blackbird Lees estate in Oxford, to be collected the following weekend by myself. I learned early to keep that little bit of distance.

"It's not what you can do that counts! It's what you can have done."

Big Ian

* * *

The skulduggery never ended and I found myself having to come up with more and more crazy ideas to solve some of the larger problems presented to a key organised criminal figure. Some of the guys in the Firm were more sadistic than others.

One idiot in particular was a cousin of Ian's, he use to tease his targets. Between that and his temper he was a walking life sentence, I hated being around him and I hated bailing him out. The more we helped the more shit he got into he was a real fuckin liability.

I got a very distressed phone call one night from Ian's 2ic Wayne pleading with me to meet with him ASAP, (two in the fuckin morning), I met him at a gamekeepers house just outside Mordiford. The gamekeeper, poor bastard was into Ian for about £900 and was late with a payment and the idiot cousin in question went round to warn him and that's all it should have been was a warning. But no, this cunt had sat the gamekeeper down in his kitchen and made him write at gun point "I'm so sorry" a hundred times on a note pad.

Half way through the gamekeeper kicked up a stink, shouting and pointing out that this idiot wouldn't really shoot him over £900, with that Ian's cousin put the back of the gamekeepers head in with a ball point hammer he keeps religiously in his belt, killing the gamekeeper outright.

Less than twenty minutes later I turn up with some very fast thinking to do, I stood back and delegated the next part. I had a dead bloke with a fuckin great hole in the back top part of his head and a note that said "I'm so sorry" written about sixty or seventy times on it, (he never got his hundred). Instantly the thought of making it look like a suicide came to mind but you'd have to be one determined, stupid or deranged motherfucker to put the back of your own head with a hammer, the guy that would try that would be the guy that failed to overdose on new blue smarties. Fortunately he was a gamekeeper and he did keep a shotgun.

I put it to the idiot, that he could put the shotgun in the mouth of the gamekeeper pull the trigger, set up correctly it might look like a suicide, my thinking being, all the mess from the shot was bound to cover up the fact his head was put in first. The note on the table was in his handwriting he owed money left right and centre and his wife had run off with a younger stag six month's before. There was a chance it would fly.

The idiot debated who should set it up and pull the trigger. At that point knowing precisely how much shit we were all in because of this cunt and having zero tolerance for anymore of his bullshit I took him outside across the road and beat the shit out of him at the same time pointing out it was his mess and that we were just along for the unfortunate ride.

Wayne and I left shortly after that leaving the idiot to execute my plan. He was violent and sadistic, lazy and a pisshead but far from stupid, he knew exactly how to set it up it wasn't the first crime scene he'd left before the law arrived.

My work was far from over with this one, I rang every bent copper I knew that night. Never giving anything away. But I needed to know how such an event would be investigated and who would be involved. Ian was on holiday and he made it clear when he left that he wanted to return to a clean house and that didn't include his cousin doing life.

I learnt long before the law has a budget for each type of crime. If a guy gets a good hiding they'd look into it but without any real leads the case would just fade to nothing after a very short period of time and the Criminal Compensation Board would give a tax free sweetener of a grand or two to ease the victim's pain and keep him sweet. Protecting the law from shit press.

So depending on the crime and circumstance, depended on how much cleaning up had to be done. All with one exception "MURDER". Murder gave the law an open purse.

I never had or have any hate or disrespect for the British lawman, the Great British Bobby. I know them to be the best in the world at what they do. A lot of the time its policy and politics that inhibits them as individuals and as Units and that could always be used against them to our advantage. Just like terrorists, immigrants and women do on a daily basis almost corrupting the laws of the land for personal gain.

But if you overstep the mark you give them almost unlimited power and money and you're fucked, because as sure as shit stinks they will get you.

With this in mind we had to keep the words "Murder and Suspicious circumstance" away from any and all reports, despite the fact I had nothing to do with incident itself by not calling the law I may as well have had and I wasn't doing a seconds bird for this shit kicking idiot, so the only option was to bail him out again.

And it WAS the only option because "Snitches are a DYING breed"

If the moron had set it up right the law would call it as they saw it. The suicide of a depressed lonely man with nothing to live for. The note would help and if they did have a quick dig into his debtors, would anyone kill a man for £900?

After asking around the nightmare got worse, the police may call suicide but the coroner on post mortem would almost definitely deduce that the gamekeeper was actually dead a good half hour before he blew his own head off. What a fuckin palaver.

I used every favour and paid a fortune in cash to sort this one. First I had to find the exact guy who would chop the gamekeeper and write the report, then I had to find where he lived. After that I had to find something on him, if there was anything then I had to use it and just to stop that being too easy I had about three days to do it all and the only reason I had that long was because there'd been a pile up involving three cars and an HGV lorry on the road to Leominster leaving four dead, so fortunately for me there was bit of a back log of bodies in Herefordshire that week.

The coroners name, for this book anyway was Mr Morris. He was 58 been doing the job over thirty years and was a perfectionist his whole life. On top of that he was squeaky clean, I guarantee if I'd had two years to find dirt on this guy I wouldn't have found any, he really was one of the good guy's. He lead a good life, put all three of his kids though Oxford University, had a little summer house in Spain and been married to the same woman for forty years. He was looking to retire early at sixty with great pride in his flawless service to his chosen profession. Unfortunately that wasn't to happen, I needed this man of impeccable morality to overlook something, to lie, to go against the scruples that had stood him in good stead his whole life.

Violence to an old professional was definitely not the way to go, that was sure to bring on too much attention. So the obvious place to start was with bribery and that's exactly where I started. We caught up with him the following night straight after he'd finished work just after 1730. We were lucky to catch him alone at that time in the mortuary car park. We used traditional car jacking tactics, as he unlocked the beautiful silver merc and got in we all got in with him , two in the back me shotgun (in the passenger seat) and jock a very heavy angry looking guy stood outside the drivers door to stop him bailing out. I really did feel for him, trapped in his car with three very large silent, angry looking men. Petrified, wondering what the hell was going on. I never remember the faces or plea's of men I've hurt only the fearful look or pathetic crouching that comes before any good hiding or punishment due. This was one face I've never forgotten, we were about to change this mans life and not for the better and it was all down to one blood happy sadistic fool.

"I need something from you" I said
"Take the car" He said "But please don't hurt me I've got no money please let me go" he pleaded.
"We don't want your car my friend" I replied softly using the word friend in a bid to try and settle the old man down. "What I need is your help"
I explained to him he was about to do a post mortem on a Herefordshire Gamekeeper.
"Yes the suicide" He said "I know the man in question he's first on tomorrow mornings list"
"That's the one" I said.
Then I went on to expain that it wasn't a suicide without giving too many details. I also explained that we weren't asking him to forge his report, but rather to overlook certain details. Then I went on to offer him £150'000 in cash and an all inclusive holiday to the Domincan Republic in the Caribbean and would you believe it, the old bastard said no!

He didn't care if we hurt him or not and yet only five minutes earlier that was his biggest concern. Figure that one out? I told him to think very hard on it and pointed out that if he went to the police about our little visit that we'd be back, only next time we'd be doing the driving. With that we all got out the car and walked away.
"Fuckin ell" Pete said "I wasn't expecting that"
Pete was a six foot four slimmer version of Shrek. His whole life revolved around violence and with no real intelligence to speak of he was easy to offend and was quick to lash out. He was too volatile for door work so Ian used him to smash people up and as muscle on occasions such as this. But thick as he was I had to agree with him.
"Neither was I mate" I replied.

Plan B at this point hadn't been thought up as I was sure my first plan would work but I needed one and fuckin fast. Once again I found myself digging to the deepest depths of my own morality, I was ok to take it to the next level but it would be a bluff on my part. As for Pete and the other guys I was with I couldn't say.

At 0245 the following morning about six hours before the post mortem of the gamekeeper, I sat on a white king size bed in the dark next to the coroner Mr Morris, his wife sleeping soundly beside him, a £150'000 in cash on his bedside with details of his free hoilday next to it and two large men stood behind me in the doorway. He woke with a hell of a start, I stopped him from sitting up too far and handed him his gold rimmed spectacles.

"No noise" I said softly "don't want to wake the missus"

"How did" I stopped him there

"We made you an offer, a good offer, no one will question your report if there's no other evidence and no other suspicion. You can rest easy knowing you did what was right for your family, do you understand?" I said at an almost whisper.

Mr Morris nodded and laid his head back slowly. I stood up and we left the same way we came in, through the front door. All that was left to do was wait.

We never contacted Mr Morris again. I felt we'd pushed our luck enough with him. We got the info we needed from a tame copper we had on the pay role at Hereford nick. By all account's all went our way and nothing more was made of it.

When Ian got back off his holiday I sat him down in his office and told him the whole messed up saga and he listened intently. After about an hour of hearing my own voice I rapped up by saying "and that's about all Ian"

"All, that's not fuckin all is it" He was real pissed off.

In my debrief to him I pointed out that with bribes and outlay the whole episode had cost just short of £350'000, money Ian now had to pay out. Even to this day I've never seen a man more angry, I was beginning to wonder if I'd done the right thing bailing his cousin out. I didn't have receipts and Ian didn't want any. It's not the kind of thing you can deduct against your tax bill. I had enough time in with Ian for him to take me at my word and I like my hands attached to my arms so I'd never have short changed him anyway.

It seemed like ages till Ian calmed down enough to talk normally and until that point I just sat there with Wayne his 2ic in silence. Sometimes it's best not to stoke the fire.

Ian flew back the day before and was picked up unbeknown to us by his cousin who had made the whole thing sound like he'd given the gamekeeper a bit of a slap, not even mentioning that he'd killed him and that's what pissed Ian off most. The money was nothing to Ian.

* * *

Working with the Firm was a constant life of violence. All problems and issues were solved with the use of uncompromising brutality. You owe money you get a slap. You rob anything, sell drugs, steal a car, smash a bar up on our manor without permission you get a leg broke in a far off field and are left to walk home.

The other side is the paid work, that's when someone pays the Firm to give someone anything from a "good hiding" to "A Lord Lucan." A couple of Ian's contacts owned fishing boats and for a small fee would drop a person off in the North Sea with cast iron bling padlocked to their wrists and ankles.

But believe it or not working in those circles had its advantages. A good friend of mine found out his daughter was being sexually abused by his EX wife's long term boyfriend. The police got involved but did very little and the mother not fully believing the young teenage girl wouldn't kick the boyfriend out. My friend was distraught and asked for my help to give the guy a beating but I had a better idea. I explained to my friend that because the Police had been involved he would be prime suspect if this paedophile got a slap. Then I suggested he take a long weekend away to Spain with his girlfriend, which he did.

With the help of some contacts and one of our guys, I got the kiddie feeler into a travel lodge just outside Great Yarmouth where he lived. It took me less than twenty minutes to get a confession, he admitted everything and told us how he'd instigated it and how he got round the girlfriend, I stopped him short of telling me what he actually did to her. I don't think I could have taken it. He spoke in tears for a good half hour and up to that point I hadn't laid a finger on him but he knew I wasn't fuckin about.

Then the crew I'd taken with me set up a camera and tripod and I left the room. Across the way from the travel lodge was a Little Chef, I went there for my lunch and waited there for three hours. Then one of the crew came in and sat with me and had a coffee and explained what had been done. I was shocked to say the least.

The five men had beaten and gang raped the Paedophile for three hours and filmed the whole event. Copies would be made he explained and his friends and family given the copies, along with the reason why. The internet was in its infancy back then but I'm told it's on there too.

I went back to the room, the pervert was in the bathroom bleeding, sobbing and whimpering all his teeth were missing at the front and his wrists and ankles were blue and cut from the cuffs. His eye was cut and would need stitching and judging from the blood on the floor underneath him that's not all that would need a stitch. The others were laughing while cleaning up and watching the rerun, they just seemed to be ignoring him as if nothing had happened. I watched part of the video and felt a strange vulnerability but despite its material I felt no pity it was less than he deserved.

My friend returned from his long weekend to find his daughter in no more danger, the target had not only moved out the house he'd left the town. I sent the police a copy of the Audio confession and all his contact details. They did nothing. The confession was also used as the video sound track.

* * *

I'd been working for the Firm on and off for five years at this point and was offered a legitimate job as a Close Protection Officer for a millionaire businessman in Hampshire about a week before the gamekeeper incident. I'd asked for time to think about it but this made my mind up for me. The CPO positon was only a six month contract but it seemed like a good stepping stone to getting out the mess I could see myself ending up in. I sat down with Ian the next day and told him my intentions. He was good about it and wished me well.

"You've always got a job here if you need it" He said

I thanked him sincerely. I had no intention at that time of returning to that way of life but didn't see the need to burn bridges. As I stood up to leave he stood with me opening his desk draw, and taking out a black zipped wallet. I'd been working with him long enough to know what it was. Money.

"No Ian no retainers mate, but thanks again," I said humbly hoping he wouldn't take offence.

"It's not a retainer mate, it's a thank you, no strings," he said "I love my Auntie Mo she's been a mother to me since my own died when I was a kid, it would have killed her to see her only son go to prison, you did well there mate"

I'd never known Ian to be so open and wondered if he would have been had we not been alone.

"What about your Cousin Ian, he is a liability to you?"

"I know" He said "And he'll be doing nothing more than shovelling shit for a long time, but he's one of us,"

There was nothing more to say, "He was one of us". Ian looked after all his boys, we all did well out of Ian and we knew it. Maybe that's why we were all so loyal. On my way out the door, I apologised for quitting. Then Ian shocked me again:

"It's not quitting, to quit while you're ahead" He said "It's prudent"

CLOSE PROTECTION

My Military career had been a good one, I'd been shot, stabbed twice, broken both legs and been caught in an explosion sustaining massive internal injuries. It was time not to settle down but calm down. I was working for the Firm in between jobs for the Company I was employed with and needed to step away from that too. I spoke to the Company I was working for, and they suggested taking six months off the Military side of things and working the Close Protection aspects instead.

I always saw CP work as Policing and not Soldiering. So did my level best to avoid it. The two are worlds apart and I believe you can only give your full attention to one or the other. That and the fact all the real CP work for Diplomats, British Royalty, Foreign Royalty, and Ministers was done by the Scotland Yard boys. Its well documented and published that the SAS have helped the Yard Boys in the past. But this is only done in the absolute extreme and expressly with the Chief Constables say so.

I didn't need the money. My own businesses were doing well. I was just afraid if I stopped the private work I'd never start again and I'd become just another "Has been". I'd seen literally hundreds of "Has been's" in the pubs of Aldershot and Hereford. Good men all and all with a tale to tell. Some old and some not much older that me, but for whatever reason had retired or been retired. I used to love to listen to the "Old and Bold". We all did, but the disrespect these men got from society and the narrow minded civilian was a crime. A crime against everything they'd done and the reasons they did it. I never wanted to be the guy that said'
"I used to do that" or "I was there"
Just to have some spotty faced little urchin but in with:
"Year whatever Granddad, blah blah blah,"
I'd heard things like that said and it pained me. A few times in the past I'd had it out with people over it but something's are worth

giving and receiving a black eye for. So with all this in mind I said yes to the job.

No Royalty for me though, my Principal was a garden variety billionaire. Self made. He'd gone from pushing a wheel barrow to owning a private jet. A very polite humble man with a Yorkshire accent in his very late sixties. The first time we met he asked me to call him Tom but I never did. He was Sir to me, that's the way we worked but it genuinely bothered him. At the end of my twelve hour shift wherever we were in the world he would invite me into his private lounge for brandy and a chat about the day.

"So, how was your day?" He asked.

The first time he asked after my very first shift, I replied'

"You were there Sir, how could you not know?"

This was another reason I avoided CP work. I wasn't best known for my diplomacy or tolerance of small talk.

"I know how it went from my point of view, but what about yours? He said.

"I don't understand what you're getting at Sir" I said turning down the brandy

"Well" he said "your job is solely to keep me safe and well, yes?" He was firm but friendly.

"That's about it," I said

"I like to think of this as the time you can voice an opinion on the day's events" He said.

I was speechless. Every CPO's nightmare and worry is the Principals demands and ways, eight times out of ten they compromise their security in one way or another and the CP team would have to constantly adjust at the last minute. Its all part of the job but it's still a major hassle. As the conversation went on I found out Tom was all for things running smoothly and would do anything to facilitate us in our duties. This wasn't going to be the arse kissing exercise I'd been dreading.

He insisted on the brandy, so I necked it.

"You're not a brandy drinker are you?" He enquired

"Not really Sir, more of a Guinness man" I said

"Have another and this time try and savour the brandy" He mused.

He poured me another. I was more impressed by the glass than the drink. It was a giant fish bowl of a glass. Even the double measure he was pouring was lost in it.

"Move the brandy round the glass" he said motioning me to copy him. "Brandy must never be chilled but gently warmed by the hands," the lesson went on. "Any good spirit will almost stick to the glass."

I held my glass up a bit mimicking him. I already knew that bit, my Granddad use to say the same about whisky.

Then he went to savour the aroma of the beverage, I thought he was about to drink it and necked mine back again only to finish and find Tom still smelling his.

"No more for me Sir I'm driving" I said, hoping it would cover my ignorance.

"Tell you what" He said "That's the quickest I've seen two grand go outside of a casino"

"How's that?" I asked

"This brandy stands at £500 a shot" He said with a smile.

I put the glass down and said:

"My round next then, I'll introduce you to the wonderful world of Irish Stout"

He smiled broadly and sipped from his glass.

***

The security at Tom's estate was unique in Great Britain. He turned his cash into assets such as art, jewellery, precious metals and bonds and kept it all in a vault under the main house.

Before our team took the job Tom gave us a personal tour of his house, grounds and the vault. He ended his tour by saying:

"If you ever steal from my vault I'll consider it my fault that the security I've put in place here on my estate is not enough, or is wrong. Then I'll claim off my insurance. However if you steal ten pence off my side board or bedside table, I'll hunt you down and drag you through every court in the country"

I almost didn't get what he was on about, then he said:

"The pennies I save are the millions I insure"

Fair play I thought but if you were to think that an invite to rob him you'd be very wrong. The security at the estate was tremendous. He had a total of six security teams. All from different companies and regions and even one from Germany.

He had a gate and fence team. They worked all three gates and maintained the perimeter fence cameras. If you weren't on the day's itinerary you didn't get in full stop.

His external roaming patrol never came into the estate and they were a local company set up by Ex Royal Marine. All they did was randomly but very effectively patrol the perimeter and were in constant comms with the local police and main house security.

The grounds team were from Germany. They all lived on the estate in servant's quarters. They ran four dog teams. One team of Dobermans and three teams of the largest German shepherds I'd seen outside of Northern Ireland.

The main house team was in two parts. A four man team worked the fault. Two inside it and two outside it. The next lot roamed and secured the rest of the house as well as working the OP's room. That had all the CCTV controls and communication with all the other security teams.

Then both Tom and his wife had separate personal security teams.

All the teams were changed at different times and all teams were completely refreshed every six months and he wouldn't have the same people back in any one eighteen month period.

***

Tom was a great guy, he worked everyday of his life. He loved to drink and he loved to gamble but he always kept a level head.

One night in Monty Carlo he'd had a great night at the poker table. It was obvious to me and all around that the other three players were linked in some way. It's not cheating to team up against another player, it's just not very sporting.

On the night in question Tom soundly beat all three even though they were all out to see him off. Two of the players took exception to Tom after the game and started making open verbal threats. This did not make for an easy night for me. Tom, the man that he was asked if he should call it a night. A CPO's blessing, but I told him things would be fine and he should just continue with his evening .

Later that night at a restaurant in the casino Tom was having supper with his wife and the two wannabe Mavericks pulled in. I'd informed casino security about the incident shortly after it had happened and unknown to me they watched these two idiots from then on. I made my way to the reception area to intercept the two men and I wasn't there to talk them out of their intentions. The second I met them at the restraunt reception I grabbed one by the bottom lip pulled his head to one side with little or no resistance and kicked his legs out from under him, in the next second the casino security team wrenched both of them away.

I looked over at Tom who winked at me and carried on his conversation with his wife. Tom's wife never knew there was anything wrong, but that's how Tom liked it. He was a hard working, hard playing man and he never bothered his wife with the details. He was a great Principal.

Tom's wife of thirty years on the other hand was a right Royal pain in the arse and I'm glad I wasn't on her security detail. She had the same two visitors at least once a week. The doctor and the vet and when they came round it was fuck about time for all of us. I was going to argue once that we worked for the old man and not her but Tom pulled me to one side and ask me to; "Please go along with it." As it gave her one less thing to complain about, I didn't argue I respected him too much.

The doctor came along to treat her long list of ailments. If there was a flu outbreak in China she got it. If the monthly women's magazines she read had a sickness and symptoms page she would get them. Each time the doctor would come running and leave after prescribing some bullshit placebo and charging an absolute arm and a leg.

* * *

The vet was no better. The old girl had two small Chihuahua's. No bigger than my shoes and they would get as sick as her. So the vet would be called. He was as much use as the Doc but a lot more entertaining.

He'd poke and prod the dogs, then diagnose some long thought dead canine illness.

He was good to watch though. He was bit of a showman and went all out to earn his money. He'd have the dogs walk and sit, then he'd get out all his vets tools, lights, pokers and such before reaching his diagnosis. Then he'd walk round the room, taking deep breaths and nodding his head and scratching his chin, keeping the old girl on the edge of her seat, before making his diagnosis final. He was great to watch. God only knows how he kept a straight face.

He knew we knew he was taking the piss and it got to a point that when we knew he was coming. We'd make a point of watching under the rouse of concern for the mutt's.

He was called out on some canine emergency one Sunday and as usual we met up in the lounge to offer our services. (Well watch the show anyway). The vet picked up the smaller of the two glove puppets and started to give it the once over. As usual he got it to sit then walk then tugged its ears. Then he stood up, put one hand on his chin and went:

"Mmmmmm, we may have a problem here"

Not the first time we'd heard that but as usual the old girl was on board.

"Really" She said "Can you help my poor Hugo?"

"I don't know yet Madam" He said.

Now that we hadn't heard before. Then just as we thought the vet was losing his thespian touch he said:

"I need a stool sample and I need one quickly"

He looked straight at me.

"Quickly man, it could make all the difference" He said.

This was great a whole new level of con was being born and by not exposing him we might as well have been in on it.

With my dignity up for grabs I took the silver shovel and brush from the fire place and went into the garden, leaving with me my whole security detail. None of us was doing a great job of keeping a straight face that day.

As soon as we got into the garden the laughter erupted and big Johnny G said:

"Give that here"

and took the silver ash pan and brush off me.

"You don't have to do that" I said thinking Johnny was doing me a favour and picking the tiny glove puppet stool for me.

"Yes I do" He replied

He walked across the perfectly laid and cut lawn to a very large pile of Alsatian shit that one of the guard dogs had left. Then proceeded to gently brush the mountain of crap onto the silver spade and garnish it with a sprig of Holly from a nearby Holly bush.

"There. Give him that" He said

I couldn't contain myself. None of us could but I couldn't resist the prank.

All of us trying desperately not to laugh and drying our eyes, returned to the lounge. Keeping the vet between myself and the old girl so she couldn't see me and my bright red face. I handed him the stool provided by one of the German killer dogs. I couldn't speak and the sound of my colleagues falling apart behind me wasn't helping.

"Thank you" He said "We may well be able to help this poor animal now"

I couldn't cope any longer. I left the room leaving the vet explaining his diagnosis, still with a straight face. Unbelievably the old girl never questioned how her poor Hugo could shit his own body weight in one sitting. How the vet kept up the facade is beyond me but after that the vet insisted on treating her precious canines Hugo and Farley alone.

* * *

Working for Tom turned out to be a great job in the end and not the nightmare I'd expected. He didn't have enemies as such, just people that wanted what he had. But the fact he would do all that he could to help us in our primary task which was to see him and his wife safe and well made the job easier and more enjoyable.

I only did the one six month tour for Tom. It had a few hairy moments but for the most part it was a very quiet tour. I received as all Tom's employees did a Christmas and Birthday card each year until 2004 when Tom died aged 71.

The Khmer Rouge

All the countries that form Indochina rely on as all Third World countries do some form of black market economy. African countries illegally use diamonds, gold, and mining concessions. Central American countries do it with cocaine and arms. Even now the countries of Eastern Europe use heroin, arms and human traffic to boost their failing economies and feed the people. All of these areas flood the sanctimonious western world with its worst political nightmares.

Normally any self respecting PMC stay's well away from material payments and sticks purely to cash. Well that's what they'll tell you. Truth be known a lot of those Companies take diamonds and gold as more than a down payment. Their in it for the money in whatever form it comes in, but aren't we all?

So when I was offered the job I never felt bad about backing an illegal logging outfit in Laos.

* * *

In 1999 Cambodia outlawed the Khmer Rouge. At the time they were no more than a fallen power that had become a well armed separatist problem for the country and an embarrassment to the new Government. The Khmer Rouge was lead by General Noun Penn at the time who in 1999 ordered the execution of two teenage American backpackers. The fabricated charge was espionage. It was the last straw for the new Cambodian Government looking to a future of international commerce. So laws were passed and it became illegal to be affiliated with the Khmer Rouge and the General was hunted down.

The problem here was; there was an estimated six million active Khmer Rouge in the country at that time. Many renounced their affiliation to the Khmer and just as many filled the prisons of the small third world country, but shit loads of them scattered off into the jungles of Laos, Thailand and Vietnam and this posed massive problems for the whole region.

For the most part they split up and went different ways, fearing capture and persecution. They lived as the Mong people of Laos did, nomadically.

An easy and abundant source of food, money and supplies for the now withering and separating Khmer Rouge tribes is the logging camps that are spread all over the jungles of South China and Indochina. They employ on average four hundred people per camp and there can be upwards of a hundred operational camps at any one point. Even though in the eyes of the world it's illegal the Governments of Indochina turn a blind eye because the industry feeds thousands of its people in the long run.

Well armed Khmer Rouge groups were hitting the logging camps at random two or three times a year. They'd steal everything and kill anyone who put up any kind of resistance and because of their logging camps position in the world opinion and politics the Government was unable to legally assist. The Lao people have a term for the Khmer Rouge bandits and directly translated it means; "Jungle Pirate".

* * *

Back then it was well above my pay grade to know how and why, but our Company got the job and had the people to do it.

Our sections objective was short, sweet and outrageously simple:

"Locate elements of the problem within a set time frame using onsite Intel, and Dispatch it"

Job done.

When we were finished if they wanted it done again the Company would supply the means again.

The team of eight I was assigned to was well trained and motivated purely by financial gain. All with the exception of one, Pagan, an Ex Royal Marine. He loved to hurt people and not always the bad people. I gave him the scar on his cheek a year earlier in Gloucester. He was a potential liability, I pointed this out to the Company but he came with the right background and nothing I could say could change the team at this late stage.

* * *

On civie street Pagan was working for a Firm from Manchester and he came on to Ian's patch (My Boss at the time) to do a number on a bloke that owed money. The same bloke owed Ian money and we ended up going together to address this guy's financial disposition. I had no problem with this the Firms from round the UK crossed paths all the time.

We got to the blokes front door and knocked, as soon as he dropped the latch I kick the door in on him. He was a big bloke and I didn't need him to get any momentum. He fell onto his back in the corridor. I walked over the top of him grabbed him by the hair and pulled him into his front room then started kicking his lights out. He knew why I was there.

I heard the front door slam followed by insane screaming from the kitchen. I left my victim in the foetal position half unconscious and moved to investigate.

I opened the kitchen door to see Pagan knocking the shit out of the bloke's girlfriend and he was doing a good job too she was bleeding everywhere. I grabbed him by the hair and the balls and smashed him off the kitchen side. Pagan's bit of a hard cunt and fought back real well. Too well. I pulled the blade I always carried in my belt and rammed it hard into his leg. It dropped him like a stone. I ceased the opportunity I put my knee over his stomach and lent over him pushing the blade into his face.

"What are you fuckin doing?" I hissed

"Let's do this later" He replied cool as a cucumber.

I wanted to cut his throat and he knew it, but he was like ice he didn't give a shit.

I got off him but never turned my back on him. Then regrettably I said:

"Go sort him out, I'll patch her up" I pointed to the front room.

I went over to the girl who'd taken a right beating, I handed her a tea towel and asked that all time arsehole question the question everyone asks someone in pain,

"Are you ok?"

She sat on chair by the door and sobbed, Pagan had broken at least her nose her cheek bones and her wrist. Everything was quiet in the room next door, too quiet. I opened the kitchen door to see Pagan stood by an open front door holding a make shift dressing to the knife wound on his face and using his other hand to push wadding onto the wound on his leg.

"Let's go" He said

I ignored him and walked into the lounge. Pagan had stamped our victim unconscious then broke both his arms against the wall. He was a right mess. I was pissed off to say the least. The idea was to shake him up a bit and get the money back. Pagan seemed to have other plans.

We left together, him with the mother of all limps and me seeing red. I drove. When I found the right spot I pulled the car up on the side of the road next to a field and got out.

"Get your fuckin arse out here." I said getting out the car.

I had one intention, beating the shit out of him for what he'd done to the girl.

"Its done now" He said calmly "Lets just go home"

I was dumb struck at his cold response. I wasn't going to get satisfaction here I was gonna have to wait. I got back in the car and drove straight to Ian's warehouse. When we got there we got out the car together and walked to Ian's Office, he wasn't there.

"Don't fuckin move" I said to Pagan. "I'll be back in two minutes."

I went for a piss with every intention of returning and finishing what I'd started by the field but when I got back Pagan was gone.

* * *

The first part of the job was to get to the logging camp we'd be basing ourselves from. We flew onto Viangchan the Nations Capital then got a light aircraft to Luang Prabang. Not quite a City more a large town in the middle of an endless Jungle.

From there it was black Cadillac's all the way, by that I mean; "We walked". A four day, hot bug invested tab got us where we were going. The jungle was so thick in places it was quicker to detour than fight through, thankfully map reading is a specialty of mine and wrong turns were kept to an absolute minimum. The small rivers were infested with leeches and we constantly had to check each other for their parasitic presences. You know you've got a good mate when he doesn't whinge about having to check you arse crack for parasites and he quickly becomes your best friend when he has to remove them.

The terrain was hard going, the area we were in had had a little rain, not monsoon rains but enough to make any muddy incline a right slippery mission and make small rivers run fast and dangerously unpredictable. Even though we moved through what was designated as a safe area we moved at a fully tactical pace maintaining tactical patrol patterns. If the Khmer knew we were coming it would take very little to ambush us at any one of a hundred vulnerable points over our chosen route.

On the afternoon of the forth day we hit the logging camp. I don't know what I expected. Maybe two smiling treefrogs chopping down trees with makeshift axes sharpened off whetstones and a horse and cart to pull logs out the way. Possibly a nailed together factory with a handful of workers in it, paid with rice and chick peas. I really can't say what I was expecting but I know it wasn't what was there.

As we approached the logging camp thought the jungle it just looked like another clearing but when we broke the tree line the clearing never ended. For as far as I could see the ground was clear. Nothing more than giant but short tree stumps and exposed earth and the occasional fire burning unwanted green litter. This was the true face of deforestation.

We made our way across the clearing for half an hour before reaching the main camp. It was a small town made of metal shipping containers and wooden huts. It had shops a bar, offices and homes. All made from abandoned metal containers with small wooden extensions. The trucks parked up were the biggest vehicles I'd ever seen. This definitely was not a small operation and as world wide illegal as the logging was this could not possibly go unnoticed. If this camp was one of many any modern day satellite could have picked this up as easy as picking up the Atlantic Ocean. It was an eye opener. It's safe to say that the local Government was not the only authority turning a blind eye.

Dave A went on ahead with our guide and into one of the offices to get details of what was to happen next. When he came back he had accommodation for us and orders for us all to stand down for the rest of the day as the guide for the next phase wasn't around. The accommodation was as simple as the rest of the settlement, we all fitted into one container, small hammocks had been hooked up under green mosquito nets for us and a long metal sink bolted to the side with a single cold water feed. After stowing our kit we set out exploring our new short term home.

During the down time the workers and their families wouldn't interact with us at all. That area of the world has certainly had it fill of foreign troops coming in and pushing their politics' and beliefs on them. Us stood there in full combats and armed to the teeth was a sour reminder of very hard times for some of these proud and gracious people. With great respect for their history and them we stayed out their way.

The next day the new guide turned up. This guy was to go with us on our patrols. Supposedly he could track the Khmer Rouge groups better than we ever could. His idea was to leave the logging camp from a different point each day, patrol the jungle in that area then come back to the camp at night. From the second he opened his mouth this was not a good plan and not one we would follow.

The clearing was so big in some points it took an hour to get to the tree line. That was far too much exposure, there was nothing to stop the Khmer engaging us from the dense jungle. We could be cut down before we got a round off. The patrols he had in mind were also to short. All we'd be doing is securing a small area. We weren't there to guard the camp or secure it. We were there to address the bigger issue not scare it off. We put our heads together and much to the guides dismay we came up with a different plan. The patrols would be three to five days long in order to cover more ground tactically, and instead of walking off the clearing we'd catch a lift from the out going dawn trucks. They could drop us off undetected at a different point each time on their way out. Then we could lie up till the sun was up and proceed from there.

This pissed the guide off no end. He didn't like the idea of staying out in the trees over night. That problem was easily solved by leaving him behind. Good guide or not, a man that didn't want to be there wasn't welcome. So we paid him well for his time and efforts in a hope he wouldn't turn grass, then I as politely as I could fucked him off.

We had good maps of the area and broke it down into plausible FUP's (Form Up Points) and patrol routes. Using geographical logic and a wealth of jungle warfare experience we located the more likely spots a nomadic tribe would set up, short and long term. Then pin pointed possible staging points around the logging camp that could be used for an all out attack. We also located good OP's they could use for recognisance and mined them. We were in full swing by the end of the second day.

After three weeks of recognisance patrols and finding very little. We change tactics. We would launch fighting patrols at likely target areas. This enabled us to branch further out. This we did with great success. On the first patrol we came across a small village our guide didn't know was there (lot of fuckin good he was). We chose not to enter the village but just watched it for twenty four hours. They had no weapons, none that threw bullets anyway and certainly no ability to attack the logging camp. So we left them as we found them. In peace.

The next two patrols provided evidence of recent settlement, whether by Khmer or Mong was impossible for us to tell. A week before we were due to go home we happened upon the beginnings of a new set up not far from a river I used as a navigation point on that side of the logging camp. It was a good days patrol from the camp and when we first spotted it there was a group of nine local male adults building it.

We set up two OP's and after only twelve hours my thoughts were confirmed. They were Khmer Rouge. Well armed and within striking distance of the camp.

JACKPOT.

They were still in the building stage and we'd established their route in and out. I chose to pull the guys back to the camp. Pagan was the only one to protest. Then I ordered the withdrawal of all the mines we'd used to boobytrap possible OP's overlooking the logging camp. Once again Pagan protested. We sat down that night to go over our next move, it was then Pagan really kicked off.

"We could have done em all today" He yelled at me.

"Sit down Pagan" Andy P said

"Why? cos you cunts have got no bottle" Pagan was getting angry.

Then Billy stood up and smacked him square in the jaw, Pagan hit the floor hard.

"Stay there and fuckin calm down" He said.

Pagan didn't move, he just sat there bleeding. Billy was as hard as they come, if you were gonna take him on you had to go, "All in"

"Why did we pull out?" Billy asked me "And why dismantle the traps?"

Billy and two of the others didn't have the experience the rest of us had but they'd done everything right.

"If in doubt, listen to those who know."

And they did, but now I needed to explain myself, so I sat them all down and did just that.

I pointed out that their makeshift camp wasn't finished so they weren't ready to start anything and that gave us very precious time to prepare. I pulled the mines back so;

A) They could recci the logging camp without hindrance, maintaining our time advantage and not alerting them to our presence.

And B) we could use the ordinance to cover our path when we withdrew after our assault. Then I pointed out the obvious; there was only nine people in their camp. They were only a forward party. So the main fighting force hadn't arrived yet and they were the targets we were really after.

"You're a clever fucker you know that" Billy said.

"I have my moments" I replied.

The rest of the night was spent refining the assault. Everyman knew his place, the kick off signals, his individual tasks, the routes in and out the RV's the ERV's. We went over the plan and the "Actions On" time and time again. We got weapons cleaned and ready, kit checked and ready for the off the next day.

The attack would begin on either Dave A's or my signal. We divided into two OP's. One on the south side of their set up and one and the west side. The western OP looked straight down their line of approach and the southern OP with the wider and better arcs of fire flanked it. We only put three guys in the western OP and the rest I had in the south. We sat for two days watching them finish the building of their new homes. Then at 1300 on the second day the main party arrived.

The final count as they entered our main killing area was; twelve women, thirty five well armed men, four Toyota's, two Landrovers, and a slack handful of small assorted livestock ranging from mules to chickens tagging along were it could. The bulk of their arsenal was on the back of the two front Toyota's that was easy to see and would be easily covered. Dave and I had expected a larger force but this lot had the means and undoubtedly the combat experience to hit the logging camp. Thirty five men! That's Company strength. In the past military miracles had been accomplished with those numbers, it was a legitimate target and they instantly became ours.

    I didn't want them to settle in and get organised. So as soon as the drivers left the vehicles and people started stretching and chatting I signalled Dave A, with that a 66 anti tank rocket launcher took out the rear vehicle. The ambush had been initiated, we hit them with everything we had.

    After an initial onslaught of high velocity rounds, grenades and two more 66's, Dave A's team gave accurate covering fire, as we left the relative safety of our ambush positions and started the full on assault Dave's team switched fire left into the trees as we hit them hard and fast from the flank.

    Rifle in the shoulder I advanced with the line, the two men right in front of me went down easy. A few shots to the chest and one shot centre of the face. Two men down.

    Most of them ran for cover behind their transport, their new houses, anywhere they could. A man went down to my left, thanks to Billy. The hardest part was not hitting the women in the commotion. Unlike the men that took cover most of the women stood and screamed covering their ears from the horrendous noise.

    Our advantage ended quickly and fire started to come back at us. It was no surprise, they were seasoned fighters some of these men had fought all their lives and they used their numbers well.

    The covering fire from Dave A's team resumed with frightening and welcome precision. My section divided as practiced, into two fire teams, one held the line the other advanced, then we switched. It was a loud, fast and violent fifteen minutes. Everyman making use of every shot. Using momentum to keep the fight in our favour and the accurate covering fire stopping their every escape. They had to fight or surrender. Not one of us stopping or doubting and believing in each other, we pushed them into the ground and forced a welcome surrender.

The incoming fire had stopped and was replaced by women screaming and men moaning. All the livestock with the exception of the chickens had disappeared. I witnessed the same thing in central Africa, what is it about chickens?

The covering fire stopped. Dave A's team would now adopt a sniper role to cover us. The women who we agreed that unless armed or endangering us directly were not to be harmed, ran to the aid of their men. Closing in on their destroyed position we took visual stock of each other, secured the area, then took it in turns to reload.

One by one those of our enemy that could stand, did, arms high and unarmed. The women continued to tend the wounded. I sent Charlie our medic to help them. I then called all the men that could move forward to the centre of their new but by now ruined settlement and made them lay on the floor face down and fully stretched out. Two other members of our team pulled them up in turn onto their knees and secured their hands and feet.

I went over to assess the situation in the main killing area. They had nineteen dead, one woman and eighteen men. One woman had been hit in the arm and five other men had non life threatening wounds. The rest we had in custody thirty yards away in the centre of the location.

I went back to the men in custody. After the others disarmed the dead and wounded, we could move freely knowing Dave A was watching. When I got back to the centre all the prisoners had been secured.

"Does any of you speak English?" I Said,

"Yes I do" came the reply in perfect English from a middle aged man to my right.

"You don't sound very local" I said "What's your name?"

"Vin Va Chi and I am local" he said. "I was educated in the UK then came back here to teach and ended up here"

"How many more are you?" I asked "Is there anyone else to come?"

"We're it" he said "There are more tribes but it's not safe to stay in large numbers anymore. What will you do to us?"

"Nothing" I replied "We'll destroy all your weapons and combat capability then let you go"

Then from nowhere Pagan said:

"You fuckin what, the job's to kill the fuckin lot of em"

"It's not happening" I said

Then trying to avoid open confrontation with Pagan, I asked him to watch the prisoners with the others. As I walked back to the wounded to check on Charlie I signalled Dave to join us. As I got to Charlie a single short was fired from behind me. I ran back the few yards to the centre of the location to see Vin Va lying dead on the floor. Pagan had executed him.

The two guys with him stood stunned and staring. As Pagan pointed at the head of the next man in line, I swung my rifle hard and caught him smartly on the side of his head and for the second time that week he hit the floor like a bag of shit. The side of his head split like an orange and he went out cold. I took his weapons off him and used the plastic cuffs I had to restrain his hands behind his back.

Dave A arrived just in time to see this all happen.

"Just to make it clear gents, I'll shoot the next man to try this" Dave A, said

Dave A and I were thinking exactly the same thing. Yes our primary objective was to eradicate the problem, but these people had lost the day, their numbers had been cut considerably in battle and those left over were now in our care.

We are soldiers, not murderers.

We would destroy their arsenal and any capacity they had to attack the logging camps using the ordinance we had. Then these people were free to tend to their wounded and bury their dead and that's exactly what happened.

We made our way back to the logging camp lifting out our anti personal mines as we went. I had Pagan kept cuffed the whole way, I knew if he got that chance he'd do me and Dave in a heart beat. Once back at the camp the injuries to his head kept him in the aid post there for the last few days. Dave had him physically secured and a guard on him the whole time. We discussed the possibility of handing him over to the local authorities, but the idea came to nothing more than chat. At the end of the day he was one of us, that being so he was our problem. Once back at the airport and in civie rig the guys refused to have anything to do with him. The journey home was a long lonely one for Pagan.

When we got back to the UK, we asked for an enquiry in to the incident. The Company informed us that because Vin Va Chi wasn't a British National any action taken had to be taken by the Government of Laos but they realistically weren't going to prosecute a man for something they wanted done. Thankfully our End Ex reports didn't go unnoticed. Pagan never worked for our Company or any other private military organisation in Britain again and last I heard, he was doing seven years in HMP Highgate for intent.

Banged Up Abroad

Before there can be any kind of significant movement by Private Military Troops a lot of time and money is spent dedicated to the gathering of Intelligence and sucking up to the British Foreign Office. Thankfully I never had anything to do with the latter politics not being my strong point. But the gathering of Intelligence had very much become a career speciality of mine.

I was asked to go down to our Offices on the Kings Rd in London for a brief on a job that had come up in Central America. Not a place I really wanted to be after the last time. The Company knew precisely how I felt about working for the Americans. To me they're a parasitic race that will do anything for personal political gain and they're not to be trusted. I've had dealings with them twice and twice it nearly cost me my life.

This job however had fuck all to do with them though, so I was in. I loved to work the jungle and Sean the guy I was going with had been a good friend of mine for a very long time.
Like all jobs the overall objective was simple, the execution of the task however, well that was never as easy as it sounded in the brief.
All the Central American countries for as long as I can remember have been constantly under international pressure to sort out their massive illegal drug export business's. Because of this the fact that nearly all the Central American countries have been on the brink of war over boarder disputes is constantly overlooked.
With all the regular troops and special police units, legitimate drugs researchers and research teams from National Geographic, not to mention the legal and illegal logging that goes on it's a wander there's room for the multi billionaire drug Cartels.

Thankfully, this time they weren't our concern either. Our job was pure recognisance and risk assessment. All Intel to be forwarded directly to the Government of Ecuador via a contact I'd met and worked with before, which suited Sean and I down to the ground. Sean had been with me in Venezuela and had no time for the Yanks either. Doing things this way almost guaranteed they had no involvement, with us anyway.

Sean and I left the Kings Road offices after a full brief of the task and our travel details. The objective was simple:

> Land in Quito, "Recci and Assess" a logistical land route from Esmeraldas to Tulcan on the Colombian boarder, advise on what it would take to secure it, then pass all Intel onto the relevant Government contact.
> SIMPLE

It meant spending approximately two weeks in the jungle, but as tourist not as a tactical Unit and that was great. We'd be able to have fires and take all the comfy kit. It was money for old rope and we were both looking forward to it. With two weeks before we had to leave Sean and I used the time to train, the job wasn't going to be hard compared to what we'd done in the past but it was by no means going to be physically easy. We got ourselves up to Hereford booked into the Marlot B&B and each day drove off to the Brecon Beacons and tabbed our arses off every week day for the two weeks we had.

We only trained on the weekdays because Hereford's great on the piss and we'd both spent lots of time there and had lots of friends, so a great weekend out was guaranteed.

The two weeks flew by and in no time Sean and I were sat at Gatwick Airport waiting to fly to Ambato then on to Quito. Once there the job went smoothly to start with. We were met by our Government liaison and he took care of the hard work, finding Visa's, transportation and movement permits. Some of the areas we needed to go onto were restricted for reasons that ranged from environmental control to areas of jungle being off limits to tourist because of the kidnap threat and you needed permits and papers to move in those areas. I don't think for one minute a kidnapper would give two shits for the paperwork, but we still had to have it.

On the second week our liaison never turned up at our RV in San Lorenzo to give us our new visas and a general update. We found out later that his car broke down and he couldn't get another till the following day. Regrettably, we didn't see not having a visa as such a big deal as we worked directly for the Government and surely they'd issue us with one when it was needed. We had a schedule for the mission and chose to carry on and not wait for the liaison. He knew where we were, he could always come find us if it was that important. Failing that we'd go and see him in his office when we got back to Quito.

With the job done in just over two weeks we headed back to Quito to meet our liaison, hand over the Intel and get home. Our Government liaison's office was not too far from the place we hired our Landrover from. We parked up, handed back the keys and decided to walk the short distance back to the office. When we got there everyone in the office had gone for lunch and we had no passes for access so we ended up having to wait.

Sean and I picked a small fast food place on the edge of the city square and decided to stop for lunch. In the same second we sat down Sean was arm locking some bloke, bending him over the table next to us and clobbering him. I didn't know what was going on. The cook and a few waiters came flying out of the kitchen and all hell broke loose.

Sean had caught the man now supporting a broken wrist, picking his pocket and the staff of the food joint piled on thinking we were drunken tourists. In no time at all the local plod were all over us and less than twenty minutes later the pick pocket Sean and myself were in the local nick.

We explained to the station commander who we were and what we were doing but when Pedro (I don't know if that was his name, but it's what we called him when he wasn't around) asked for proof, all we could show him was out of date visas. This just put us in more shit.

It was a Friday and unbeknown to us at the time the Station emptied its cell's on a Friday into the local prison to make way for the busy weekend. Pedro took our expired visas and said he'd look into it. Whether Pedro knew it or not while he was looking into it Sean and I were being shipped off on a bus with three wheels to a prison five hours away in the middle of the jungle.

Santa de Mingo prison was a shit hole. Its home to over five hundred hardened criminals, doing time for everything from drug dealing to kidnap and torture to mass murder. I think Sean and I had more teeth between us than the rest of the prison population put together. They were however good enough to put us in a room together. We still had to share it with sixty other stinking, heavily tattooed, Spanish speaking psycho's, but at least we were together.

The prison itself was a square U shape three stories high, sealed at the top with a twenty foot chain link fence, then the whole lot was surrounded by a perimeter fence twenty feet high and a good forty meters from the walls, with lookout posts on each corner. Quite a simple set up, but the guards had a; "zero tolerance for escape policy", that meant they would shoot you the second they thought you were gonna make a break for it.

The exercise yard was in the centre and could be accessed from two doors on each wing. All the windows had bars and the external doors were made from thick steel, but inside the prison it was just walls and door ways, no gates or bars separated the rooms or the wings for that matter.

The building was old, the walls cheaply white washed and plaster fell off regularly, the rooms on the top floor flooded in the heavy rains and the plumbing, well it was as old as the building. The toilets were rows of long drops on the ground floor, no cubicles, you just squatted and made polite conversation with the gringo taking a shit next to you. Each floor had showers sometimes they worked sometimes they didn't, sometimes the water was clear other times it was a rusty brown colour, either way they were more likely to give you tetanus than clean you. The bedrooms were simply large rooms with bunk beds in rows about a metre apart, each room housed about fifty five to sixty inmates. There was no bedding, no toilet roll and no running drinking water. Overall it wasn't that bad, I'd stayed in worse.

The Prison ran very much day to day, what was tolerated on Monday you could get a beating for on Tuesday. The guards walked around turning constant blind eyes to the drug abuse and punishment beatings dished out by the cons and two guards had openly set up shop in the exercise yard selling contraband, none of that bothered me though, I just rolled with each day.

My main concern was food and where we got it from. There didn't seem to be a mess hall of any kind or any cookhouse, I joked with Sean saying:

"Maybe we have to catch kill and eat the weaker guys".

He didn't see the funny side. Sean's main concern was being gang raped in the shower. I told him; if it's coming its coming, do what you can if and when. Sean wasn't comforted.

The food came in on a truck once a day. The prisoners surrounded the beaten up old wagon and literally fought for a single helping. The first day I got nothing I wasn't sure of the rules. That didn't happen again. I was more than happy to fight for food, of all the reasons to fight in a place like this, of all the reasons to get stabbed in my sleep, food made more sense than the others.

Sean was on a downer from the minute we arrived. We tried to put our case to the guards but they just mugged us of saying we'd be collected soon. A week later I was beginning to doubt they'd even looked into it.

There was a definite rank structure in De Mingo, lead by large street gangs and drugs Cartels. Tattoos generally told them apart. There was nothing that couldn't be got if you had the price or connection. Whores came in daily, drugs were everywhere and some of the prisoners even had guns. Pistols stuck in their belts for all to see and again the guards turned a blind eye.

Stabbing a man in the back, chest or stomach carries an instant charge of attempted murder. So people with a grievance went round stabbing their victims in the face. Half the prison had received some kind of facial trauma at some point. We bumped into a European guy in there called George. He was in for drug smuggling and wasn't getting out any time soon. He too had some great facial scars. Sean bought up the worrying subject of being raped. (He seemed consumed by the fear of it) George told Sean not too worry too much about it. If it was going happen he could little to stop it, but generally he said "the Spiks believe male rape to be a North American black thing."

Sean asked me one day:

"If it looks like I might get raped, would you stand by me in the fight?."

"Fuck off" I said "If in the unlikely event it did happen, you'd get over it. No point us both having our arse's stretched"

As much as I was joking this didn't fill Sean with confidence. Depression seemed to be hitting Sean. I couldn't work him out, we'd been in tighter spots than this. This was a holiday compared to some of the shit we'd endured in the past.

Two weeks had passed and still no sign of Pedro. Prison life was largely routine. Get up, wait for food, fight for food, walk around the compound, go to bed.

I played a lot of volleyball with the other cons. At first I volunteered to join in, after a while they'd look for me to play. Prison volleyball is a rough game, I spent just as much time pushing and shoving my own team as I did the front row of the opposition, you have to be very alert in the front three as anything vaguely ball shaped is fair game, this includes the human head. I lost everyday at arm wrestling to whoever was on the table, I've always sucked at it, I don't know why I bothered. Wrestling was popular, I won more than I lost thanks to a well established Judo background and to my surprise the other inmates didn't seem to mind, not once was I threatened after a win, if anything it did Sean and I good that I won a few. I kept my moral high by keeping busy. I also made a point each day of pestering the guards to help us find Pedro.

But all the time Sean was getting worse, I couldn't get him to involve himself, I tried to get him to read a book or play chess in the yard, anything to give his mind a temporary escape but he wouldn't and it was starting to affect his health. He was losing weight at a rapid rate and hadn't eaten for a few days.

One day I got into a fight and not in the food ruck either. It was over a simple thing. A guy stole one our chess pieces for his own board. I say "Our" board, I played chess with the same old gringo everyday. He didn't speak a word of English but the rules for chess are universal so I spent a good three hours everyday on the chess board with this old bloke.

I gave the Bishop thief a good right hook and when he went down I took a step back. As my target stood up Sean hit him from nowhere, I thought he was gonna kill him, it was all I could do to get Sean off him. Sean was losing it. I was worried for my friend. Even more so now that he'd made an enemy.

The only book I could find in the library in English other than the Bible was a science fiction book call "Enemy Mine". It's about a human and an alien stuck on a planet together during a human alien war. Not a particularly educational book, but good brain bubble gum all the same.

I sat Sean down everyday and read to him. At first he wasn't interested and I couldn't get him to sit still long enough to read to him. I had to all but force him to listen, it was as if I had to re-establish his trust, it was very confusing for me we'd known each other for years. After a few days he did sit and I would stutter though the story, then we'd discuss different aspects of the book. After a few more days we had our own little book club going.

It was the only thing I could think of to put Sean's mind anywhere but in that prison. After a time I could read it from cover to cover in about two hours and Sean sat though it everytime.

I don't know if it had anything to do with the reading but after a week Sean seemed to come right, he'd come and watch me play chess with my old gringo, I even taught Sean to play. But more importantly he was eating and sleeping again.

Three weeks into our incarceration God dangled a carrot I couldn't reach. I was playing chess with my gringo and I saw Pedro walking on the other side of the fence. Leaving the game I ran at full pelt across the yard. When I got to the fence I started banging on it to get his attention. He stopped and looked at me as if I was a mad man. Then after long seconds he threw his arms in the air and said:
"Hey English, What are you doing here? I gave orders for you to be released"
"When?" I said
"The same day I arrested you" Pedro replied
"Can you get us out now?" I was eager to push the point
"No problem" He said "I'll be right back English"
Then he walked off. I ran to find Sean and tell him the news. I wish I hadn't. Sean got so excited he burst into tears and collapsed on the floor. He'd had a hard time with this God forsaken place, I never fully understood why.

It was ten more days before Pedro came back. In that time Sean went from bad to worse. He stopped eating again and got into petty fights with anyone for any reason. I backed him every time even when he got angry towards me. He doubted I'd even seen Pedro, he said I'd made it up to get at him. He was almost delusional. After a week I started to doubt myself, then I took a smack from a guard I was losing my temper with when trying to push our case. Sean was not himself. I thought it was a miracle one of us hadn't been stabbed because of his behaviour. His biggest fear was being raped, mine was going home blind in one or both eyes.
I found out later from one of the guards that released us, our guardian angel was the old gringo I played chess with, he'd made it clear Sean wasn't to be touched. We never even spoke we just played chess, I never knew the old man had that sort of clout but I'm thankful he did and I'm glad I can play chess.

After thirty eight days in Santa De Mingo Prison Sean and I were released and picked up by our Government liaison. Sean never said a word all the way back to Quito. When he did speak later that night after a glass of wine and a meal it was to give me a very unnecessary and tearful apology.

"Fuck off" I said "Lets get another drink"

He smiled straightened himself out and followed me into a bar, there we drank like Lords at the Governments expense. I never expected an apology from Sean and I didn't want one. It never crossed my mind to let him go it alone in Santa De Mingo nick, not even when I was warned he was on the right path to getting us both killed. When the veiled threat came I violently pointed out to the guy that if he had ideas that way he'd better make it count, as the opportunity for a second chance would never come.

I think Sean being so down gave me strength to do more for myself and the two of us, I do know for sure I never would have left his side. We went in together and we were coming out together, dead or alive but together.

The Ecuadorian Government was happy with the work we did do and paid well. It was also completely unsympathetic to our ordeal. We'd been caught in a Central American legal administration loop hole. I know now that if I'd had a hundred US dollars in my pocket the whole thing would never have happened. That said no one was to blame directly.

I never pushed Sean as to why he found it so hard, it didn't matter we were out now life could go on. A week later we returned to the UK and after a full debrief from the Company and the standard "You silly bastards" speech from the Foreign Office we let ourselves loose on the great City of London for a night out. This whole episode had the potential to go so many other ways, both of us are thankful it didn't.

KEEP YOUR CHIN UP

Russ Gowans

ABU SAYYAF

The events of November 2003 could and really should have their own book. It was quite possibly the most frightening and violent time of my life. It took a lot of reasoning and self control to come back from it. It also has a lot to do with the way I view certain elements of the world today. But this book is about my life and not any one aspect of it. Although a horrific time and a time probably best forgotten I hold the experience close to me and use it to give me strength against the obstacles and problems that life throws at me. I've used this chapter to glance over them.

* * *

The Regional Government of Sabah in collaboration with the Philippines Government under President Arroyo was by no means a new client to our Company. They paid well and on time. What more can a man ask for? The work always varied but it was always interesting and challenging. For the most part it was "Recognisance and Training", but as the world terrorist threat thickened the work branched out into consultancy and specialist armed response in support of local forces.

A paramilitary group called ABU SAYYAF was and still is a massive problem to the region as a whole. In 2003 Intelligence suggested the Terrorist Organisation had base camps on several small Islands and a main camp was suspected to be on an island north east of Sabah called Basilan with more in depth positions on the island of Palawan to the north east. Our target at this time was on Basilan.

The mission objective was straight forward:

Located Abu Sayyaf Camps and Outposts in the area with a view to locating a Mr Gailb Andang (a senior Commander within the group). Report all Locations and Movements and give detailed reports of Enemy numbers and Armed Assault Capability.

Leaving the coalition of the Philippine and Sabah Governments to formulate and execute a plan that suited their needs.

It might sound simple but that's a lot of work and a lot of ground to cover even for hand picked professionals with what we could only hope would be up to date Intelligence.

* * *

My first task was to put together a team of guys that best suited the job, but despite the abundance of out of work troops in the UK, that's not easy to do well. I put word out through the usual channels that we needed Infantry men with experience in Jungle Warfare and Long Range Patrolling. Within a week I was mobbed with applications, at least five hundred of them. For the most part they were good professional guys that applied with good experience and water tight references and if I had the funds I could have used them all to rule the world.

But it's the wonnabes that make for the best reading, the guys that sat on their arses doing nothing in the Army and still believed they were the Muts Nuts, the same guys that went back to their home towns on leave and told other peoples war stories in the local pub, surrounded by his old school mates that worked in local warehouses, each of them hanging on every word of every lie. One bloke from Hemel Hempstead's covering letter for his application read:

"From Royal Green Jackets (RGJ) Support Company,
I went to RGJ Snipers, I didn't need the course cos
could already shoot,
Then I done one tour of Northern Ireland where I did Special Ops,
I got out after three years cos it wasn't challenging enough and
there was too many rules"

Instantly, this guy seemed too good to be true. Was this bloke that good that he'd had a star career in just three years and found the world of Special Operations so boring that he'd left the British Army in search of more challenging goals?

I didn't think so! and neither did anyone else in the Company and after two quick phone calls the truth was found. He had served in Northern Ireland and did start in Support Company, but spent all his time on Guard Duty due to his lack of social control and general lack of professional ability.

He wasn't the only Walter Mitty, there were loads of em from all manner of Bullshit backgrounds, but he's the only one I met in person. It was in a night club in Watford "A lack of social control" they said. That was true enough, everyone liked a good time and we all act up a bit at some point, but this bloke came under the "complete wanker" tag. I was thankful for the vetting process we had and my ability to spot a Bullshitter a mile away.

After three months of endless selection, interviews and training a competent and confidant team came together. I'd worked with most of the guys myself in the past, I wouldn't say I got on really well with all of them socially, but the men I chose were the best men for the job and knowing them I knew I could rely on them, not just under fire but just as importantly during the down time. Those I hadn't worked with came highly recommended by respected and tested sources, but all the men came from a British Special Forces background.

The team consisted of ten men. All Jungle Warfare Instructors from Infantry backgrounds and all specialists in one area or another. We had three comms specialists, two medics, two combat engineers and out of the ten, four were sniper trained, all had a detailed knowledge of the other man's specialist ability and all had worked operational long range reconnaissance.

After three months of recruiting and training we had a sound and solid team. No bitching backstabbers, no one man Rambo's, but a good "One in, All in" team and unbeknown to us all at the time, we needed to be.

The next task was to get into threatre, meet the client's appointed liaison and get started.

It was November in the UK and freezing cold. Although it wasn't the hot season in the Philippines it was a lot hotter than the UK. So when we met the Government liaison the first thing I asked for was some time for the team to acclimatize. As it was the client needed time to set up our communications and frequencies anyway and that gave us a week. Not as much time needed to properly acclimatize but more than I was expecting. The guys were all physically and mentally able and I knew it wouldn't be too much trouble.

In those seven days we never stood idol. Paddy took us for PT every morning and we each took it in turns to lecture on our specialist areas and share tricks of the trade with each other. We also used the time to perfect our patrolling and "Action on" Drills.

When the time came our FUP (form up point) was another very small island to the south of Basilan. When we arrived by helicopter the night before our insertion our equipment and boats were already there and set up. As was, a small Sabah regular Army contingent. We spent the rest of the day and that night checking weapons and equipment ready for the off just before dawn the next day.

The boat trip was under an hour. We had three boats to carry ten men and kit, it was a squeeze, but we got it all in. We approached the south shore of Basilan at dawn the sun seemed to rise slowly, it was gonna be a very hot day. We braced ourselves and hit the beach, the landing went like clockwork. We pulled the boats off the beach and hid them deep in the jungle tree line all within minutes of landing. Then we set up a small fully tactical camp with an admin and sleeping area and a mined perimeter. This would be manned by Milly and Paddy while the rest of us patrolled. We gave it the call sign "Costa Rica" after the beach resort. It was a great place to store excess rations and ammo and also set up comms. This would be our safe area. As soon as we had set Costa Rica up, we kitted up ready to walk the trees.

Eight of us left the sanctuary of Costa Rica at 0830. The sun was up but at that time it wasn't too hot or humid. Following given Intelligence our first objective was a ridge line five miles north of our position. It took no time at all to settle into our patrol disciplines, allowing us to move swiftly. Once at the ridge we followed it east another mile. There, sooner than expected we encountered what we suspected to be Abu Sayyaf for the first time. It was a result. Realistically we could have walked round the jungle for weeks and not found a thing.

The guys moved well, no one spoke, it was all hand signals. Everyone knew what everyone else was doing or would do given any situation, we moved in almost complete silence. It's always a pleasure to work with true professionals.

The small outpost we now approached never knew we were coming. The section went to ground and Sean and I moved forward to a better vantage point.

A small contingency of eleven men, living in tents, they were lightly armed and well fed, with no apparent leader. We set up an OP (Observation Point) in a slightly better position and watched them for the rest of that day and night. At dawn the following day we moved on as silently as we arrived having gathered the Intel required. The small outpost never even knew we were there.

The next objective took us a lot deeper into the jungle island. Everyman on the team was at the top of his game. We now had established enemy to our rear and imminent contact in front. The patrolling had to be meticulous and silent. After an hour we stopped for water, checked map references and confirmed comms. All was well back at Costa Rica.

The day went on, patrolling one hour at a time then resting up to rehydrate and check maps and comms. We weren't expected to reach the next target area until the following day. As night fell on the second day we set up a harbour area and took the watch in turns through the long hot night. Off the ground and under a mozzy net, you're wet, you sweat and you powder your feet every chance you get, just a small part of the jungle routine.

At dawn on the third day, we got up, washed and had breakfast all in complete silence. Then got together once again to check routes and confirm comms with Costa Rica. All still being well we chose to follow a small stream so far, then cut east to our next objective. The jungle was thick and the stream would make navigation easier. Like the previous day we patrolled an hour then drank and did all the usual checks.

Around noon on that third day all hell broke loose. We were ambushed from an incline on our right flank by what was obviously a numerically superior force.
Instantly, everyman jack went to work. Every one of us knew we had to hit them hard and hopefully in their main killing group. To run forward or turn back would only result in us being cut to ribbons by the ambush cut off groups. Two areas of this attack we could destroy with ease once the back of their offensive was broken.
As an infantry section we immediately turned to our rights and fought onto the incoming fire. Our enemy was a hell of a lot closer than it should have been and it would be to their down fall. They were less then twenty meters away. Slightly uphill. I didn't need to give fire control orders, none of us did. From the moment we turned into them as long as they were firing we could see em clear as day and pick them off with surprising ease.
Their Ambush was a sham from the start, the bulk of their fire was ineffective and they screamed and shouted like Celts attacking a Roman Legion. Always on the lookout for the man giving the orders so as to put him to bed first, I gave up after a few seconds, it was impossible to tell who had control on that side. As we gained ground Sean and I came shoulder to shoulder.
"I nearly fuckin shit myself" He shouted.
It was the first time anyone had called out anything I could understand. Then all of a sudden the inaccurate rounds coming our way stopped. We kept taking ground. Inch by inch, yard by yard, quicker now that the incoming rounds were at an almost standstill.
Why had it stopped?
As I came up on the enemy position the reason looked me straight in the face. The four soldiers in front of me and Sean had

all run out of ammo at the same time and so had to reload at the same time. Leaving nobody to give covering fire for this segment of the ambush. Sean and I literally walked up to them and took full advantage.

With a firm foothold on the main killing group, dividing and concurring the rest of the ambush was a matter of time. We divided into four man fire teams and systematically took them apart. Over the next fifteen minutes we took day and took prisoners. Our two fire teams reorganised just past their position coming together as one again. There we reloaded and dealt with our teams injuries, the largest of which was our radio.

Looking back over the ambush sight I could see why they were so close. They were after ambushing a small trail that could be seen clearly about a hundred metres away. But they went off as soon as they saw us. Inexperience, stupidity, panic. Who's to say?
All the prisoners were cable tied and secured and the twelve dead were wrapped in their own ponchos ready for extraction. Anywhere else in the world I could have argued things went like clockwork and I could have done there but for one very unforeseen issue. The troops that ambushed us, the troops we had just engaged and overcome, the troops twelve of which we'd just killed, weren't, Abu Sayyaf. They were AMERICAN regulars. United States Marine Corps "USMC". This was going to be a very big problem and every one of us knew it.

Their Commander and 2ic being dead I found their Radop and asked him some very important questions. The first of which was:
"What the fuck are you doing here?"
As we reorg'd that was one of two questions on everyone's lips. The other one being:
"How the fuck do we get out of this?"
But we never asked them that one.
The young radio operator gave me his number rank name and Unit. I explained who we were and what we were doing there hoping

he'd lighten up and talk to us but he never did. None of them did. They all believed they were POW's, and acted accordingly.

I called the rest of the team together for a bit of a hurried Chinese Parliament and we went through the limited options we had and then glanced over options we could create. Basically what we came up with was:

-Kill em all, and leave the way we came. Who would know?
-Surrender to um and hope to get a lift home.
-Or let them live, leg it back the way we came. Leave them to explain and hope we get away.

After reviewing our maps and theirs and working quickly through notes we found on their dead Section Commander we deduced that if they did get a "Contact Report" out, and they more than likely did they couldn't get any close support to that location for at least twenty five minutes, provided they had nothing already closer to hand. Air support was almost imminent but we could lose ourselves easily under the thick jungle canopy. With all this in mind we quickly formulated and executed a working plan.

Sean and I secured the remaining prisoners all the time talking to each other and giving the Yanks false Intel. Johnny and Terry took the working parts out of every weapon they had and threw them deep into the bush, then their radio was taken by Taff and Neal down to the trail and booby trapped. Not in a way to kill but just to delay. They would need that radio but we didn't need them getting it too soon. With everything in play and the Yanks secure. We bailed.

We had little or no time to lay false trails and booby traps and in all honesty we didn't want to kill anyone else, (as late as that ideal was,) any damage limitation we could lay down now was good news. The rolling idea was to go out the way we came. Leaving nothing for the USMC to follow. We'd take our path as close as we could to the outpost we OP'd on the way in so any hunter force that did follow us would engage the ABU SAYYAF Cell, hopefully giving us time to lay low and extract ourselves by boat at night.

We got the head start we wanted. It was an astonishing six hours before the first helicopter flew overhead. Not a chance in hell it would see us at the speed it was doing. But they kept coming, we counted seven in total. How many troops were here? That seemed a shit load more support than a jungle patrol would normally receive even from the worlds most expensive Army.

Our plan seemed to be going well. We kept good discipline never panicking and maintaining a good speed. That night we laid up in a harbour area not far from the one we'd used the night before, there we licked our wounds, cleaned our weapons and ate. I felt sick to the stomach, the fact that the Americans were there meant shit was gonna follow us all the way home.

At sparrows fart the next day we moved on in silence once again. The day went to plan, we left no trail and bought our pace to an almost standstill to get within a few meters of the outpost. Once we'd cleared their position we picked the pace right up to get along the ridge we'd followed on the way in.

We stopped short of Costa Rica. Not having had any comms with them for the last twenty four hours made it impossible to know if they'd been compromised. It was decided that Taff and Neal would go forward and assess the situation, the rest of us would lie up and wait.

Neal returned less than an hour later. It was all bad news.

The rest of us followed him to a vantage point were Taff was waiting. From Taff's would be OP we could see a stretch of beautiful tropical beach at least two miles long and on it was what looked like the whole fuckin US Marine Corps. Landing craft, helicopter support units and worst of all for us, Navy. Worst because that was our only way out.

In the middle of it all the news got worse, our boats had been pulled out onto the beach, all our comms equipment and everything we left behind was all under armed guard including Milly and Paddy. Both of my troopers were on their knees with black hoods covering their heads. The guards with them armed not just with guns but with batons as well. Even from our vantage point it was obvious my men had been though the mill already.

We pulled back to talk and tried and get an angle on the situation. To come up with options and find answers to questions.

"How long can we evade capture?" Taff said

"It doesn't fuckin matter" I said "We're going nowhere without Milly and Paddy.

Could we rescue them? How could we get off the island? The questions came thick and fast and the answers didn't seem to come at all. After nearly three hours of quiet debate we unanimously chose to join Paddy and Milly, it was the one option that kept coming up.

Even if we could get off Basilan none of us was prepared to leave them behind. Eight of us with all the ammunition in the world couldn't openly take on what was in excess of a Battalion of men and armour and if a rescue attempt for our Brothers in Arms was successful, we'd most certainly be hunted down and slaughtered while extracting.

Like Terry pointed out, surely if we handed ourselves in the Americans would have to contact our client and they could vouch for us. As for the ambush, they engaged us and came second that's not our fault.

That said, something told me it was going to be our problem.

With the votes in we agreed to hand ourselves in right then. Leaving our weapons and equipment at the new OP. We walked down to the beach, hands in the air and with a good gap between each one of us. We walked eight abreast towards their sentry at the end of their set up.

As expected, when he saw us he started panicking and yelling all sorts of shit and in no real order:

"Get down, halt, stop, stand still, Sergeant Come quick"

It came flooding out. We all stopped where we were about fifty meters from his position. We'd been seen. Now the trick was not to get shot by some trigger happy Yank mourning the death of a comrade he never really knew. All of us put our hands on our heads then dropped onto our knees and calmly waited for the chaos to begin. As the Marine Corps Platoon ran up the beach towards us I couldn't help but second guess our decision.

In no time at all we were surrounded by that typical American overkill. Breathing hard they smothered us. I waited for someone to say something.

"Fuck, don't move" Neal said "If they all start shooting from there they'll kill each other,"

We all started laughing at Neal's ability to point out the obvious, there must have been at least twenty men around us all stood no more than three yards away. Pointing their M16s as if they were afraid that if they did open fire the bullet wouldn't reach us from any further away.

As funny as we found it our nervous humour was short lived. It sent them into a manic football hooligan type frenzy. In the same breath as Neal's comment, we were head bagged violently and pushed to the floor. That's when the first beating started.

It was all boots. My hands were still free at this point. I grabbed at legs and kicked back. Someone grabbed the side of my headbag and pulled me backwards to the floor. The kicking continued, I felt ribs on my left side break and was lucky not to lose my front teeth. The heel of someone's boot found my nose and my right cheek bone. More heels found my stomach and chest and solid toes hacked away at my ribs. It was short and brutal and over within a couple of minutes.

When the kicking stopped I was restrained, as the inevitable heavy duty cable ties bound my wrists together behind my back. The hood stayed on and was tightened at the neck. At this point I wasn't that worried I'd taken worse beatings, it wasn't even as bad as I'd expected.

I could hear Taff yelling abuse then with a thud that almost turned my stomach he was silenced.

I was dragged backwards across the sand for a few minutes. Then put in a kneeling position and my head pushed forward into the sand. I couldn't hear the others and as the rush of adrenaline subsided the stiffness and pain of the stress position kicked in. I could taste blood in my mouth and feel my eye's swelling up from the beating. I could feel the chill of the evening as the sun set, but that chill was replaced by the fear that came with the tide licking at the back of neck.

I could understand the hiding from the troops. The twelve men that died in the ambush would have had friends in the Corps and feeling and tempers would be running high.
But the stress position and the occasional boot on the back of my neck pushing me further into the sand didn't make any sense. It must have been an hour by now. My ribs and neck were killing me and the water was now in my ears and in my nose. Everytime I went to move I was stopped. I was struggling to control my fears and I could feel fear taking hold of me. I let my mind wonder to my team, how were they all holding up?

The water got higher and I was holding my mouth at a funny angle to breath. Once again I tried to move and once again I was stopped. It was getting cold now and my body started to shiver. Then the water got so high I couldn't keep it out my mouth any longer. I gagged and choked then shook my body violently to try and change position, but the boot on the back of neck stood firm as did the knees in my ribs. Every time I made a little room someone would grab my restrained hand and set me straight back. The salt water and sand was everywhere, my nose ears mouth and now the back of my throat. I tried swallowing and holding my breath. Nothing was working. I tried to speak but the water stopped me. I felt my whole body panic. I had sand in my eyes. Breathing now was impossible the water was over my chin. I wasn't getting any air what so ever. My lungs felt like they were ready to burst, tried again to kick and wriggle, the water in my lungs made me gag, my head know completely submerged. I started to panic. As I did I was pulled up out the water by the back of my hood. I instantly tried to take a deep breath but was greatly inhibited by the thick black hood. I tried again and again to catch a breath but my head was plunged mercilessly back into to cold salt water.
Time and time again this happened, never quite being allowed to take a full breath then held to the point of drowning. To make things easier for my torturers they pulled me out onto the break and

keeping my feet from the sea bed, they continued. I fell into unconsciousness a least twice only to be revived to relive more of the same hell.

I don't know how long it went on for but when they finally finished I was dragged up the beach and tied to a fuel drum. Legs out in front of me arms stretched out behind me around the rusting oil drum. It was night now and cold. Very cold. I was too exhausted too be scared and I drifted of into a deep dreamless sleep.

A searing pain woke me the first time. Someone kicked me in the ribs that had broken earlier. They said nothing the whole point was to keep me awake I knew this but I was fucked and within a few minutes I drifted off again. The same thing happened moments later and went on all night. I was so tired.

At one point I woke up being moved into a different position. I was dragged by my ankles, I kicked and wriggled but I was easily subdued with a swift kick to the balls. I wasn't dragged far before we stopped then my feet were strapped to a horizontal wooden pole about two feet off the floor. Hands still behind my back, hood still tightly over my head I was shitting myself. I knew what the pole was for, I'd seen it used as corporal punishment in the Yemen and after the vulgar use of water torture the evening before I knew these animals would do it.

I'd never been so scared in my life as I was at that moment. I knew whatever happened next would affect me physically for the rest of my life. I knew water torture could instigate claustrophobia and anxiety attacks later in life, I also knew I could get round that if it happened to me, but the pole, the pole could leave me crippled for the rest of my life. I began to cry quietly.

* * *

The Bar

The bar was to raise the feet so your torturer could beat them with ease. People were lucky to get away with broken feet. Often it did so much damage to the ankle joint and tendons victims hobbled and needed walking aids for the rest of their lives. The bones didn't break under this method of torture. They shattered.

* * *

I was shaking uncontrollably, partly due to the cold but mainly out of fear. I knew I had to be cold but I couldn't really feel it. I couldn't even feel my broken ribs. My body was numb and my heart was racing. I couldn't even think of anything to say and all I could hear was the blood pumping though my body. I lay still, eyes shut as tightly as I could hold the lids together, tensing every muscle in my body and holding my breath waiting for the first strike.

I needed to breathe before it came. Quickly I exhaled then sucked the cold air back into my lungs taking as much in as I could then I held it again and tensed my body in anticipation of the beating to come. But it never came. I waited and waited then after a good while my breathing returned to normal and once again I drifted into a dead mans sleep.

It was still dark but by the rising noise levels around me dawn couldn't have been far away. I could hear sentries being changed and talking in the distance, too far to make out words but it was talking. I could smell food being cooked and exhaust fumes from diesel engines being run.

Over the next hour things got louder. I could hear orders being barked. Heavy metal doors being slammed and all this time I was being left alone. It was obvious that the division was on the move. But what would happen to me and where were my guys? They could leave us here for dead and no one would ever know. The Yanks had that power and those morals.

Even though killing everyone in the ambush was an option, it was just that, an option. We'd never have done it. We don't do that. But if you put the extreme on the table you can avoid it. Use it as a good behaviour beacon. Americans have no such moral value. As far as they're concerned if it's on the table it's a viable option. That's not just my opinion. That's common knowledge.

My ribs began to hurt again, the adrenaline had subsided and the night chill was giving way to tropical morning warmth. This was not good news. The air became thick with diesel fumes and I could hear heavy engines revving up. I counted four helicopters fly over. Whistles being blown and men shouting orders. The division was leaving in quick time.

I lay there bound tightly to that fuckin bar with my hands deep in the sand behind me. Despite the pain in my side I tried to sit up. I was instantly met with a large boot to the middle of my chest. It pushed me back slowly but firmly into the soft sand underneath me.

"You lot are going nowhere" Said a calm deep American accent.

Even though the words "You lot" selfishly stripped me of the feelings of loneliness and isolation. Fear and anticipation ran through my body once more. My feet were still strapped to that bastard pole and I knew our captors weren't bluffing.

The sun and temperature rose quickly and the beach became quiet. The sound of rotor blades and engines got further and further away. Until the only thing I could hear was the sea and the breeze in the palm trees. After a while I could feel my clothes drying and I started to sweat. I knew I was in direct sunlight. Not a problem yet but that would change fast. No one had spoken to me all the time this was going on. I knew I wasn't on my own I could hear movement and distant conversation. The wait was too much. The anticipation was getting harder to control. I took the deepest breath I could cleared my dry sand filled throat and said:

"What do you want?"

"A cold pint and two paracitamol" Sean said

The instant relief I felt, I couldn't help but laugh, I could hear Sean giggling away too.

"How are you mate?" I said with new found energy.

"OK I think" He replied "I've not long woke up"

His night had taken a different route to mine. He was beaten unconscious at the start and spared the water. I decided not to share my experience.

"Stop talking" the familiar calm American voice interrupted.

I repeated my question. I got no answer. I lay still and quiet, sickly comforted knowing Sean was close by.

The day was uncomfortably hot when my hood was pulled off. The daylight was blinding, I couldn't open my eyes and focus for a good few minutes. When I did the first thing I saw was the soles of Sean's feet strapped to the same bar just off to my left, obviously our torturers were right handed. Sean's hood had been taken off as well and he to was trying focus on our surroundings.

Two men stood at either end of the bar both dressed in Military greens but neither man sponsoring any badges of rank or Unit. Both men were holding meter long, two inch thick bamboo canes. Dread ran through my whole body again and I could see the panic in Sean's eyes.

"Hello mate, do you come here often?" I said to Sean.

I looked at him and smiled best I could. Trying to hide the terror I was feeling.

"No, and I'm not fuckin coming again" He replied. No humour in his voice this time just panic. He also knew full well what the canes were for, he just hadn't cottoned on until that very moment. We both looked at the two guards whose faces never changed, they didn't engage us in anyway not even a glance. Both men looked down the beach to my left my eyes followed theirs and for the first time I noticed the rest of the guys.

They were spread out down the beach. Staked out in fifty meter intervals the same way Sean and I were. All with two guards a piece. My observations were interrupted.

"Come on mate, don't lie to me." Sean was trying to talk to one of the guards. "Today's gonna hurt init?"

Sean was using his humour to disguise his fears. I looked to the guard for some response. I got nothing.

"Why haven't you asked us any questions" I said.

I got no response. The guards just kept looking down the beach.

"We work for the Government of Sabah and the Philippines" I went on.

Still no response, not a flicker.

"What's the matter with you two fuckin homo's?" Sean intervened.

One guard turned his head to look at Sean then turned and looked back down the beach.

"Oh you can hear me then you fuckin Yank prick?" Sean was losing it.

"Leave em to their games mate" I said to Sean, "We'll wait for the organ grinder"

I was still hoping for someone in Command to explain or at least let us explain.

Sean lashed out in another episode of insulting sarcasm.

I looked back down the beach to see three men walking up it. Taking the time to stop at each set of guards and presumably to give instructions.

Sean had no shortage of insults and couldn't seem to stem the flow of them either. I didn't interrupt he was as afraid as I was. This was just his way of dealing with it.

The three men also dressed in anonymous green but obviously in charge reached us about ten minutes later. These were the men that called the shots, that knew the big picture, these were the men I needed to speak to. As they got to us the larger of our two guards pointed at me and said:

"That's the one you need Sir"

Just the fact that he singled me out made my blood chill and once again my body went numb, I knew I didn't have long to explain, I'd have to make every word count, but before I could say a word the dark haired one of the apocalyptic three said:

"Start with him then".

As he finished the sentence the bamboo cane struck the soles of both my feet.

I screamed and curled up. Head on my knees, hands bound behind my back. The cane hit me again. I screamed again. An unbelievable pain ran sharply up both my shins to the knees.

I could hear Sean reach a whole new level of insult as he screamed at my assailants to stop.

The cane stuck again and this time I heard the thwack as it made contact. This time I let out no cry, I just shut my eyes tightly gritted my teeth and winced through the next few minutes, praying all the time for shock to set in. but it never came.

When they stopped, I was at the peak of exhaustion. Every muscle in my body had tensed to its snapping point. Tired, dehydrated and unable to move all fear left my body and I fell unconscious.

When I woke the hood was back in place tightly over my head. My legs were still elevated and the sun was, hot hot hot. My mouth was dry and my lips were cracked. I couldn't really feel my beaten feet but the pain in my ribs and knees was phenomenal.

"You still there Sean" I said loudly, praying he was. The thought of being alone right now was unbearable.

"Yes Mukka" He replied "How are you?"

"I've had worse" I said. In a vain and wasted attempt at humour "How are you?

"Fine mate, they only did you and Milly" He said.

"Stop talking" Said one of our guards.

"You can fuck off, you hillbilly cunt" I spat the words out as pure venom. It was only then I realised that my fear had been replaced by anger.

I heard him step closer. The back of my hood went tight as he grabbed it. I could smell tobacco on the his breath through the mask, this was no Soldier.

"Things can get worse." He whispered harshly.

He was right, they could get worse and I knew it. He let go of my head and it hit the sand like a dead weight I lay still and silent. The strength that anger gives deserted me and fear took its place once more.

I drifted in and out of consciousness for how long God only knows. I remember three times being woken by the distant screams of my Brothers in Arms. Every time I asked the same questions to our jailers.

"Why haven't you asked us any questions?"
"What do you want?" and
"Are you aware we are here legally and legitimately?

But they all met with silence. This had gone beyond simple revenge for the death of the men in the ambush. I doubted these men were even military. CIA, NSA maybe, but not Military. We were there on legal and legitimate terms and conditions and I'd offered that information freely but with no joy. I could see no happy end in sight and no working options, I remember hoping for one last minute with my son and swore that if I got it I would hold him forever.

My hood was ripped off for the second time and the binds on my feet were cut. I looked over at Sean whose hood was still on. The guard stood next to him raised his cane high above his head. He didn't hit Sean across the feet as he did me but bought the cane down hard right across both of Sean's shin bones. Sean screamed and the cane came down once more.

I opened my mouth to shout some kind of protest, but as I did to my horror I was dragged back down to the water by two other guards, no stress position this time they just held me under the cold salt water, facing up. Held there to the point my lungs felt they would collapse and as my consciousness ebb away and just before complete darkness, up for a breath, hood back on, tightened at the neck, then under again and again and again.

Time escaped me, I don't know exactly how long it went on for. My torturers changed at least once. Sometimes I got two breaths sometimes three and I lost consciousness I don't know how many times, I was finished.

It was dusk when they dragged my body back up the beach and strapped me back to that fuckin bar. With the thick black hood wet, even out the water I was struggling to breath. I was just living, if I had what they wanted they didn't want it, I had no answers and no more energy to protest.

The torture went on for another two days. The bar, the water and in between time the personal attention. At one point my hood was removed after the water, I was put on my aching bruised knees and kneeling in front of me was one of my captors with a pair of U shaped pliers.

"Open up" He said with a smile.

Allowing me to kneel up was a mistake, he should have kept me on my back. Fear provided the energy and experience provided the power and accuracy. As he came closer I struck him hard with my forehead catching him right on the bridge of his nose. It burst like a ripe tomato, blood splattered over both our faces as he went sprawling backwards.

"Explain that to your kids you Yank cunt" I rasp at him.

Within a second, I was back in the sand and the boots came in. I curled up and took it silently. My ribs were getting worse but I didn't care. After yet another brief violent beating I was dragged by my swollen bleeding feet back to the bar. I knew what was coming and I could do nothing, nothing at all to stop it.

Sometime later the same broken faced agent returned. He ripped my hood off, grabbed me round the throat and pushed me hard into the sand. With my hands bound behind my back and my feet strapped to the bar I was helpless. He punched me repeatedly in the face, then pulled a pair of pliers from a pouch on his belt and went to work.

I tried everything I could to keep my mouth shut, but he pinched my lips with the pliers and pushed the end so hard into my right cheek at the corner of my mouth, I thought it would rip right through. My resistance was very short lived. The second my jaw gave way he started gripping and pinching like a madman, four, five times he tried for a good grip of a tooth, he got my tongue my lips and gums and eventually secured a back right molar.

He gripped hard, his broken and swollen red face full of hatred, then with straight arms and the full weight of his body he jerked forward. The pain was unreal.

The tooth gave way and my cheek split at the corner of my mouth. Blood filled my mouth and throat again and again, I thought I'd drown in my own blood.

"Tell your kids about that, Limy cunt" he said, then he spat on me and kicked me in the side of the head.

A short while later still bleeding profusely I was dragged up the beach to where Taff was, he was in a terrible state, other than Sean he was the first one of us I'd had close contact with since this hell began, they'd shattered both his collar bones and he was bleeding heavily from the wounds.

"This is next for you" snarled his torturer.

Then with that the two men dragged me a little further up the beach, cut my hands free and put my left hand on a large rock. At first I couldn't work out what was going on. I was tired and confused then one of the guards pulled out a long heavy blade and started shattering my fingers one by one with the back of the Army issue machete. I thought I'd lose all my fingers altogether. It took them and their games a good twenty minutes to finish a job that could have been over with in a second. Up to that point I thought the hard extraction of my tooth was the worst pain I could endure, how wrong I was, at least with that act the guard was angry. With my hand the tortures laughed about it and mocked Taff's fear and my pain. How much more could I take?

On the forth day we were all put together for the second time since the ordeal began and made to sit in a circle on the beach, all of us facing in. Given the circumstances of the first time we were all tremendously on edge. Our boots were returned to us with comments like:

"See if they still fit" and "You won't need these again".

Basic rations and water were left out for us. Then medical supplies made available and we were told to help ourselves. Emotions ran hard and fast. Lots of anger, hate and frustration polluted our reunion. Was this just another torture method? Show us something we needed give it to us then take it away. The thought crossed all our minds. None of us could physically do anything about it. We all struggled massively to walk, it was easier to crawl on all fours like dogs. I struggled to eat the food because of the swelling in my mouth and I couldn't do a thing with my shattered hand.

All of us without exception had broken bones below the knee, the bar had done its job well. Amongst the list of injuries sustained were;

Sean had both cheek bones broken in the initial contact and Paddy had a broken jaw. All the fingers on my left hand were broken as was my right cheek bone and three ribs, not to mention the dentistry work I'd need. But the worst by far was Neal, he'd lost his right eye on the final afternoon of our ordeal when Neal was made an example of. Neal was, for want of a better term, a fuckin hard bastard. His guards had mistakenly let one of his hands go and that's all he needed to wipe two of them out even with the injuries to his feet, but out numbered he was brought down quickly. Then they dragged us together and sat us in a line in front of him and made us watch as they put him on his knees, removed his hood and cut his eye from his head with what looked like nothing more than a leatherman multi tool. During this heinous crime the only thing that was said to us was:

"Be warned"

We were all beaten men, both inside and out. We'd had little sleep, very little water and no food in four days and nights. All I wanted to do was sleep and cry.

We sat on that beach for most of that day not a word from our captors. Our liaison turned up in a helicopter that afternoon to extract us. It was all very informal and confusing, not a word of explanation. We were literally piled into the chopper and flown back to our FUP and given better medical attention. We stayed on that small Island for the next two days being debriefed, and treated for dehydration then fed before being taken back to Sandakan in Sabah for more medical attention and a more in depth debrief.

At no point during the ordeal were we asked for information or given any kind of explanation as to why the ten of us had spent four days and nights being beaten and tortured. The top scoring theory was; we were being softened up before being passed on to be interrogated.

It's easier to get information out of broken men.

After another week recovering at a Base in Sandakan, we were taken to Kota Kinabalu for a few days. Neal needed special attention for what was left of his eye and Sean's legs were fucked. From there we flew to Kuala Lumpur, all the way using old wooden crutches to aid us walk. But not Sean, he had a wheel chair. The trauma to his shin bones was immense and even though the events on Basilan were now almost three weeks away at this point, Sean's leg showed little sign of healing.

From Kuala Lumpur we took the long flight to Vienna Austria and to our surprise and worry, there we were taken into custody and extradited 1st class to Gatwick London.

At Gatwick the surprise continued. The ten of us were taken straight into a Customs and Excise interview room. A small bald man in a pin stripe suit stood in front of us. Some of us standing some seated.

"Right gentlemen" He said "let's get some details"

He then proceeded to ask our names, address's and such. I noticed he wasn't writing anything down.

"Sir" I said "We're all fucked, this has not been a picnic are you gonna take our details down or what?"

The small Government man looked up at me, pushed his spectacles back onto the bridge of nose and said:

"Young man, I have all your details written down here and if any of you give me any other answer than what I've got written here. I'll lock you up until the enquiry and that could be six months from now. Do you all understand?"

Defeated, each of us nodded in total agreement.

After taking our details he then took our passports. Taff asked for a receipt and our inquisitor informed him and us that a passport was a privilege not a right and if the Government deemed it so, we would get them back after the enquiry.

He then went on to explain that this wasn't an isolated incident and we were not the only lost souls to fall down this road. Not just in the Philippines but all round the world. The long and short of it was;

American troops should not have been there. By order of a treaty with Malaysia they weren't allowed anywhere in that area in military numbers exceeding thirty two and even then, only in an advisory capacity. But they were and unfortunately so were we.

Within six months of being back in the UK the Foreign Office returned our passports along with a list of restrictions and conditions. Another list of places I couldn't go. Unfortunately only eight of us needed them, two of our number took their own lives in the time between the happenings on that beach and the enquiry. I could never get that to settle with me, I never understood why they did it.

One of them came home one night after a party at a friend's house, alone he took over a hundred pills and washed it down with a bottle of Vodka, his wife returned after a weekend at her mothers to find him dead on the couch. The other droves his car off a cliff edge in Cumbria the day after he put everything he owned in his wife's name.

We'd survived a horrific event, we'd lived to not tell the tale, we had won the day and we'd done it together, I never understood why they couldn't talk to one of us if things were so bad.

I went to both funerals but I had no answers to any questions asked by their wives and children. I knew those men as warriors, fighters. Not as men who'd throw their lives away. They both had plenty of hooks to keep them in this life. I can't imagine how they were feeling or what was going through their minds but I've prayed I never experience their last frame of mind.

Two weeks after we arrived home this was officially released by News VOA com:

Philippine authorities have captured a senior leader of the ABU SAYYAF terrorist group, which has links to al-Qaida. Galid Andang, also known as Commander Robot, was wounded and captured in a gun battle on December 7th with Philippine security forces on Jolo Island in the south Philippines.

Abu sayyaf shares al-Qaida's extremism masking as religion. Its goal is to establish a radical fundamentalist Islamic state in the western Mindanao and the Sulu Islands of the Southern Philippines.

President George W Bush said: "The United State stands with the Philippines in the war against terror. Both our nations are threatened by terrorism, and we are determined to fight that threat until it is defeated. Our diplomats and law enforcement and Intelligence officers are working arm in arm to disrupt terror plots, to cut off terrorist financing and to bring terrorists to justice."

Hunting With Giants

I first met the Prince (Mark P) after getting knocked off my bike by some piss head on a wet day in September. The Insurance company said they'd sent my bike to his garage in Radlet for the repair work, ironically I found the name of his business very easy to remember and despite the spanner even his company logo looks familiar at a glance.

In no time at all Mark and his crew had the bike repaired and me back on the road. I'd spoken to Mark a few times on the phone but never met him until he delivered the bike back to me at my Tattoo Studio in Hemel Hempstead.

Not best known for my light hearted phone manner or my patients I was instantly relieved I'd been polite to him in my daily hassling phone calls. Even though I was pissed off with my Insurance company, them never answering the phone or returning my calls Mark never let me let that spill over onto what he had to do. He has the gift of peace. Whatever mood you're in he can give you peace of mind without giving you any bullshit. It's hell of a thing to witness.

Mark is a mountain of a man, a typical very large Eastern European. At that time he hadn't told me where he was from but from all the time I'd done in that part of the world, well lets say although I couldn't pin point exactly where he was from it was obvious to me he wasn't Italian.

When he dropped the bike off we chatted for a while about the bike and his work and over a brew he showed me a small tattoo on his left arm that he wanted covered. The tattoo wasn't tiny it just looked it on his arm, it would have been fine on any normal sized guy and the artist that did it should have advised Mark to that effect. I told him I could fix it and Mark said he'd book it in with me when he had time. Then finishing his brew he shot off on his yellow Bandit.

Mark popped in a few weeks later, we chatted some more about what he wanted and then started the work on his arm. He was happy for me to freehand it on and as usual that bit of artistic licence worked out for the best. The big guy got a custom piece of his own something no one else would have. It took three or four sessions and in that time I got to know Mark better. He came out with us on our Christmas piss up and was there for one of my birthday bashes, we even ventured into London a couple of times to piss it up there, where he met other friends of mine. He stayed at my house, met Angela and Jim and in less than a year it was like I'd know him all my life. He's such a genuine and likable man its hard to imagine anyone not getting on with him.

Like all great events I don't remember how it first came about, but Mark invited me to Hungary in Eastern Europe on a hunting trip with him and his best mate Ged. Ged was another one of life's true gentlemen. A colossal man, like Mark he worked hard and played hard and took great pride in his family and his work. I met Ged for about an hour the first time at an open day summer fair and in spite of us both being pissed out of our brackets we seemed to get on well.

It took nearly a year of clay pigeon shooting, tattooing, barbeques and beer to arrive, but eventually the Eastern European hunting trip was on and like every other opportunity in my life I grabbed it with both hands. Unless you count rabbits, fish and people, I'd never hunted before, I didn't know what to expect, but knew I could handle myself in the field and I knew I was in good company.

We drove to Luton airport. Lyn, Ged's wife, gave us all a lift. Everyone refers to Lyn as; Aunty Lyn. She's a very caring and compassionate person, she's one of those people who sees the good in everybody, even as I left my house she had a little check list for me.

"Got your passport your toothbrush and something warm and dry?" She said.

Even with all my experience in the field I never take offence to people asking such questions. It's always nice to be looked out for.

Lyn got us there in no time and after a short flight we landed in Budapest some time late that night.

Marks cousin Peti picked us up from Budapest airport and took us to his house a short drive away. If there was an economic crisis in Hungary you wouldn't know it in this home. Peti and his two boys, a couple of fine young men with promising football careers came out to meet us and have drinks giving Mark and his cousin time to catch up before we moved on. Six large glasses of home made red wine and a wad of cheese, meat and bread later we moved on. Gently.

From there we went to the Prince's Auntie's home. God bless this woman. We turned up pissed as crickets at two in the morning on our best behaviour and this lovely old girl got up and prepared us food and greeted us with more homemade wine and "polinka". Even though she had set us a table and prepared us a feast she never sat with us, she was just happy we were happy and it would have been impossible not to be, the woman breathed pure kindness.

* * *

Polinka
It's the local moonshine. It's not made from anything, it's sent by the Devil to prove to men that drink that they can't really drink. It's crystal clear and has to be served in glass because it melts plastic. I remember describing the shot as like;

"Licking the balls of a dead yeti"

I'm sure it could fuel rockets and I know it can strip paint, But as much as I struggled to swallow the potential, "brain damage in a glass", I could not turn down this wonderful ageing Saint of a woman.

* * *

That night at Mark's Auntie's, Ged and I shared a large double bed and the Prince stayed on the couch in the room next to us. Me and one of the largest human beings I've ever met had to share a double bed. I could only hope he didn't miss his wife to much. Ged slept like a vampire on his back with his hands across his chest. I on the other hand slept like an epileptic octopus. I'm sure if the wine hadn't flowed like it did, I'd have ended up on the floor.

The following night we went to Mark's nephew's twenty first birthday party. The son of Peti, our host when we first arrived. The venue was large and apart from me and Ged the hundred and fifty invited were all related. It was a great crowd. As the alcohol flowed my Hungarian got better. The Prince had to intervene a few times as me and the person I was speaking to were laughing at two different conversations and Mark thought it good to put us on the same page. At one point even Ged and I were speaking fluent Hungarian to each other. Three bottles of Jagermister, twelve litres of wine and a shit load of Hungarian traditional dancing later,

"Enough said."

The next day we took the long drive up to the Prince's hunting lodge. Between the garlic, paprika, spicy sausage and polinka the van we were in stank like a Guardroom sleeping billet on a Monday morning and yet it was only the three of us in it.

When we got there I was impressed. The white walls of the lodge with the black beams on a back drop of conifer forest was a beautiful site, it almost held an English Tudor aura. The lodge catered well for the necessities. It was warm and clean with plenty of room I had my own bed and I didn't have to shit in a hedge. It was perfect. Our butler there was a an old old man who'd been hunting since the stone age called Solly, he had a single English phrase that brought a smile every time he said it:

"Alright, Mr White"

Said slowly in a deep Hungarian accent it became the words for the weekend.

At the end of the first days hunting we travelled through the mountains to a small village where Peti had another house. There with all the hunting crew from the beaters to the butlers we ate like Gods and drank like Goats. I sang in fluent Hungarian made up new verses to "Old King Cole" and met people I would never forget.

I was also introduced to tripe stew. I ate everything except the tripe, as did Ged. Whoever said it was ok to eat that part of whatever it comes from should be shot. It's like being gang raped in the mouth by something dead. Having said that the Prince loves it and was happy to finish mine off.

It was a fantastic night. At one point we were even joined by the local police who I believe were related to our host at some point down his linage. I've no idea how we did it, but we drove back through the mountain and back to the lodge without a single hitch, I half expected to have to push the van or walk home but instead things went remarkably smooth and an hour after leaving the village we got back to the lodge for a welcome nights kip.

At first light we got up and hunted again, I was amazed at the shear size and power of the wild boar it was daunting to say the least. This animal lives to live. Their not killed easily and can turn on a man in a heart beat. I put a 308 round behind the shoulder of a large male from less than twenty yards. It scrambled to its feet and ran off. Big Ged hit one twice, once in the shoulder and once in the head. The beast rolled backwards down the hill, got up and buggered off. If you didn't hit this truly wild beast spot on, it was legging it. This animal is a true adversary.

After a few days in the mountains of northern Hungary, hunting, drinking, eating and hunting again the three of us made the long drive back to the Prince's village. By the time we arrived we were all starving. We sat down in the restaurant part of the local pub and ordered food. I ordered steak and potatoes, so did Ged. Mark ordered the tripe (fuckin savage). After a fifteen minute wait the waitress informed us that the only thing left on the menu was the tripe stew. I wasn't surprised with the prince out of town who else would eat that shit? Ged and I looked at each other looked at the waitress, politely declined and ordered a beer each instead.

That night we played cards with the locals and drank our body weight in red wine and soda. About three in the morning we returned to Marks auntie's house and once again bless her heart she got out of bed made food for us and insisted we drink her Polinka. How could we possibly turn her down?

The next morning on a massive hangover we toured the sights of Budapest. Like London it's full of great architecture and history. Modern battle damage still scars the walls of ancient buildings. The Prince takes a lot of pride in his knowledge of his native country and was a fantastic tour guide. Between Communism and Revolution this proud country really has been through the mill. Yet its people are among the friendliest I ever met, all three of us were fed and watered at every house we stopped at, we were treated like celebrities and accepted like family.

We stopped at the home of Marks oldest friend for lunch, for a feed the likes you only expect to see at Christmas, we sat and talked a mixture of English, Hungarian, Russian, Serbian and Shite. The kids with a larger English vocabulary than me kept the conversation going between us when the Prince was otherwise engaged in conversation elsewhere, once again we drank copious amounts of red wine and soda and we were still there at supper time. Like with all the people I've met through the Prince they were so friendly welcoming and happy I felt I'd known them all my life.

The next day we returned to the UK on the red eye, and fuck we had red eyes, we were all picked up at Luton airport and I was dropped off at home back to my Angela. I had missed her the whole trip, it was a first for me. I'd spent a lot of time away in the past and never missed anyone except my son, now I missed a woman. My life was changing all the time and all for the better. The whole Hungarian experience was full of firsts for me. It was a long weekend of high velocity rounds and high octane alcohol. I can't wait to return.

Over the following years I got to know Mark and Ged as good friends and two years later Mark, Ged and Aunty Lyn flew out to Africa for my wedding, it was a memorable two weeks. My new wife and I took great pleasure in showing our friends around, new friendships were forged in that short time and fond memories taken away by all. Each one of my friends left their mark in our new house and Africa left a mark in their hearts in sure.

On the 15 May 2008 the world lost a good man Mark lost a best friend and a family lost a great father, Big Ged had a heart attack and died at work. People came from far and wide to Ged's funeral. I believe it's true that good men live on in the hearts of others. This is certainly true of Ged who is spoken of with the greatest fondness. In his short time he'd touched the lives of hundreds of people from all manners of backgrounds and through this giant of a man new friendships have blossomed. Mark P (the Prince) and I remain great friends to this day he is a great friend to my family who love him for the giant of happiness he is. He is another person I was fortunate enough to meet at the right time in my life.

WANKER

A Life Lived

I've fought two wars and eleven major Military Campaigns
I've Sent three passports back because they were full and thrown one away to get home quicker
I've married out of pity and divorced out of need
I'm now married to a woman I love.

I've fathered three children, I've fathered girls, I've have a son
I've changed nappies and dressed gun shot wounds, carried limbless friends off the battlefield and carried my kid's home from school
I've stood shoulder to shoulder with friends under Artillery bombardment.
I've had a white wedding.

I've been shot, stabbed and tortured.
I've nursed loved ones
I've warn foreign uniforms and fought for foreign causes
I have fought for Queen and Country

I've been drunk on all five continents, fought on four and loved on two
I've earned a fortune and blown it.
I've won gold medals.
I've fallen at the first hurdle

I've kayaked great rivers and climbed vast granite faces
I've broken bones and hearts
I know loneliness, I've met fear.
I've cheated and lied cared and cherished.

I've jumped from planes at night and ridden great beasts
Swam in tropical oceans and frozen on glaciers
I've known desire
I've accomplished dreams

I have fought with man, beast, element and emotion
And won and lost to them all
I've heard my children call my name and been woken by the woman of my dreams
I know love,
I have lived, I aim to live.

Gaz lynch

Light At The End Of The Tunnel

After the events in Basilan I made the decision to leave the Company and concentrate on life in the UK, my Tattoo studio was doing well as was my other business enterprises and I had more than enough money to buy a new bike and a house for me and my son. I was looking forward to a change of pace in my way of life.

Over the year that followed the Basilan incident my life changed dramatically. I was struggling with the events that happened on that beach half way round the world and even though divorced, Jims mother was constantly acting up, she had four boyfriends that year, two I had to warn off for her when they threatened her round my boy. She'd also moved five times, her life was about as stable as the Palestine Israeli peace talks. I had a lot of shit of my own to deal with as well as sorting her life out for the safety of my son,

I was also finding it hard to slow myself into the monotony of civilian life. It was my son and my love of Tattooing that harnessed my thoughts and kept me straight during that hard time.

By the end of that year Jims mum moved in with yet another boyfriend, (which was good, it meant she'd leave me the fuck alone) and things were coming right in my mind.

My wars were over. My ego I felt was satisfied and my way of life had settled down to a dull roar. My son was turning into a fine young man and business was good, loads of cash coming in and plenty of guys in the pub and the gym to call mates. I know everyone in the town.

All manner of people were coming to me for help; school leavers with hard times, Bouncers, Publicans, Professionals out of their depth,(surprising how much shit a Fireman, Copper or Builder can be in) even local drug dealers trying to get even. Anybody who had what they believed to be a real problem had come to me at some point over that period.

I've always been renowned for helping my friends. Going out of my way to see them well, but hangers on, like all business men I only helped if I gained.

A state of mind founded between my time with the Army and my time with the Firm. I will stand by you to the bitter end if I know you as a friend, other than that you have to have something to offer.

"There's no friends in business"

Even though I was still doing small bits for the Firm at the time, (the money was good) I was very much without leadership and direction. My life was in my hands and I loved it.

Never being one to let distraction get in the way for long, by that I mean women, drugs and the bullshit influence of wannabe gangsters, I was free to set my own course.

* * *

I use to have this neighbour, a West Ham fan who fancied himself as a bit of a villain. He was a nice bloke but he had to taken with a pinch of salt. A few times he'd bang on about "A Job" he'd done at the weekend, it was all bullshit of course but it passed the time to listen to him. His favourite brag was about how he "Robbed the IRA," as he would put it. I pointed out to him on more than one occasion that if he'd hit the IRA one of the most powerful terrorist organisations in the world, he'd be dead by now. As it happens the money he made from his hit on the IRA coincided with the sale of his house in Little Gadston.

The man was a full time bullshitter, in all my time working for the Firms not a single person he mentioned knew him or of him. A mate of mine Dave C told me that this neighbour of mine was the worse type of grass, because he was the type of guy to run off at the mouth about things he'd heard and if he ever got pulled in for it there was no chance he'd get charged because he wasn't there but the pinch would add credibility to his story to his mates, it was just the type of talking he did that drew attention from the law, attention nobody wanted.

After listening to Dave I started giving my neighbour a wide birth, he was everything Dave had said he was. One day my neighbour caught me outside my house and proceeded to tell me about his latest job. I had to walk away. The bullshitter had crossed the bullshit line in a great big bullshit tractor. He was now telling me he had done the very job me and two others had done a week earlier.

That afternoon after I'd mugged him off, he came to my front door with a nose full of cocaine pushing for a fight, as good as Eddie Kemp thinks he is, he's never been that good. On two other occasions he'd backed down from me and the pair of ball he was showing now was purely cocaine grown, but I wasn't about to prove it to him in front of my Son, who was sat six feet away in my front room. There are parts of me that wish I'd just smacked him up on the door step but all that would have done was draw attention to myself proving Dave C's point, so I bit my lip and let it go. I tried for weeks after that to get hold of him, but like all real challenges in his life, Eddie steered away.

* * *

My small business empire was thriving. It wasn't much in the grand scope of things but it was all cash and it was all mine. Life was cooshdy and everything was going my way.

Then I met my Angela.

How easily she changed my life, I didn't even see it coming, I didn't even put up a fight to try and save the harmony of my life. At the time I let this beautiful woman into my life, I was too long in the tooth to bullshit. If she asked I answered, I'd never done that before. In the passed the secrecy of my life sent a lot of women packing which suited me fine. But something about Angela made me put all the cloak and dagger to the side. On a few occasions she found out about events in my life from friends in Hereford purely by accident. Things I would never have volunteered due to their nature, but friends talk to friends and girlfriends listen. But my Angela didn't vex she took it all in her stride. She never judges me just takes me for the man I am to her. Meeting Angela granted me a very rare opportunity for people like me, the opportunity to find happiness, trust and love. An opportunity not to be taken lightly an opportunity I would grab with both hands.

Whilst courting, Angela and I flew up to Edinburgh, a place she long to see. Neither of us was disappointed by what it had to offer. It was early December and freezing cold, we wrapped up warm and drank mulled wine under the Christmas lights watching kids ice skate in the park, with the silhouette of the great castle in the background.

Enjoying the romance and slow pace of the evening I watched my Angela cup her warm wine in both hands and use the steam to warm her cold nose I knew then I'd be with this beautiful woman for the rest of my life.

I let my world go. The criminal underworld the drink induced good times, the violent paydays and other peoples wars. I literally turned my back on my way of life. It was taking me nowhere I hadn't been before, I was in a rut given to me by my past and although I was content there Angela could never have been happy or fitted in, so I walked away from it all without ever looking back. The people I grew to know and love respected and supported my decision and the underworld I worked for never hit me with the concept,

"Once you're in, you never leave"

I was renowned for surgical clandestine violence. They didn't want me on their back anymore than I wanted them on mine, so I got a good clean break, just what we needed.

A year after we met and six months after we got together, Angela moved in with me and my son. Angela never had to try and fit in with Jim. My son was fascinated by Angela and her white African background. He loved to hear her talk about the wild and the way of life in her homeland. Life in our home was peaceful. Jim is a very respectful, compassionate and smart young man and the three of us were very happy.

Meeting Angela's family was more daunting for me than I let on. The only experience I had with "In laws", was my ex's bitchy, money grabbing family and a culture that thrived on mother in law jokes. So I was on the back foot to say the least, as much as I wanted to be with Angela if I didn't meet the family requirements it probably wouldn't happen.

We flew out to Johannesburg and then got a connecting flight to Gaborone in Botswana. The idea was to connect again to Francistown where I would meet the folks and her older brother. However, the plane crashed on the runway at Gaborone and it looked like we'd be there a hell of a lot longer than we wanted to. Deciding not to wait Angela and I hired a car from the airport and started out on the five hour drive to Francistown.

We arrived in Francistown at about nine o'clock that night, Angela's folks had been at the local rugby club most of the day on the piss with Angela's brother and his mates. As much as they wanted us to join them I made the command decision not to meet them for the first time on the piss. I didn't really want their first impression of me being influenced by my "Who can piss the furthest trick", so we booked into a hotel and got our heads down till morning.

The next two weeks with Arthur and Brenda my potential new in laws was one of the best holidays I've had, and it was easy to see where Angela's relaxed and confident view on life came from Arthur took me to play golf with his friends. I don't think I've ever tried so hard at something I suck at.

At the end of the first week they took us to a fishing camp on the Zambezi River. A friend of theirs, Larry took us out on his boat and accommodated us at his beautiful riverside house there. I'd spent a lot of time in Africa over the years, Somalia in 1993, Rwanda in

1994, Ghana, Kenya and the Sudan after that, but this was the first time I had time to appreciate Africa and its natural beauty.

It goes without saying that I got the third degree about my intentions towards Angela, but it was done well and with Arthur and Brenda being the people they are it was impossible to take offence. That and Arthur has guns. The man has trouble reading the paper in the morning yet he can shoot the eye lashes off a shit house rat at fifty yards.

Arthur is the true mark of a hard working family man. He is a man I've grown to love and respect over the years I've known him, and he's one of the few men I've met in my life who really is fearless.

After two weeks we returned home with a library of tales to tell and a new found love for a foreign land. We returned back to the UK and slipped quickly back into the rat race. After a while Angela was being hassled by my very jealous ex wife and her daughter. The ex had done this before to a landlady I had, she made things so difficult for my landlady and her kids that she had to cancel my tenancy agreement. The police were powerless and said they couldn't help.

It was well within my ability and recourses to sort it out myself but how do you tell your son later in life you had his mother dropped in the North Sea with a twenty kilo plate for a float.

To make things worse a very bitter and twisted former mother in law kept sticking her ore in as did all the ex's sisters.

But the thing that worried me most was the mental stability of Jim's mother. She suffers from Munchausen's disease. In the past she'd thrown herself down stairs and even cut herself one Christmas in front of my friends, all because she wasn't the centre of attention. Her favourite trick was to crash cars. In the time I knew her she'd written off two new cars and attempted suicide at least twice and all to get attention.

It got worse when I first left her and my concern was that she might go proxy and things would start happening to Jim. Once again the authorities couldn't or wouldn't help. In the end I had to make it very clear to her that if anything did ever happen to my boy she would come a very distant second in the events that would follow. Thankfully, she heeded my warning but the bitchiness and slander towards Angela continued. Again the police were powerless.

British Police are dogs without teeth.

We rose above the pettiness of the Hemel Hempstead York sisters. If anything their attempts to put a wedge between us pulled Angela and I closer together. Angela could have walked away at any time and sought out an easier life but she didn't. She loved me. In a very short space of time I realized she was more to precious to me than any other woman I had ever met before. I had fallen in love.

Jim got a baby sister on the 2nd August 2006 and Angela and I married on 2nd April 2008 four years after we first hooked up. We had a white wedding in Africa on the grounds of our Lodge. Friends of mine flew all the way from the UK to celebrate the occasion. They all stayed for two weeks and we used that time to introduce them to Africa. It was a honeymoon to remember.

Jim's mother wouldn't let him come to our wedding, she said she was getting married in the same week, even after giving her a year's notice. She said it was the only slot the registry office had and she wanted Jim at her wedding! I never believed her, she'd pulled the "I'm getting married again" card more often than she crashed cars. Almost a year on and she still isn't married. Jim missed a wonderful and special time all for a woman's self induced scorn.

After a rollercoaster life with no real direction or long term goals other than that of looking after myself and my son Jim I had found real love, a light at the end of a maze of dark tunnels, in the form of a beautiful woman. Angela. My wife.

In the March of 2007 after two great holidays there we emigrated to Angela's homeland. All with a view to starting a new life away from the rat race. Our first priority was to buy property. Africa is a beautiful place despite its troubles and with people leaving like rats from a sinking ship there was an abundance of land for sale. After six months of looking Angela and I fell in love with a beautiful small safari lodge. The first thing we did after we bought it was close it, giving us time to make it our own and do things our way.

Living in a black market economy has been one small challenge after another. Corruption lies on every street corner as it does on every corner of the world. I've not yet met a local official anywhere that wasn't after a backhander or who wouldn't abuse his powers to line his own pockets. It's just like every Central American country I've worked in.

The general population here is a very resourceful civilian culture. They have a saying here:

"We'll make a plan"

and they do, every day just for the essentials. Even the white population here will make a plan to rip you off, as several have tried to do to me over the last two years, fortunately for them with no success, but the standard of living here is high and the way of life relaxed. A good day here is a great day and the bad days are the same wherever you are. I enjoy it here.

Having used firearms for one resolve or another in my past I'd hoped too leave them alone, I turned down one offer after another to go hunting and was happy with the excuse:

"It wasn't my thing".

Until one day I accepted an invite to go out with a friend of mine Premesh D. We took his Landrover onto a farm just outside of the city and it was there I shot my first Impala, two in fact. Since then Premesh and I have hunted a dozen times and I would go out everyday if I could. It's refreshing for me to know that after everything I've done and everything I've seen, that life still has more to offer me, more to enjoy.

On the 20th July 2008 we had another baby girl. A new sister for my other babies. Life is better than ever. The lodge is coming together slowly and my old way of life is little more than a fond memory. I can honestly say I have lived every minute as if it was my last but I find myself now living every minute looking forward to the next one.

This book covers the major events in my life but it's the smaller things in life that link them together. I had a job as a driver for Jewson Hire for a while and not being one to stand still I went on to manage my own branch in Enfield North London, there I got to meet unemployed Soldiers from all Regiments and Corps, many I eventually employed though my Company Olive branch, a small but very busy PMC.

I also went on to own my own small plant hire company that hired everything from electric screw drivers to eight ton diggers and sell it on for a good profit.

I worked for Buildbase in Oxford, through them I met French Company that employed my services for two years.

Martin Welsh from A Fine Tattoo in North Camp gave me my first professional Tattooing job that lead to me opening my own studios some years later and even a job packing box's for the little red book company lead to greater things.

I treated all my successes and failures equally as opportunity and it served me well. I hope now to pass that enthusiasm and drive onto my children and live a long peaceful life away from the petty influences and mistakes made in my younger days.

AN OBSTACLE IS ONLY SEEN, WHEN YOUR EYES ARE TAKEN OFF YOUR GOAL

Beni Bennit

End Ex

Some of the better anecdotes come from the bar or long nights on stag and they always end up with a good laugh at someone's expense. Each one told a thousand times and each time something new is added to keep it up to date and make it more humorous.

One of my favourite anecdotes told with such energy by its victim happened in Kenya. Two off duty Safety Staff walked up to a vantage point to watch the Live Firing Exercise they'd been training troops for all week.

They took their horror box's (Lunch box's provided by the cookhouse and prepared with the same care and detail as a Christmas food fight) and their water bottles then started out on the five mile walk to the range.

About a hundred metres from the range the two troopers heard a loud throaty roar. In the hot sun of Africa both soldiers instantly thought "Lion!" One of the troopers without giving it a second thought took off back the way they came at full pelt. The other not wanting to come second in this particular race sprinted after him.

The two troopers slowed to a fast Tab after nearly a mile and made there way bristly back to the Barracks. Jointly deciding to abandon their afternoon plans they spent that afternoon in the NAAFI watching the TV.

When the troops finished the exercise the safety staff that took the succession of live fire attacks approached the two would be spectators and asked what they'd been up to.

"We came out to see the exercise" One guy said "But there was a pride of lions in the bush between us and the range so we thought better of it and walked back here instead"

"That's was histories fastest fuckin walk" Said a voice from the back. "We saw you two legging it down the road at formula one speed through our binoculars"

"You'd run too if a pride of roaring hungry lions was hiding in the bush next to you" Said the other runner defensively.

"It wasn't lions" said the onlooker "it was a wild cattle bull, they make that noise to scare other bulls way".

Red faced, It was an event the two DS Staff would never live down.

* * *

Other good anecdotes come from wind ups. The best thing about them is they can be done over and over again to anyone that would fall for them.

Just before I first got to Battalion someone had passed our Admin Sgt his static line hook as he jumped from a C-130 at night.

The static line pulls your parachute out. The hook on the end hooks onto a wire cable in the plane and remains there when you jump pulling out the chute when you leave the plane. If you've got the hook in your hand logic dictates the parachute can't open.

Fortunately the hook handed to the nervous Sgt was a spare and his chute opened as normal but the look on his face must have been priceless and chute or not he must have shit himself all the way down.

* * *

The professional error too is always good listening, you learn from it because you never want to be the wanker in the story. I did a Rigger Marshals or Heli handling course taken by the SSM of 63 Sqn Dave. In one of the theory lessons he explained how a helicopter becomes a giant ball of static electricity and because of this the chopper has to be earthed before it can be touched. To do this you're given a "Static Probe." it's a wooden handle with a metal hook at one end that runs thought the wood and out the other side connecting to chain that drags on the floor and in turn earthing the helicopter to make it safe to handle.

The only problem with this simple but purely ingenious device was;

Guys kept leaving the static probe attached to the Heli hook when the Chopper flew off, leaving the Heli Handling Team with no hook for the next load.

Dave told us of a Gurkha Heli Team that had lost three hooks in one day. The guy who got the forth hook had the bright idea that if he kept the chain in his pocket so he wouldn't lose the last of the static probes in the teams equipment box.

Later that day, poor Johnny Gurkha stood under a Chinook that had been in the air for over an hour, charged with enough electricity to power a small village and dutifully hooked the strap holding the load, the chain still in his pocket.

A 100'000 volts shoot right passed the testicles of the brave Gurkha Warrior and out the heel of his boot shooting him thirty feet across the ground.

The way Dave put it had us in stitches but he knew none of us would leave a probe behind or put it in our pocket.

I got money says that Treefrog never had kids.

* * *

It's true the Army does a lot for a man and in some respects too much. Like so many others I joined at an early age so when I left I really had no idea what civie street was about and didn't understand some of the simplest of things with regards to local Government and so would make innocent mistakes. A friend of mine Tommy whose not the sharpest knife in the draw at the best of times made innocent mistake after innocent mistake, but his crowning moment was the dawn of his bodyguard career. After leaving the Forces, Tommy chose to follow the life of a CPO (Close Protection Officer), an area of employment he was more than qualified to do. Following standard procedure when looking for any job he put out a few CV's and made a few phone calls. One of these calls was to an add that read'

"We need Escorts."

By the end of the day Tommy had a job. All he had to do was Escort a client to a dinner dance. Tommy said the night went well, the old girl he was looking after was polite and didn't seem to keen on talking to anyone but him, (which is strange for a Principal). What he found stranger was, at the end of the night when he escorted her to her hotel room, expecting to sit outside all night, his Principal invited him in and started hitting on him. It was only then he clicked that it wasn't a bodyguard service he was working for but a male escort agency.

Depending on how many pint's he's had depends on how the rest of the night went when you question him about it, but it was an innocent one off and when I last spoke to Tommy he was working for a Sultan.

* * *

If you talk long enough in any group of guys women will come out in the conversation at some point, usually coming second to male ego and wit. Sorry girls that's just the way it is, and having bumped into a few hen nights in London I know you lot are not much better.

One night in the Traf our local Aldershot haunt, Big Sid was telling us about how he loves riding the rodeo with the chicks in his local village. It's a simple manoeuvre guaranteed to get any man swiftly evicted from the bed of the hardest core dog. Basically when you've had enough and you need a quick out, you get your new short term girlfriend on all fours. Then locking yourself in nice and tight and tell her something charming like:

"You don't sweat much for a fat bird" or

"Don't you ever clean your house" and my favourite:

"The lads said you were shite in the sack".

This ultimately leading to a fuming female trying to buck you off. The rodeo bit comes in the hanging on.

Later that week at the Unit Bob has had to call in sick. No problem but at lunchtime he still wasn't back. When we went for lunch

Bob was in bed the quack had given him one week's bed rest. We crowded round his bed and asked him was wrong. Not that he would get any sympathy but its good to know what you're about to take the piss out of. Bob explained:

He'd gone into the town the previous night to meet a girl he met at the weekend, but from the off she was boring him to tears. He went through the motions, they had a few drinks and a bite to eat, then as many an Aldershot dog does she was happy for him too spend the night. Without being too graphic the second half of the night was no better than the first half and Bob found himself needing an out. Amazingly, the only thing he could think of was Big Sid's rodeo play, and with that urged the two of them into the rodeo position. Then he put his charm to work by saying:
"You're not very good at this given the amount of practice you've had are you?"
Then he held on for the ride, but the ride never came, instead his date for the night simply opened her legs, grabbed his balls and yanked them as close to her chin as his painfully stretched sack would allow without coming completely off. Then she rolled wincing Bob off the bed and proceeded to beat him with bedroom furniture. Bob made the agonizing trip back to the block and the rest as they say is history.

A lot of us went out of our ways not to upset the hard core Aldershot Dogs. Some of them were as hard as the guys. The thought of upsetting one when you're naked doesn't bear worth thinking about.

***

ALDERSHOT DOG GOES TO HEAVEN

After four decades of putting out for British Airborne Forces. Fist fighting Fanny passes away peacefully in her sleep. At the pearly gates she confronts Saint Peter not even sure she'll be allowed into Heaven.

"Of course you're welcome Fanny" Says Saint Pete, "You have served the trooper well in your life, you have earned the right to paradise, we have a special spot for you on cloud fourteen, but be warned your old life in over, if you fraternise with any of the Paratroopers in Heaven, its straight to Hell for you no second chances"

Not wanting to do anything to jeopardise her chance in paradise Fanny quickly makes her way to cloud fourteen and settles into her new life, sitting on the porch of her new house stoking her new cat, singing and making merry with the Angels. This truly was her paradise.

After several months of this Fanny had found true peace and the scars of her life on earth slowly faded away. Then one day she hears the familiar deep humming sound of a C130 and is shocked to see a Paratrooper descend and land on cloud fifteen.

In a panic she runs to the Pearly gates to seek council from Saint Peter desperate not to lose her new found utopia. When she gets there, out of breath and bordering on hysterical she explains what she has seen.

"Cloud fifteen you say?" Says Saint Pete "Don't worry my child, that's not a Paratrooper, that's God, he just wishes he was a Paratrooper"

(It's just a joke)

* * *

I could write another book just on other guy's anecdotes and old squaddie jokes and it would probably make for better reading. The chapters of this book however have followed my life through times that directly influenced who I am today. That said it's true of all of us that stories we hear and characters we meet and aspire to influence our everyday state of mind and in turn contribute to the happy or tragic endings to the choices we make.

I don't believe the men we are at twenty are the same man we are at thirty. I don't believe the single man is the same Father or the

Father the same Grandfather. Although in each case they are the same person. We mature as we age.

Despite some of the events, mine is not a tragic tale. For the first time in my life I like the man I am. I'm no longer a man of circumstance and situation. Any issues I ever had with my past have been long since exorcised, to a point that on the rare occasion they crop up I merely brush them off and carry on with my life.

I know well the handful of friends life has blessed me with and it's down to the events of my life both the good and the bad that I know how best to serve them as a friend. Giving them unconditional love and support and wishing them all my peace of mind,

It is the friends we make in life that keep the most powerful emotion at bay. Loneliness.

Despite my studies and love of Philosophy and Theology I would not consider myself a religious man, but I do hope there is a God. There are questions I would have him answer and conundrums I would have him solve like; how is it a world of brutal violence is held together by love and compassion? How did he think that shit up? I would also let him know that I forgive him, but until that time, I just have to keep:

Counting my blessings, not my troubles!

FRIENDS

You can never pin point when it started
But you pray it never ends
You'll only ever meet a handful
But you'll always call them friend

Gaz Lynch

GLOSSARY

A
ACC	Army Catering Corps (Fat Splasher's)
Arty	Artillery. Big Guns that can ruin your whole day.
APM	Anti Personnel Mine, can also ruin your day
ATMP	All Terrain Multi Purpose Platform, six wheeled overlander.
Actions On	Tactics carried out, upon unforeseen events
A Lord Lucan	When a guy disappears/or is made to
AWOL	Absent without leave

B
Box head	A German
BOWO	Brigade Orderly Warrant Officer.
Brick	Section in Northern Ireland
Bird	Jail time.
Biff chit	Sick note
Block	Barrack Room, Soldiers residence.
Blade	Member of British SAS
BFA	Blank firing attachment
BMP	Soviet Troop carrying vehicle
BRDM	Soviet Troop carrying and Recon Vehicle
BOO	Brigade orderly officer
BMA	Brigade Maintenance area

C
Colly	Colchester
Chorley	Blank training grenade
Cas Evac	Casualty evacuation
Compo	Army Rations
Craphat	A soldier not of Airborne Forces
CO	Commanding Officer, (Lt Colonel)
CSM	Company Sergeant Major (your top dog)

CP	Close Protection
CPO	Close Protection Officer
CMH	Cambridge Military Hospital
CFT	Combat Fitness Test
CQB	Close Quarter Battle
C130	Hercules Aircraft

D

DIBUA /DIB	Defence in built up areas
Doss Bag	Sleeping bag
DPM	Disruptive pattern material
De Bus	Get off, Get out
DI	Detective Inspector
DZ	Drop Zone. Wet, Rocky, Potholed place Paratroopers land on.
Drill	Marching as an individual or body of men
DFC	Draw fit and check equipment
Digs	Place to stay
DRA	Defence Research Agency

E

EOD	Explosive Ordinance Disposal. (Bomb Squad)
ERV	Emergency rendezvous
IED	Improvised explosive device
Eager Beaver	Army forklift truck

F

Full Screw	Full Corporal
FIBUA/FIB	Fighting in built up areas
FUP	Form Up Point
Firm	Name used to describe groups within the organised criminal underworld
Fan Dance	March that covers all the peaks (Fans) in Brecon Beacons

G

Green Back	US Dollar

Griz	Push through discomfort
Greenies	81mm Mortar Bomb

H
Hat	Short term for Craphat
Harbour area	Tactically Secure area in the field
HALO	High altitude low opening. (Special Forces jump)
H Hour	Time the action starts
Horror box	Army packed lunch

J
Jump window	Period in which you could jump at anytime

I
IRA	Irish Republican Army
INLA	Irish National Liberation Army

L
LPBG	Leading Parachute Battalion / Battle Group. (The first in.)
Landy	Landrover
Link	Belt Ammunition.
Lightweights	Green Army issue trousers warn on camp

M
Maggot	Sleeping Bag
MT	Motor Transport Dept

N
NCO	None Commissioned Officer
NATO	North Atlantic Treaty Organisation
NAAFI	Navy Army Air force Financial Institution

O
OC	Officer Commanding, (a Major)
OR's	Other Ranks (Not Rupert's)

P

Principle	Person you Bodyguard
Paddy	Irish Civilian
PMC	Private Military Company.
PSC	Private Security Company
Pips	An Officers Badge of Rank
Pad	Married Soldier
PTI	Physical Training Instructor
Pit	Bed
PJI	Parachute Jump Instructor
Stand to	jump to a tactical state of readiness
Port	Left hand side
Proff'd	Got for free
PRI	American NAAFI
POW	Prisoner of war

R

Rat Pack	Army Rations
RAOC	Royal Army Ordinance Corps (Blanket Stacker)
R.S.M	Regimental Sergeant Major. Highest rank for an enlisted man.
R&R	Time off
RUC	Royal Ulster Constabulary
RE	Royal Engineers
RP	Regimental Police
RV	Rendezvous point
Recci	Recognisance
Replen	Replenishment
Rupert's	Officers
Rodney's	Officers
Radop	Radio operator
RPG	Rocket propelled grenade

S

Stand to	Order that brings all men to arms
Stickman	Sergeant Major/ RSM

Score	Twenty quid
Squaddie	Young soldier
Stag On	Guard Duty
SIS	Secrete Intelligence Service (MI6)
Splitarse	Female Soldier
Starboard	Right hand side
Star Item	Expensive/Specialist bit of kit
SSM	See CSM
Sky pilot	Vicar or priest

T

The Trees	The Jungle
The Shot	Aldershot
Tabbing	Tactical Advance to Battle. A body of men moving on foot in full kit. Usually Very quickly.
Teeth Arms	Front line troops
Treefrog	Gurkha

U

UDA	Ulster Defence Association
UFF	Ulster freedom fighters

W

Wank sack	Sleeping bag

Back Cover

This is one mans remarkable journey through a life of violence, love and friendship. Son to a violent drunk he literally dragged his way through childhood, forced to create opportunity and make his own way, constantly battling against circumstance, society and even his own family. His forced enlistment into the British Army and his choice to embark on a special forces career gave him great foundation, but after ten years like so many others of his kind it left him with few options, pushing him once again into the firing line only now for the highest bidder. Foreign Military, Government or Civilian the work was as constant as the trouble to be had with it. This accurately documented account of his life is both humorous and tragic, it dispels urban myths and enforces politically frowned upon public opinions and is made all the more shocking by murder, deceit and open treachery by untouchable powers. This book is guaranteed to make you think about the world we live in and those chosen to keep and disrupt its delicate balance.

John Pollock. Free Press

Until I met the author himself I didn't know one man could do so much with one life. This book will either make you grasp all of lives opportunities with both hands or it will turn you into a hermit too afraid to venture out. A fantastic read.

Peter Jasons MM